Still A BAPTIST

... neither angry nor ashamed of it

JERRY D. LOCKE

Still A BAPTIST

...neither angry nor ashamed of it

JERRY D. LOCKE

ISBN# 978-1-61119-180-6

Printed in the United States of America.

Printed by Calvary Publishing
A Ministry of Parker Memorial Baptist Church
1902 East Cavanaugh Road
Lansing, Michigan 48910
www.CalvaryPublishing.org

FOR BAPTISTS
BY BAPTISTS

Calvary
PUBLISHING

A ministry of Parker Memorial Baptist Church
1902 East Cavanaugh Road • Lansing, Michigan 48910
Phone: 517.882.2112 • Fax: 517.882.2317

www.calvarypublishing.org

Contents

Dedication 7

The Picture on the Cover 8

Preface 9

The Wild, Wacky 21ˢᵗ Century Church World 15

The Glorious Beginning of the Churches of the NewTestament 41

The Characteristics of New Testament Churches (Part 1) 67

The Characteristics of New Testament Churches (Part 2) 85

The Blood-Bought History of Baptists 113

What Do Baptists Believe? 163

In Search of the Body of Christ 207

Why Is the Church Still Important? 233

Calling God's Churches to Revival 253

Who are independent Baptists? 265

Postscript 285

Bibliography 309

Other books by the Author 317

Dedication

To all the Lord's churches for whom I had the privilege of serving as pastor:

Oak Grove Baptist, Caddo, TX, 1966-1968
Bible Baptist, Electra, TX, 1968-1969
Belt Line Baptist, Garland, TX, 1969-1976
Northway Baptist, Humble, TX, 1976-1983
Lake Worth Baptist, Fort Worth, TX, 1983-2016

And

To the great Baptist men who helped shape, clarify and codify my ecclesiology:
Al. C. Locke, Sr., (1918-2003)
Calvin "Cal" Sims (1910-1977)
B. F. Dearmore (1898-1969)
J.D. Johnston (1920-2017)
Edgar C. Carlisle (1923-2014)
Kermit Johnson (1919-1986)
M.L. Moser, Jr. (1925-)
Wendell McHargue (1933-)
Edwin Zellner (1933-)

The Picture on the Cover

This painting of a baptism at the turn of the twentieth century was authorized by Southwestern Baptist Theological Seminary, Fort Worth, Texas, under the presidency of Dr. Ken Hemphill and prepared by artist Kenneth Wyatt to remind Southwestern of its sacred mission. Used by special permission of the seminary, February 7, 2017. Paige Patterson, President

July 10, 2017
Good Morning,
    Kenneth will gladly give you permission to use the painting for your book.
    Thank you for your interest in Kenneth's work.

Kenneth Wyatt Galleries
Jeanetta Bradford
310 Comanche Tr.
Tulia, TX 79088
806-995-2811
www.kennethwyatt.com

Preface

The title of my book, *STILL A BAPTIST,* needs a brief explanation. For generations my family has been found among Baptist people. It is a story of God's amazing providence which carries with it divine privileges and responsibilities.

The first record of my Baptist heritage is October of 1882. The Missionary Baptist Church of Christ of Mineral Wells, Texas, was organized (this is now the First Baptist Church) and among the charter members was my Great, Great Grandmother Tabitha Jowell (1815-1896). A few years later, an anti-missionary element got into the church and it was disorganized (the term used in the church minutes); then two weeks later re-organized. Among the nineteen members in the re-organization on October 17, 1891, were my Great, Great Grandmother Tabitha Jowell, and my Great Grandparents Matthew Beal Locke (1835-1915) and Mary Caroline Jowell Locke (1834-1897).

My grandfather, Jesse Quinton (J.Q.) Locke (1877-1967), the youngest of eleven children, was saved in 1892 at the age of 15 at a Baptist meeting. It was held under a brush arbor near the Indian Creek School house, west of Mineral Wells, with George Webb Slaughter preaching. G.W. Slaughter (1811-1895) was ordained a Baptist minister in 1844 and was said to have baptized over 3,000 persons and ordained more preachers and organized more churches than any other person in the state of Texas. According to my granddad's diary, he was baptized in Walter Whatley's tank by Rev. J.D. Clough. I suppose he was the Baptist pastor who organized the meeting. My grandparents, J.Q. and Alice Locke, joined the Rock Ford Baptist Church on July

15, 1923, according to his diary, but the church died three years later. My dad, Alfred Conner Locke (1918-2003), the youngest of nine children, recalled,

"We never attended church in these years on the farm. We started attending singings at Valley View school house on Saturday nights. It was there that we met Clint and Delia Herring. He asked us to come to church at Salesville (Baptist Church) *the next Sunday night. Papa and Mama, Quinton and I went and I was saved that night, May 16, 1937. Quinton was saved also that night and my Mother and Dad joined by statement. My mother shouted when she saw our decision."*

That is something to shout about! My dad and his brother became Baptists when they were baptized at the Walker stock tank outside of Salesville, TX, June 20, 1937.

On June 18, 1938, my dad's brother, Quinton, married Vivian Wilson. Dad became the last child at home, but only for a little more than a year. Vivian had a cousin, Mary Florence Hudspeth (1921-2013), whom she introduced to my dad on July 8, 1939. Seventy-seven days later my dad and mom were married on September 23, 1939. One wonders how the conversation went when my dad asked my mom's father if he could marry his daughter. I am sure some thought it might not last. Man, did it last — 64 years — 'till death did them part.

After my parents were married, they lived on the old home place on Turkey Creek with my grandparents and farmed with his dad for a year. His new father-in-law, Claud Hudspeth (1888-1982), worked on the Tarleton College Experimental Station where my dad was hired in September of 1940. All those years of working and learning back on Turkey Creek paid off with a decent job in Stephenville to support himself and his new bride paying him $60 a month.

After moving to Stephenville, they joined Washington Street Baptist Church in November of 1940. While at Washington Street Baptist, dad taught the young people's class in Sunday School, led the singing and was ordained as a deacon in September 1942, but that didn't last long. Within only a few days, my dad was sure God was calling him into the gospel ministry.

Dad wrote a letter to his parents dated October 6, 1942. J.Q. had saved this letter and it is now in my possession. He wrote,

"I have accepted the call to the ministry. Been fighting it for some four years. Will have help teaching from Bro. Rippetoe. Have been filling in for him when he could not be here. Bro. Rippetoe made the announcement at church last night. I feel so much better now. Both of you pray for me that I might carry out this work the Lord would have me to do. I know you would, without me asking."

On November 28, 1943, my dad was formally ordained to the gospel ministry by the Washington Street Baptist Church, where Ernest Rippetoe (1892-1962) was pastor. A. A. Davis (1900-1978), pastor of the First Baptist Church of Nowata, Oklahoma, and lecturer of "The Trail of Blood," preached the charge. From 1944 to 1952 Dad pastored six churches, as many as four at one time. I discovered America in 1945 and was named after one of my dad's older mentors, Jerry L. Davis (1863-1956). In September of 1952 he became the pastor of Lake Worth Baptist Church in Fort Worth, TX., where he would minister for the next thirty-one years.

I trusted Christ as my Saviour on the first Sunday evening of 1956 at the age of ten and was baptized within minutes of my profession of faith in Jesus Christ, thus becoming a

Baptist.

While I was originally a Baptist by divine providence and because of a strong family heritage, I am now a Baptist by a strong and growing personal conviction. At age eighteen, that conviction was born when I surrendered my life to God for ministry. Shortly after, my conviction grew as I was educated in a small Bible School which was under the authority of a Baptist church.

My conviction was tested when I was ordained to the gospel ministry at the age of twenty-one by fourteen Baptist preachers. During the fifty years (minus five months) that followed while pastoring five Baptist churches in Texas, the last was at the Lake Worth Baptist Church for thirty-three years, my Baptist roots grew strong and deep.

My Baptist conviction has not diminished now that I have entered a new season of ministry as the minister-at-large for Lake Worth Baptist Church, as the staff writer for LWBC Publications, and preaching by invitation at Baptist churches near and far.

Through it all, I am *STILL A BAPTIST* … and, amazingly, I am neither angry nor ashamed of it!

While I have written several books on various topics (a shameless plug to check out LWBC Publications @ www.lakeworthbaptist.org), I am persuaded this one will likely corner the market. Seriously. The reason for that belief is no one is presently writing much at all on ecclesiology – the doctrine of the church. When I was educated in Bible college and became a pastor in the 1960's "church truth" was a part of the Baptist landscape. The lines of distinctions were clearly drawn. Most Baptists knew who they were and they were neither angry nor ashamed of it. In my research, I uncovered a seventy-five-year-old warning from a little-known Baptist writer who commended his brethren for fighting against "theological liberalism" but charged that they had been flatly indifferent to "ecclesiological liberalism." We are presently paying the price for that indifference!

In writing a small book on the church, I am under no delusion that it will settle this matter for everyone. My hope is it will declare truth, expose error and challenge every reader to adjust their beliefs to God's Word. When it comes to Baptist church-truth there are too many "mugwumps" in our ranks. A "mugwump" is a fence-sitter. A "mugwump" is someone who sits on a fence with his "mug" on one side and his "wump" on the other. I pray this book will be a fire that burns down the fence some professed Baptists are presently straddling on this most important Bible doctrine.

To suppose that the name "Baptist" means that all Baptist congregations believe and conduct God's work alike would be an obvious misrepresentation. Baptist churches are vastly different. There are Baptists who are SBC, GARBC, WBF, BBF, IBFI, GIBF, and those who are independent from any affiliation. There are some churches who still carry the Baptist name who are no longer Baptist in their doctrine and practice. Those who are dropping the name Baptist from their identification may be moving away from long-held Baptist teachings.

I have gone to some lengths to quote prominent Baptists of the past, with the year of their birth and death, to affirm that certain Baptist positions have been long held by prominent leaders in our ranks. The current Protestant view of many modern-day Baptists exposes who has changed from the historical Baptist position.

Throughout this book, I would have preferred to avoid using the term "the local church." Among true Baptists it is only used for clarification, while it is used by others to imply there is another kind of church. To say "local church" is like saying "widow woman," "free gift," "past history," "false pretense," "added bonus" – all redundancies. The only kind of churches in the New Testament were local. The word "church" is consistently used in the New Testament to indicate an assembly of baptized believers in Christ united together in a single location for worship, fellowship and ministry.

One final disclaimer. I have long-time friends and acquaintances who are Baptists in conventions, associations and fellowships. I have other friends who are in groups that are much too organized for the appetite I have acquired during my lifetime as an unaffiliated Baptist. Those who know me hopefully know my heart and recognize the love I have for "the church of the living God" and the men who are pastors and missionaries. To the best of my ability I have attempted to remove any disrespectful, dishonest, or destructive language that would be unbecoming to our Saviour Jesus Christ. It is not my goal to win an argument or to extend any debate, but that we all might be consumed with the simple desire Paul expressed under the inspiration of the Holy Spirit; **"Unto him *be* glory in the church by Christ Jesus throughout all ages, world without end. Amen"** (Ephesians 3:21). This small book is not an *attack* from an enemy, rather an *analysis* from an observer and an *affirmation* from one who is *STILL A BAPTIST... and is neither angry nor ashamed of it.*

Jerry D. Locke (1945-)
August 2017

CHAPTER 1

The Wild, Wacky 21ˢᵗ Century Church World

My earliest memories are "church memories." Life in Texas in the late 1940's and the early 1950's was centered around the church. That was true for most of America's families, but ours was Baptist church-life on steroids.

Two years before I was born, my dad was pastoring his first church, the First Baptist Church of Morgan Mill. He preached there one Sunday a month and, also, eight miles down the road at Sap Oak Baptist one Sunday a month. Smaller churches in those days often met each week for Sunday School, but only had preaching once a month.

In the summer of 1943 my dad became the pastor at West Side Missionary Baptist Church in Tyler, a half time church, so he was driving 200 miles from Stephenville to Tyler twice a month. He had given up a good job paying $75 a month and taken a four-day-a-week job paying him $1.50 a day which allowed him weekends off so he could do ministry. The next year, December 1944, the Leagueville Baptist Church, Murchison, called my dad to preach there on Saturday nights and Sunday afternoons, twice a month (on the weeks he was in Tyler), while at the same time he was preaching the other weeks at the two churches in Erath County. I was born in Stephenville, Texas, in March of 1945 and in September of that year the First Baptist Church of Brownsboro called my dad to be their pastor two Sundays a month. So dad resigned Morgan Mill and Sap Oak and moved our family to Tyler in October, 1945 when I was seven months old. Now it gets even more crazy. Keep up.

In May, 1947 both First Baptist Church of Brownsboro and West Tyler Missionary Baptist Church of Tyler, called my dad to be their full-time pastor. He accepted the full-time work of the Tyler church. In October of that year the Union Hill Baptist Church, outside of Brownsboro, called dad for the other two Saturday nights and Sunday afternoons. From October 1947 until September 1952 my dad pastored the West Tyler Missionary Baptist on Sunday mornings, Sunday evenings and Wednesdays and the Leagueville Baptist and Union Hill Baptist on two Saturday nights and Sunday afternoons each.

I wish I had asked dad what he did in his spare time. I am sure he was preaching somewhere on the four 5th Sundays during the year!

Added to my dad's pastoring, he was preaching summer revivals, where I and my two older brothers would do special singing accompanied by my mom on the piano.

While other people were not getting the frequent-flier miles that we were getting from going here and there, most were going to church every week. Humorist Will Rogers once quipped that highway engineers in Texas constructed roads for Texas Baptists to wear out going to and from church. Sunday was the Lord's Day. Businesses were closed, churches were opened and people gathered. Church was the place to be. The singing was the lively Stamps-Baxter kind. The women could hit those high notes and the men were low-down bass singers. They all sang by letter – they were taught to open up and just let 'er fly. It wasn't uncommon to see the older ladies who dipped snuff sitting by the open windows for obvious reasons – they needed a place to launch their mouth full of spit. The preaching was KJV-only and it was hell-hot and heaven-sweet. I still remember as a boy the scores of people who were baptized in Chapman's tank (pond for you northerners) after the annual summer revival. Ten-day revivals were not uncommon. Those were the days.

But those bright days began to dim in less than a couple of decades.

When I became a pastor at the ripe-old age of twenty-one, things were changing in the church-world. The year I was ordained as a Baptist pastor, 1966, a Methodist professor at Emory University made headlines when he declared, "God is dead." Really? Philosopher Friedrich Nietzsche had announced the "death of God" poetically in his book, *Zarathustra*, in 1884, and like most things, it took a while to make it to church. That announcement made the cover of *Time* magazine on Good Friday of that year. It's religion editor, John T. Elson, believed he identified the nation's shifting theological mood from the complacent faith of the 1950s to the metaphysical confusion of the mid-1960s.

Fast-forward five decades, the period in which I have been privileged to serve as a Baptist pastor. Spiritual, moral and theological life has now become completely unhinged. Without worry of contradiction, we have never seen what we are seeing today.

Now there is no real truth; everything is relative. Truth is determined by ever-changing public opinion, so, there is no ultimate standard of authority. We debate and then pass laws legalizing what societies for centuries deemed immoral or illegal. Bodies of the unborn are disposed of as medical waste under the protection of our highest court, with some baby parts sold for scientific research. For the first time in human history, marriage has been radically redefined to include people of the same sex. There is now no ultimate parental authority. It has been given up to the government by default. Radical feminism is very much alive and mad about it. No longer is any one allowed to judge another person's religious or non-religious beliefs. Any assertion of biblical morality may now be considered "hate speech." Missionaries are seen as "destroyers of culture." God's laws are out, personal preferences are in. Thugs who destroy private property and commit crimes are classified as "protestors." The "deconstruction" of literature, history, science, morals, and values has left us with only a corpse of the truth. Those who are determined to hold on to any trace of the "old ways" are marginalized as naïve, old-fashioned, outdated and need to get out of the way of progress.

And that's life outside the church.

What's happening in the church world?

The Dismantling of Denominations

If you are observing the church-world around you, Methodists, Assemblies of God, Presbyterians, and, yes, Baptists, are going under cover. Churches who once proudly identified who they are and what they believe can hardly be found today with a blood-hound dog and court-ordered search warrant. The purveyors say they are dropping their denominational identity because it *might* turn off unchurched people who *might* come to their meetings who *might not* like their label. One pastor, who dropped the Baptist name in favor of the ambiguous name "Church for the Communities" admitted, "One of my members told me the other day that if he had known we were a Baptist church, he would not have joined."

Even the term "church" is now only carefully used by some, preferring a less intrusive term like fellowship or other vague non-starters.

Check out the ambiguous hipster church names in your area where people are encouraged to worship. Their trendy nameplates sound more like upscale subdivisions than churches trying to lure suburban residents to Sunday morning worship. There are plenty of *Pointe* names: *Crosspointe, Gracepointe, Lifepointe.* By adding the unnecessary "e" everyone is immediately alerted that these churches are more sophisticated than others. Some are more straight forward like *New Life* or *The Way.* Others are more mysterious like *The Table, The Grove, Elevate, CrossWinds, The Well at Springfield, Tapestry* or *The Gathering.* Saying nothing says everything!

One satirist quipped, "Perhaps the concept has not been taken far enough. Get some focus groups together to discover everyone's favorite warm fuzzy words and then name churches after puppies, comfort foods, or characters from Sesame Street. I think *Chocolate Cake Chapel* or *Bert and Ernie's Bible Fellowship* have possibilities. Churches that really want to market themselves need to learn to run with the big dogs. Maybe even seek corporate sponsorship. How about *Nike Christian Church*, with the big swoosh painted on the door? Would a church named *Big Mac Methodist* have golden arches on the front lawn? The water image being appropriate, there could be an *Old Navy Baptist Church.* And wouldn't *FedEx House of Prayer* suggest a place where your petitions would absolutely reach the intended address? Would a *Taco Bell Temple* have services in Spanish?"[1]

This craze would be laughable, but it reveals a far deeper problem. The inmates are running the asylum. Where will this stop?

It reminds me of an old story involving the owner of a

---

1   Charles Austin, *The Bergen Record (New Jersey)*, October 12, 2000.

fish store who painted a new sign, "Fresh Fish Sold Here." A friend objected to the word "here"—where else was the fish being sold? The owner took out that word, making the new sign, "Fresh Fish Sold." Another friend objected to the word "fresh"—no one expects to be sold stale fish. The owner took out that word, making the new sign, "Fish Sold." Another friend objected to the word "sold"—no one gives away free fish. The owner took out that word, making the new sign, "Fish." Another friend objected to the word "fish"— everyone could smell it a block away. The owner took out that word and the new sign was blank. The story ended with a statement that the fish store owner went out of business because he didn't advertise.

Many church people don't know who they are and, sadly, they often don't know they should care to know who they are.

The Disinterest in Discernment

If Jesus[2] and the apostles[3] warned of "false teachers" and "false prophets" in their day, why are we reluctant to believe they are still around in our day? And where are the brave pulpits who identify them?

"A new way of 'doing' church is emerging. In this radical paradigm shift, exposition is being replaced with entertainment, preaching with performances, doctrine with drama, and theology with theatrics. The pulpit, once the focal point of the church, is now being overshadowed by a variety of church-growth techniques, everything from trendy worship styles to glitzy presentations to vaudeville-like pageantries. In seeking to

---

2   Matthew 7:15; 15:14; 24:4, 5, 11.

3   Philippians 3:2, 18; 2 Peter 2:1; 1 John 2:19; 4:1; Jude 4; Revelation 2:20.

capture the upper-hand in church growth, a new wave of pastors is reinventing church and repackaging the gospel into a product to be sold to 'consumers.'"[4]

"Go and sin no more" has been replaced by "Judge not, that ye be not judged."

Do we need true revival? Certainly. Where does revival come from? God. Well, how do we get ourselves in a place to receive revival from God? We find the Truth, repent over its loss, submit to its authority, begin to live our lives accordingly and God will bless. God blesses truth! **"Ye shall know the truth, and the truth shall make you free"** (John 8:32). Truth can also make you mad. **"Am I therefore become your enemy, because I tell you the truth?"** (Galatians 4:16). Jesus identified the problem for us. **"And this is the condemnation, that light is come into the world, and men loved darkness rather than light, because their deeds were evil. For every one that doeth evil hateth the light, neither cometh to the light, lest his deeds should be reproved."** (John 3:19-20) **"This then is the message which we have heard of him, and declare unto you, that God is light, and in him is no darkness at all. If we say that we have fellowship with him, and walk in darkness, we lie, and do not the truth: But if we walk in the light, as he is in the light, we have fellowship one with another, and the blood of Jesus Christ his Son cleanseth us from all sin."** (1 John 1:5-7)

If people do not turn *to* truth then, the only option is to turn *from* truth.

---

4   Steven J. Lawson (1951-), *The Priority of Biblical Preaching: An Expository Study of Acts 2:42-47*, Bibliotheca Sacra Journal, April 2001.

The Departure from Doctrine

There are some modern-day church leaders who see doctrine (which simply means "teaching") as a barrier to church growth. This is especially so of theology (which means "the study of God").

The largest church in America is a model of a modern, doctrine-less church. Over 40,000 people regularly file into the Lakewood Church in Houston to hear its famed celebrity-pastor Joel Osteen. Osteen's older brother Paul, a surgeon who left his practice to join the church staff, said, *"There is a disconnect between religion and what people need,"* he said, calling some sermons in traditional churches impenetrable, *"almost goofy. What people want is an unchurch,"* Paul Osteen said. *"They don't want pressure. Joel makes faith practical and relevant. Make church relevant,"* he says. *"Give them something to be able to take away. I find today people are not looking for theology. There's a place for it, [But] in your everyday life you need to know how to live."*[5]

Christian philosopher, G.K. Chesterton, believed, *"Theology is simply that part of religion that requires brains."* That's part of the problem. Silence, when it comes to doctrine, is not golden, most of the time it is yellow!

Steve W. Lemke (1951-), Provost at New Orleans Baptist Theological Seminary, related a personal story about how things are now when it comes to doctrine. *"One recent event in a seminary Theology class illustrates this anti-doctrinal spirit. In the midst of a Systematic Theology class that was discussing a theological issue in some detail, one student exclaimed in frustration, 'I didn't come here to learn all this theology. I came*

---

here to learn how to grow a church.'"[6]

One of the biblical signs of the last days is a "falling away" from truth and Scriptural teaching.

"Let no man deceive you by any means: for *that day shall not come,* except there come a falling away first,…" (2 Thessalonians 2:3)

"Preach the word; be instant in season, out of season; reprove, rebuke, exhort with all longsuffering and doctrine. For the time will come when they will not endure sound doctrine; but after their own lusts shall they heap to themselves teachers, having itching ears; And they shall turn away *their* ears from the truth, and shall be turned unto fables." (2 Timothy 4:2-4)

"Now the Spirit speaketh expressly, that in the latter times some shall depart from the faith, giving heed to seducing spirits, and doctrines of devils; Speaking lies in hypocrisy; having their conscience seared with a hot iron; Forbidding to marry, *and commanding* to abstain from meats, which God hath created to be received with thanksgiving of them which believe and know the truth." (1 Timothy 4:1-3)

Apostasy isn't something that happens overnight. Over an extended period of time a person's faith becomes eroded, weakened, damaged, then ultimately destroyed.

The loss of biblical truth has filtered down to all divine institutions – the family, government and the church.

Consider all the changes in church-life over the past few decades.

---

6   Steve W. Lemke (1951-), An address at Mid-America Baptist
     Theological Seminary, *Maintaining Baptist Distinctives Conference,*
     April 2005.

Churchless Christianity

We are now two or three generations into the idea that you can be a follower of Jesus without any connection to a church. Here is how one person sees it now. *"As I've matured spiritually, I realize that it's not about religion at all. It's not about the traditions of a particular religion. It's not about who dunks and who sprinkles. It's not about KJV or NIV. It's not about who drinks wine and who doesn't. It's not about who sings hymns and who sings contemporary music. Pews or chairs. Fancy buildings or the old Ace Hardware store. It's all about a relationship with our Lord and Saviour Jesus Christ! It's about us digging in the word and doing what it says. It's about spending time with Him and getting to know Him, and learning to listen when He speaks."*

Such a person isn't listening to God very well when it comes to all the Scriptures about church-life. From late in the gospels and throughout the book of Acts and beyond you don't find a single person who professed to be a Christian that did not have a church-life, with the possible exception of the thief on the cross (and he had a legitimate hang up).

"Non-church" is just a step closer toward "anti-church."

The Plague of Pragmatism

I agree with Southern Baptist pastor Mark Dever (1960-) who said, *"Today, many local churches are adrift in the shifting currents of pragmatism. They assume that the immediate felt-response of non-Christians is the key indicator of success. At the same time, Christianity is being rapidly disowned in the culture at large, as evangelism is characterized as intolerant and portions of biblical doctrine are classified as hate speech. In such antagonistic times, the felt needs of non-Christians can hardly be considered reliable gauges, and conforming to the culture will mean a loss of the Gospel itself.*

As long as quick numerical growth remains the primary indicator of church health, the truth will be compromised. Instead, churches must once again begin measuring success not in terms of numbers, but in terms of fidelity to the Scriptures. William Carey was faithful in India and Adoniram Judson persevered in Burma not because they met immediate success or advertised themselves as 'relevant.' Part of what it means to recover such tenacious faithfulness in our day is that churches must swim against the tide of pragmatism and seek to be faithful to all that God calls His church to be in Scripture. We must make faithfulness to God's Word our measure of success, including faithfulness to what God's Word says about how our churches should be structured and governed."[7]

No Baptist-Name Baptist Churches

A trend started in the early 1980's of congregations moving away from denominational identity. It has picked up steam in the following decades with some congregations dropping the denominational name while maintaining some relationships with their original denomination for its greater mission.

Among them are a large number of Baptist churches. Most of those deleting any reference to "Baptist" in their official name, affiliation, or website have sincerely held reasons. They say the "Baptist" name carries too much baggage. The argument is that removing the name "Baptist" makes a church more accessible to some who would shy away from the Baptist label. So, to be able to reach more people the name must go. Who doesn't want to reach more

7   Mark Dever (1960-), SBC Life, *The Church – A Display of God's Glory,* December 2010.

people? Who doesn't want to talk about Christ, rather than explaining away the negative perceptions of the people called Baptist? If Kentucky Fried Chicken can become the less offensive as "KFC" then why can't a church take a new brand? You may find some of the answers in the later chapters of this book.

One pastor who recently removed "Baptist" from his church name said, "I'm not dying on the hill of being 'Baptist'. But I will gladly lay down my life for the truth of the BIBLE."[8] Those are not mutually exclusive terms – Baptist and Bible. Baptists are Bible people and Bible people are Baptists. And, people before our times were willing to die for being "Baptist" because of the Bible.

In a recent search of the conservative *Southern Baptist of Texas Convention*, which has 2,300 churches in their organization, I found through their "Find a Church" link on their webpage that within 20 miles from where I live there are 173 affiliated churches. Seventy-four did not bear the name "Baptist," but did readily identify as "Bible," "Community," "Family," "Fellowship," and/or "Chapel."

If you follow this logic, churches would have to constantly check the local, national and global opinion polls and make the changes demanded by the consumer-minded potential church-goers. I suppose the church sign could be a large white-board with erasable markers to make the process easier.

Some Baptist churches are presuming our "Baptist" name is a non-essential. Where will this end?

---

8   Pastor Greg Locke (1976-) Changed the name of his church in
     Mt. Juliet, TN, from *Global Vision Baptist Church* to *Global Vision
     Bible Church* in 2011.

"Red-Letter" Christians and Churches

This is a modern, non-denominational movement which emphasizes the New Testament verses printed in red letters, the words attributed to Jesus. While many Christians throughout church history have defined themselves as emphasizing the teachings of Jesus, this modern movement believes Christians should be promoting biblical values such as peace, building strong families, the elimination of poverty, and other important social justice issues. They believe that these are the issues that Jesus spoke of directly, and therefore these issues should be political priorities. They believe other issues such as the question of homosexual rights and abortion are viewed as important but often over-emphasized by both liberals and conservatives.

The Church with No Name

This is no joke. There is a house church movement called "The Church with No Name." This denomination publishes nothing about itself, does not advertise itself (except in announcements of "Gospel Meetings"), does not seek publicity but rather avoids it, and, in many if not most cases, declines to give out information about itself to researchers. There are numerous web sites about the denomination, mostly by former members. The denomination itself hosts no public web site. They are a very secretive "Jesus only" sect and have flown under the radar for over a hundred years.

Megachurch Mania

Super-sized drinks and giant-screen TVs are no match for the modern megachurch. At one time megachurches were any congregation with attendance over 2,000. It is not uncommon now for these new mega monsters to have

20,000 plus at one location on any given weekend with multiple-services.

People are attracted to the stadium-size facilities that include large lobbies, food courts, coffee houses, book stores, sport facilities – the list is endless. When it comes to their gatherings, the services are professional productions led by dozens of paid staff whose specific job is to do church. Their ministries are a virtual Club Med: poetry workshops, creative writing, singles groups, job fairs, vocational training, music lessons, additional support-groups, and even auto repair clinics.

As one visitor admitted, "In some ways you can maintain a sense of anonymity if you want to. It's very non-threatening."

The down-side is what potentially happens to smaller churches that cannot compete. Randall Balmer (1954-), a professor of religion at Columbia University, compares some mega-churches with a giant chain store *"that comes into a town and puts all the little stores out of business."*[9]

Their sense of superiority and self-importance was shown by one megachurch pastor who declared in a sermon, *"If you don't go to a large church, you are so stinking selfish… and don't care about your kids."* He said kids need to go to a large church so *"they can make friends,"* and *"go off to college and make friends."*[10]

Multiple Services

To maximize the use of their facilities and to expand their outreach, many churches offer multiple gatherings for their church, sometimes offering different styles of worship

---

9   Randall Balmer (1954-), *More Americans Flock to Mega-Churches*, www.abcnews.go.com/US/story?id=93111.

10   Andy Stanley (1958-), North Point Church in Atlanta, Sermon February 28, 2016.

(usually called traditional and contemporary). Many even have a Saturday night service for those who cannot or will not attend on Sunday.

There may be some latitude about when and where a church chooses to gather, but there are questions to answer. Is collective worship and fellowship of a church required? The Greek word for "church" is *ekklesia*, which denotes a "gathering of baptized believers in one place at one time" (1 Corinthians 14:23). The church is seen in scripture as a "flock" (Acts 20:28), a "building" (Ephesians 2:19-22), a "body" (1 Corinthians 12:14-27) and a "household" (Ephesians 2:19).

And what about a weekly Saturday meeting of the church? That does not follow the pattern of New Testament churches (Acts 20:7; 1 Corinthians 16:2; Revelation 1:10).

The innovation of multiple services was first introduced by Roman Catholics as early Mass.

Many churches affirm that as long as you stay with the *message* of the gospel that has been clearly defined in scripture, people are free to create new *methods* to accommodate the current culture. What people are failing to understand is every decision has a theological implication.

Satellite Campuses Craze

Imagine a gathering with a large video-screen viewing a live service originating in another location across town or in another state or even in another country. Welcome to the modern world of satellite campuses. The rough and tough circuit-riding preacher of the 1800's is now a celebrity, pretty-boy, closed-circuit, live-streamed, video-talker in skinny jeans.

Even if the motive is to reach more people, the end does

not justify the means because the end doesn't square with the "gatheredness" of what it means to be a church. And furthermore, the video multi-site gatherings elevate a man who is declared to be a better preacher or presenter than some less capable person on staff. It all has the distinct smell of idolatry, self-promotion and pride.

Southern Baptist pastor Bob Pearle (1953-) weighed in on this new phenomenon. *"This trend tends to franchise the church like a fast-food restaurant chain, placing one church over other churches. What benefit exists to the mother church of having all these satellite campuses except possibly to gratify the ego of the senior pastor and enhance his prestige in the world? The Free Church movement was based on the biblical model found in the book of Acts where an autonomous church was planted, a pastor was chosen, and the church set free to spread the gospel. What we are witnessing today with the connectionism of satellite campuses is what led to the rise of episcopacy and ultimately the papacy."*[11]

Multiple Bible Translations

When I began my ministry you had the choice of two Bibles – the King James Version (1611) or the Revised Standard Version (1952), excluding the Catholic Douay-Rheims (1609 translated from the Latin Vulgate into English). Now there is a flood of modern Bible translation: ASV, RSV, NASB, NEB, REB, TEV, GNB, NRSV, NASBU, NCV, NET, NIV, NKJV, NWJV, NWT, ICV, RV, AB, JB, NAB, NJB, MLB, NIRV, CEV, HCSB, ESV, and more. While all the modern translations generally claim to be a "Standard" Bible there has not been a real standard since the King James Version.

---

11   Bob Pearle (1953-), *The Vanishing Church*, p. 26.

Most publishers now have their own copyrighted modern translation for monetary profits. While they are touted as the most up-to-date, accurate work from ancient manuscripts, biblical doctrine is often seriously affected by many of them. The King James Version is the only translation without a copyright and most major publishers do not print them for purchase.

Bible translations either move us further into the truth or further away from the truth. Bible translations are not neutral when it comes to their influence.

These Bible translations are available as family Bibles, study Bibles, pocket Bibles, little Bibles, big Bibles, paperback Bibles, leather-clad Bibles, white or pink or blue or black Bibles. The other day I saw an advertisement for – wait for it – a *Duct-Tape Bible.* I guess you could call it, *A Bible for Bubba.* Added to these printed Bibles, we can now carry with us digital Bibles on our mobile devices. There is no shortage of spiritual food for English speaking people in the Western world. 40 million copies are sold every year, plus all the international sales.

All these different Bibles have not resulted in a greater knowledge among modern Christians. Studies show the current generation is the least literate when it comes to the Bible. More Bibles actually has not resulted in stronger, but weaker Christians. Our knowledge of the Bible is less than any generation before us. Is it fair to say this is the result of too many translations? The saying goes, "A man that has two watches never really knows what time it is."

The Confirmation of Cults

Non-0rthodox groups who imagined themselves as the restoration of true Christianity were at one time recognized for what they were – cults. Over time they have developed a more positive image and they are being recognized and received as main-line religious groups. They are now seen as another choice for someone seeking a spiritual experience. Mormons, after 180 years, are viewed as mainstream and no longer relegated to some forsaken desert. Even a non-Christian cult like Scientology has an acceptable status because celebrities and movie stars are found among its membership.

The Ecumenical Surge Continues

The modern ecumenical movement had its roots in a conference in Edinburgh, Scotland in 1910. It was initiated to promote a unified message of the gospel of Jesus Christ in foreign countries. It morphed eventually into the World Council of Churches. Any theological emphasis has shifted more toward social action, humanitarian relief, and social justice issues.

An example of the ecumenical reach occurred in June 2016 at the annual meeting in Portland, Oregon of the Presbyterian Church, USA. Wajidi Said, co-founder of the Muslim Education Trust, led the attendees in the General Assembly meeting in a Muslim prayer. *"Allah bless us and bless our families and bless our Lord. Lead us on the straight path— the path of all prophets: Abraham, Ishmael, Isaac, Moses, Jesus, and Muhammad."*

There is an unquestioned move toward the "One World Church," as predicted in the Bible. The ecumenical movement is no longer just a Christian conglomeration, but includes all faith systems from all nations – Islam, Buddhism, Hinduism, and every kind of cult and ism.

Proliferation of Parachurch Organizations

Bible Societies, student ministries, for-profit publishers, benevolent ministries, radio programs, prison ministries, camps and conference centers, recreational ministries, missionary organizations, mission boards and clearing houses have taken the church-world by storm as a supposed "arm of the church."

Baptists rejoice over the people saved by the preaching of the gospel, regardless of where they hear it (Philippians 1:15-18), but when it comes to "doing church" we should be fully committed to the New Testament as our only guide. What some have not considered is that these non-church organizations take people and money that should be devoted to God's churches – the only organization Jesus founded – and use them to further their vision.

More than thirty-five years ago, W. A. Criswell (1902-2002) offered his viewpoint on parachurch organizations.

- There is no real authority for such groups in the New testament.
- Most often they do not assist the church significantly.
- The church by its very nature is committed to minister to people from all races, cultures, economic potentials, and possibilities. Special interest groups are out of place in the church.
- Energies siphoned away from the local church and expended in parachurch organizations would be employed more effectively through the local church, the avenue ordained by God for the work of God.[12]

www.Virtual Church

A 21st century phenomena is the virtual world of church.

---

12   W.A. Criswell (1909-2002), *The Doctrine of the* Church, p. 23.

Some people are getting their church fix in their home or office before a computer screen.

In January 2017, a California congregation opened the first 24-7, 365 virtual reality church in 3D. Its purpose is "to meet the needs of people in marginalized groups seeking a place of faith that is genuinely welcoming of everyone." It has an online virtual campus, complete with 3D buildings — renderings from a worship space to residential apartments — which users can wander around through their avatar — a 3D graphical representation of a person. A member of the host church said, "My ministry here is radical hospitality. By the Grace of God, I strive to make other avatars who come to this simulation feel welcomed and aware that they are deeply loved by God, regardless of their appearance and experience in both (the virtual world and real world)."

They virtually "gather" and chat back and forth by typing or speaking into their computer microphone, they "tithe" through PayPal or some other form of e-giving, and they "fellowship" through Facebook.

What a wacky, weird world!

Could anyone possibly see this coming? Actually, someone did. It was a relatively unknown man, Dr. R. K. Maiden (1858-1939), co-founder in 1896 of *The Word & Way* Baptist publication. More than seventy-five years ago he warned, *"I have no disposition to exaggerate current conditions and trends, but am deeply concerned. Our Baptist Zion is either unaware of the menace of 'ecclesiological liberalism' or else supinely (flatly) indifferent. The chief concern so far shown among us seems to be with 'theological liberalism.' This, too, is a menace of prodigious proportions. But this giant heresy is being recognized for what it is and is being courageously opposed and exposed, while little is being said or done in defense of New*

Testament ecclesiology – the New Testament Church. I do not hesitate to go on record as firmly holding the belief that Baptists have more to fear from 'ecclesiological liberalism' than from 'theological liberalism.' If, as true Baptists believe, Baptists have a heaven-given mission 'in' the world and a message 'for' the world, and would faithfully perform their mission and deliver their message, at all cost they must maintain their separateness, loyalty, and integrity."[13]

That is the current problem – ecclesiological liberalism. For those not into theological terminology, "ecclesiology" is the doctrine of the church. While many churches and pastors have alertly kept the front door guarded and locked against *theological liberalism,* the back door has been left unlocked and open to the intrusion of *ecclesiological liberalism* where anything and everything goes.

The Delusion of Degrees

Some current self-appointed experts are suggesting that Christians should prioritize certain doctrines, identifying them with various degrees of importance on some kind of descending scale.

For more than ten years I have served as a volunteer chaplain at a local hospital. I have found the busiest and craziest place in the world is the Emergency Room on the weekend. It would be utter chaos if they did not follow a protocol they refer to as "triage," which comes from a French word (trier) meaning "to sort." The idea of Emergency Room Triage is to figure out the ones with the most urgent need. Does the person who comes in under full cardiac arrest get the same treatment as the one with a broken arm? Trained personnel evaluate the situation and treatment is ordered

---

13   R. K. Maiden (1858-1939), *Re-Thinking Baptist* Doctrine, p. 157.

accordingly.

Some suggest that we follow a similar triage when it comes to biblical truth.

- First level: Salvation truth: Who Jesus is and what He came to do.
- Second level: Areas where there are debatable disagreements: church-life, baptism, communion, women preachers, etc.
- Third level: Areas of differing interpretations, second coming, separation, etc.

This serves as an interesting illustration, but truth isn't always that easy to compartmentalize. Who's to say if we should move church-truth to a second level, since **"the church is the pillar and ground of the truth"** (1 Timothy 3:15). Churches in the New Testament were made up of those who professed personal salvation, this would then merge first and second level truths together. Christians and God's churches are charged to **"earnestly contend for the faith which was once delivered to the saints"** (Jude 3). Truth is often like the threads of a fabric, when you tear one area, another area is damaged and compromised. No one would doubt the supreme importance of Christ's work on the cross, but how could Christ's work that He continues today in His churches be thought to be of lesser importance? Mark Dever (1960-) warns, *"A distorted church usually coincides with a distorted gospel. Whether it leads to such distortions or results from them, serious departures from the Bible's teaching about the church normally signify other, more central misunderstandings about the Christian faith."*[14]

A church posted on its website that they had eight

---

14   Mark Dever (1960-), *The Church – The Gospel Made Visible*, p. x.

essential beliefs: God, Jesus Christ, the Holy Spirit, the Bible, Humanity, Salvation, Eternity. This was followed by a very neat and tidy statement, "In these essential beliefs we experience unity; in the beliefs we consider 'non-essential', we have liberty; and in all our beliefs we show charity."

Most of us would confess we struggle to separate beliefs into the "non-essential" category. The delusion is that we are able to assign something as either essential or non-essential. Just because something is not salvation-truth does not mean it's not important. We should regard the church as important because of its importance to Christ. Christ founded the church (Matthew 16:18). Christ loved the church and gave Himself for it (Ephesians 5:25). Christ purchased the church with His own blood (Acts 20:28). Christ commissioned the church to preach the gospel and promised to be with her to the end of the world (Matthew 28:18-20).

"That believer's baptism and other distinctives have no status as elements of saving faith does not render such elements as optional or nonessential in any sense. They still exist as a part of God's positive commands for the formation and order of the church."[15]

The Distancing from Distinctives

Baptist historian, Jack Hoad, says, *"Despite their history of faithfulness, there are many Baptists today who are ready to throw aside their heritage as a worn out garment, no longer useful to the owner."*[16]

There are pastors who make an attempt at humor by saying they are "recovering Baptists." That is not the least bit funny to me. Too much blood was shed by our spiritual

15   Tom Nettles (1946-), *Why I Am a Baptist*, p. 13.
16   Jack Hoad, *The Baptist*, p. 2.

ancestors to make such a trivial statement. Steven J. Lawson
(1951-) observed, *"The preaching of the cross is foolishness not
only to the world but also to the contemporary church."*[17] That
was stated more than fifteen years ago. What would he say
today?

Southern Baptist pastor and distinguished seminary
president, John A. Broadus (1827-1895) wrote a booklet in
1881 he entitled, *The Duty of Baptists to Teach Their Distinctive
Views.*[18] Broadus listed only the following four distinctives.

1.   We hold that the Bible alone is a religious authority;
     and in regard to Christian institutions the direct
     authority is of course the New Testament.
2.   We hold that a Christian Church ought to consist
     only of persons making a credible profession of
     conversion, of faith in Christ.
3.   We hold that the officers, government, and
     ceremonies of a Christian society, or church, ought
     to be such, and such only, as the New Testament
     directs.
4.   We hold that these societies called churches were
     designed as shown in the New Testament, to be
     independent.

My, how different things are today.

Why would formerly identified Baptist pastors and
churches be distancing themselves from the "Baptist" name?
How could removing the name more closely identify them
with the New Testament? Several years back the *Fort Worth
Star Telegram* ran an article entitled, *Church in Disguise*, that
carried the subtitle, "Some Baptist congregations are filling

---

17   Steven J. Lawson (1951-), *Bibliotheca Sacra 158* April-June 2001.
18   John A Broadus (1827-1895), *The Duty of Baptists to Teach Their
     Distinctive Views.*

up pews by cloaking their denominational identity." One pastor confessed, "We don't play up our Baptist name."[19]

Congregations are not dropping the name "Baptist" because it has been stained by some of its users; rather so they can be more accepted and less offensive. It would be too much for some to bear any shame for being a "Baptist."

Forty years ago, I became best friends with a World War II Purple Heart recipient. He had lost an eye in combat as a Marine which made him less than attractive with that glass eye always staring back at you. But this war hero had my deepest respect and friendship as few men have. We golfed together (I was witness to his hole-in-one, which I have yet to achieve), vacationed together, printed my first book *Now That You've Believed* together, prayed together, studied together and preached together. I was with him in his final days on this earth as he succumbed to pancreatic cancer. And yes, I preached his funeral for his precious widow. I was never embarrassed to call him my friend because of his unique appearance. His wound and injury were part of his special attraction.

It is strange to me that some who say they are Baptists seem embarrassed by our unsightliness. The Apostle Paul received the same kind of treatment from the Galatians (Galatians 4:15-16) and the Corinthians (2 Corinthians 12:15).

The Determination to be Different

Some do not know better because they were raised apart from any sound teaching. Others know better, but for their own reasons have given up their biblical heritage. And there are some of us who know better and are determined to

---

19   Jim Jones, *Fort Worth Star-Telegram*, January 16, 1999.

remain faithful.

You may be wondering about the trends just mentioned. "What's wrong with changes in the way we do church?" The answer is, "Nothing, provided what is done squares with Scripture."

The desire to reach the world with the gospel has been turned into a mad dash to find what the unsaved world likes and do that, and to see what the saved in the church will tolerate. If they want more casual, and less formal – no problem. If they want less preaching, and more affirming – no problem. If they want less responsibility, and more freedom – no problem. But there is one problem. That problem is the unsaved and unchurched end up dictating the nature and order of the church.

There is certainly nothing wrong with having church buildings with air-conditioning, pleasant lighting, and sound and video systems. What is wrong is to turn church ministry into a business and the worship service into a well-produced entertainment event.

A church's purpose is simple: the Glorification of God (Ephesians 3:21).

A church's priority is staggering: the Great Commission (Matthew 28:18-20; Acts 1:8).

A church's program is seeable: the Great Commandment (John 13:34-35).

A church's parameter is stated: the Grand will of God (Romans 12:2).

God's work must be done God's way with God's resources by God's people for God's glory to receive God's approval.

CHAPTER 2

The Glorious Beginning of the
Churches of the New Testament

At the early age of twelve Jesus made a remarkable statement in the form of a question. It was Jesus' only recorded words before He began His public ministry at the age of thirty. This question is preserved for us in Luke 2:49. Jesus asked, **"...wist** (know) **ye not that I must be about my Father's business?"** In this question are clear statements regarding His...

- *Deity.* Jesus' first recorded words are a declaration of His Sonship. "My Father" was a clear statement of Jesus' knowledge of His eternal deity.
- *Duty* is seen in the word "must." Already at the age of twelve, Jesus had assumed the burden of His purpose and mission.
- *Design.* The weight-bearing words in Jesus' question are "My Father's business." What was the Father's business for Jesus? What would be the Father's eternal design for Jesus? What was Jesus thinking of; not just at age twelve, but through his entire life on this earth? Robert Coleman, in his classic *The Master Plan of Evangelism*, says, *"There was nothing haphazard about His life – no wasted energy, not an idle word. He was on business for God (Luke 2:49). He lived, He died, and He rose again according to schedule. Like a general plotting His course of battle, the Son of God calculated to win. He could not afford to take a chance. Weighing every alternative and variable factor in human experience, He conceived a*

plan that would not fail."[1]

So, what did that plan involve? By reading the gospels it is fair to conclude that Jesus had two primary things He would accomplish while He was on this earth. They would be the sum of the Father's business. It was His daily motivation for the thirty-three years of His life and His three-and-a-half year earthly ministry. Every action, every deed, every sermon, every prayer, every step would in some way contribute to the accomplishment of the Father's business. Not for one moment did Jesus lose sight of these two overriding assignments.

The Father's Business for Jesus was His Death

Jesus' death, not life, was His mission. It would forever be the most important event in history. Jerry Bridges (1926-2016) says, *"The gospel is not only the most important message in all of history; it is the only essential message in all of history."*[2]

His was no ordinary death because Jesus was no ordinary man. He was the God-Man, God come to earth in a human body without a sin nature. Jesus' death would be the death of the cross, the shedding of His precious and pure blood, the pouring out of His life. For Jesus, the Father's business was His own death on the cross. F. J. Huegel (1889-1971) says, *"It was for this that the only-begotten of the Father had come. All else was secondary."*[3]

The author of the famous hymn, *Amazing Grace*, was John Newton. In his old age his memory began to fail him, yet in his aged condition Newton said, *"Although my memory*

1   Robert Coleman (1928-), *The Master Plan of Evangelism*, p. 18.
2   Jerry Bridges (1929-2016), *The Discipline of Grace*, p. 46.
3   F. J. Huegel (1889-1971), *The Cross Through the Scriptures*, p. 71.

is fading I remember two things very clearly. I am a great sinner and Christ is a great Saviour." And what a Saviour He is!

The Father's Business for Jesus was the Development of His Disciples

From the gospels, we can draw a very clear second conclusion: Jesus was in the disciple-making business. Isn't it strange – we say we love Jesus and are in obedience to Him, yet we don't seem to value what He valued. How can we say we claim to be following Jesus, when our way of living is counter to His model?

The word "disciple" means both a "learner" and a "follower."

After praying all night, Jesus **"called unto him his disciples: and of them he chose twelve, whom also he named apostles"** (Luke 6:13). Mark's gospel adds, **"And he ordained twelve, that they should be with him…"** (Mark 3:14). When you look at the list of the disciples who became apostles (which means "sent ones") there was not a super-star among them. They were common men called by an uncommon Lord.

Think about it – the natural result of Jesus being occupied with His death was because it was His death that would give life to those who trusted and followed Him. It wasn't dying for the sake of dying. It was dying for the souls of people. It was dying for His disciples. It was dying for us.

To all of this "disciple talk" most Christians are willing to give their hardy "Amen!" But before getting too far down that road, let's tap the brakes and slow down.

It's great to endorse discipleship in general as something about which Jesus was constantly thinking. But we need to bring this into clearer focus. Jesus was not just preparing the apostles as men and as disciples. Jesus was preparing them as His church. When Jesus called the twelve disciples and ordained them as apostles 1 Corinthians 12:28 tells us they were the first to be set in the church by God.

The word "church" first appears in the New Testament from the lips of Jesus. They are recorded in Matthew 16 in a conversation with His apostles.

"When Jesus came into the coasts of Caesarea Philippi, he asked his disciples, saying, Whom do men say that I the Son of man am? And they said, Some *say that thou art* John the Baptist: some, Elias; and others, Jeremias, or one of the prophets. He saith unto them, But whom say ye that I am? And Simon Peter answered and said, Thou art the Christ, the Son of the living God. And Jesus answered and said unto him, Blessed art thou, Simon Barjona: for flesh and blood hath not revealed *it* unto thee, but my Father which is in heaven. And I say also unto thee, That thou art Peter, and upon this rock I will build my church; and the gates of hell shall not prevail against it" (Matthew 16:13-18).

From this first mention of the "church" in the Bible we can learn the following.

First, the "I" statement established who was the founder and the foundation of the first church – Jesus Christ. This "I" is the great "I AM," the eternal God who came to the earth in human flesh. "I" is a word about a Person.

Second, the "will" statement is not just a word that has future implications, but a word of divine determination. "Will" is a word of promise.

Third, the "build" statement suggests His initial and on-going work. "Build" is a word of procedure. The church didn't just happen; Jesus Christ carried out a divine plan to build it.

Fourth, the "my" statement declares ownership and authority. "My" is a word of possession.

Fifth, the "church" statement is the word that will determine the biblically correct understanding of what a church is. When the Apostle Matthew recorded the word for Jesus' "church" it was *ecclesia.* It is a compound word, *ek*, meaning "out of," and *kaleo*, meaning "to call." Together the "church" was seen as the "called out" ones. They were called out by God and to God. They were called out from the world. They were called to associate and assemble with other believers. "Church" is a word of purpose.

Sixth, the phrase "and the gates of hell" were a prediction of evil forces that would stand to oppose and hinder the church. These words underscored an evil and prevailing power that is encountered by the church.

Seventh, the phrase "shall not prevail against it" are words assuring the perpetuity of the church.

The Origin of the New Testament Church is Divine, not Human

Far beyond a mere man-made organization, the church of the New Testament was divine in its origin.

- It had a *divine Architect* who planned it. It was the "church of the living God" (1 Timothy 3:15).
- It had a *divine Builder* who constructed it. Jesus said, "I will build my church" (Matthew 16:18).
- It had a *divine Purchaser* who bought it. Christ purchased it with "his own blood" (Acts 20:28).
- It had a *divine Commissioner* who sent it. Christ gave all authority to His church to preach, baptize and teach (Matthew 28:19-20).

- It has a *divine Spirit* who empowered it (Acts 1:8; 2:1-4).
- It has *divine Truth* to sustain it. It was and still is "the pillar and ground of the truth" (1 Timothy 3:15).

The Lord's Church is not an Old Testament Institution, but a New Testament Institution

While in Acts 7:38 Stephen spoke of Moses and "the church in the wilderness," we are not to understand this was in any sense a church like we see in the New Testament. Rather "the church in the wilderness" was the assembly of Jews that made up the nation of Israel during their wanderings in the wilderness. Paul stated in Ephesians 3 that the mystery of the New Testament church **"from the beginning of the world hath been hid in God...is now revealed unto his holy apostles and prophets by the Spirit; That the Gentiles should be fellowheirs, and of the same body..."** (Ephesians 3:9, 5-6).

The Church was Founded During Christ's Ministry, not on the Day of Pentecost

Christ founded the church on the day when he called the Twelve Apostles and ordained them (Mark 3:13-19; Luke 6:12-17). 1 Corinthians 12:28 says the apostles were the first to be set in the church by God. **"God hath set some in the church, first apostles..."**

It is commonly believed among most Protestants that the church was founded on the Day of Pentecost by the baptism of the Holy Spirit, and that every believer now becomes a member of the universal church they call "the body of Christ." The problem with that thinking is there is not agreement on who constitutes this universal church.

W. A. Criswell (1909-2002) taught, *"The New Testament speaks also of the church as the body of Christ which includes all of the redeemed of all ages."*[4] Those who hold this view have an interesting and substantial quandary. When were the redeemed of the ages before Pentecost baptized into the body of Christ? Was it retroactive? Charles R. Ryrie (1925-2016) says the body of Christ *"is that spiritual organism of which Christ is the Head, and is composed of all regenerate people from Pentecost to the rapture."*[5] C. I. Scofield (1843-1921) called the universal church *"the true church."*[6]

Was the church founded on the Day of Pentecost? It doesn't seem so.

- What are we to make of Jesus' promise in Matthew 16:18, where He said, "I will build my church"? While the word "will" could be understood as future, the word "my" connects it with Christ.
- They had the "gospel" before the day of Pentecost (Mark 1:1).
- John the Baptist had prepared the material through his baptism of the disciples who were set aside as apostles by Jesus (Acts 1:21-22).
- What did Christ mean when He said, "Tell it unto the church" in Matthew 18:17 if there was no church before which matters of discipline could be brought?
- Was not the church in existence in the upper room when Jesus "took bread, and blessed it, and brake it, and gave it to the disciples" (Matthew 26:26).
- Hebrews 2:12 says Christ sang in the church, which clearly refers to Jesus singing with the apostles at the conclusion of the institution of the Lord's Supper

4   W.A. Criswell (1909-2002), *The Doctrine of the Church*, p. 11.
5   Charles R Ryrie (1925-2016), *Ryrie Study Bible*, p. 1843.
6   C.I. Scofield (1843-1921), *Scofield Reference Bible*, p. 1249.

(Matthew 26:30).

- The Great Commission was given before Pentecost (Matthew 28:19-20). This commission was not given to the apostles as men, but to Christ's church. Jesus promised to be with them (as the church) to the end of the world (age).

- Before Pentecost, church business was conducted to replace Judas (Acts 1:15-26). It is fair to note that a treasurer is not a scriptural office and a business meeting is not a scriptural requirement for a New Testament church, but it seems they were following reasonable order.

- On the Day of Pentecost, people who believed and were baptized were "added" to the church that already existed (Acts 2:41). How do you "add" to something that does not exist?

Baptists have believed it is more biblically consistent to declare that Christ personally founded His church.

"It is certainly true that Christ in His own personal ministry established His church." L. R. Scarborough (1870-1945)[7]

"Out of the material prepared by John the Baptist, Jesus organized and founded His church during the days of His personal ministry here on the earth." Roy Mason (1894-1978)[8]

"The church whose charter is not issued by Christ, and whose credentials are not in Christ's handwriting, must, sooner or later, see the handwriting on the wall. Every man-made church must share the fate of man, and since it has been appointed unto all men once to die, so shall it be with the works of their hands." J. W. Porter (1863-1937)[9]

---

7   Roy Mason (1894-1978), *The Church That Jesus Built*, pp. 24-25.
8   Ibid, p. 24.
9   J.W. Porter (1863-1937), *The Baptist Debt to the World*, p. 40.

God the Father Envisioned the church
God the Son Equipped the church
God the Spirit Empowered the church

The Nature of the New Testament Church is Local and Visible, not Universal and Invisible

As we have already seen, the Greek word *ecclesia,* translated "church" in the King James Version of the Bible, means a "called out assembly." The following is a list of the 115 times the word "church" or "churches" occurs in the King James New Testament, translating the Greek word *ecclesia.*

- The first is Matthew 16:18.
- The second and third are in Matthew 18:17(2).
- Acts twenty-three times (2:47; 5:11; 7:38; 8:1, 3; 9:31; 11:22, 26; 12:1, 5; 13:1; 14:23, 27; 15:3, 4, 22, 41; 16:5; 18:22; 19:39, 41; 20:17, 28).
- Romans five times (16:1, 4, 5, 16, 23).
- 1 Corinthians twenty-two times (1:2; 4:17; 6:4; 7:17; 10:32; 11:16, 18, 22; 12:28; 14:4, 5, 12, 19, 23, 28, 33, 34, 35; 15:9; 16:1, 19[2]).
- 2 Corinthians nine times (1:1; 8:1, 18, 19, 23, 24; 11:8, 28; 12:13).
- Galatians three times (1:2, 13, 22).
- Ephesians nine times (1:22; 3:10, 21; 5:23, 24, 25, 27, 29, 32).
- Philippians two times (3:6; 4:15).
- Colossians four times (1:18, 24; 4:15, 16).
- 1 Thessalonians two times (1:1; 2:14).
- 2 Thessalonians two times (1:1, 4).
- 1 Timothy three times (3:5, 15; 5:16).
- Philemon one time (1:2).

- Hebrews two times (2:12; 12:23 future assembly localized in heaven).
- James one time (5:14...italicized..."church" was added by the KJV translators).
- 1 Peter one time (5:13).
- 3 John three times (1:6, 9, 10).
- Revelation twenty times (1:4, 11, 20[2]; 2:1, 7, 8, 11, 12, 17, 18, 23, 29; 3:1, 6, 7, 13, 14, 22; 22:16).

Of these 115 times, there are five ways "ecclesia" is used.
- "Ecclesia" was used 1 time to refer to the assembled nation of Israel, "the church in the wilderness," as it is called in Acts 7:38.
- "Ecclesia" was used 2 times of a civil assembly that administrated the affairs of the city of Ephesus (Acts 19:39, 41). (Note: In Acts 19:37 it is not "ecclesia" but "hierosulos" referring to pagan temples.)
- "Ecclesia" was used 98 times to refer to a local, visible congregation.
- "Ecclesia" was used 11 times in a generic, non-specific, institutional sense, with no special congregation in mind, but not viewed as universal or invisible. "When the 'church' (ecclesia) is used of an institution, it does not mean one big universal church but an institution made up of individual churches. When we speak of 'the home' or 'the school' we do not mean one big universal home or school. Nor is there one big church."[10]
- "Ecclesia" was used 2 times in a prophetic, future assembly (Ephesians 5:27; Hebrews 12:23).

10   Joe T. Odle (1909-1980), *Church Member's Handbook*, p. 14.

Buell H. Kazee (1900-1976), professor at Lexington Baptist College, Lexington, Kentucky states, *"ECCLESIA was a Greek word that would have been understood by all who used this universal language in the days of the apostles as meaning a visible assembly even after it had acquired a Christian significance. Christianity did not change the meaning of the word but adopted it as a fit description of its divine institution."*[11] *"In Christ's day the Greek term ECCLESIA was commonly used as we use the term ASSEMBLY today. When Christ applied this term to HIS assembly, He in no way changed the ordinary Greek usage…To speak of an invisible assembly which cannot assemble, is a contradiction of terms, and obscures what Christ intended for us to understand by His deliberate choice of the term ECCLESIA."*[12]

The Church is Local and Visible

A church in New Testament times was an assembly of baptized believers in a physical location who were carrying out God's work on the earth.

Most Protestants teach that the church is both universal (catholic) and local; that it is both invisible and visible. The reason the theory of a universal church is so popular is *"it demands nothing of any one, antagonizes no one, and accomplishes nothing…while the local church, which had done all the work, gets only scorn and disrespect."*[13]

The first church Jesus built became known in the book of Acts as the church (assembly) at Jerusalem. Afterwards, other churches were founded in other locations and were

11   Buell H. Kazee (1900-1976), *The Church and the Ordinances*, p. 16.
12   Willard A. Ramsey (1931-2011), *The Nature of the New Testament Church on Earth*, p. 4.
13   Davis W. Huckabee (1934-), *The Origin and Nature of the Church*, p. 5.

known generally by their cities or region—the church at Corinth, the church at Ephesus, the churches of Galatia, etc.

Dr. B. Gray Allison (1924-), Founder and President Emeritus of Mid-America Baptist Theological Seminary, concludes, "*The ecclesia is a local church. This is what Christ meant when He used the word. Would the apostles have been able to understand any other meaning? What other kind can minister the Word to lost persons as well as minister to the physical needs of poor people and those who are ill? What other kind can preach the Gospel? The New Testament churches were independent, but helpful to other churches. (see 2 Corinthians 8:1-7).*"[14]

Throughout this book I would have preferred to avoid using the term "the local church." Among true Baptists it is only used for clarification, while it is used by others to imply there is another kind of church. To say "local church" is like saying "widow woman," "free gift," "past history," "false pretense," "added bonus" – all redundancies. The only kind of churches in the New Testament were local. Throughout this book, the word "church" is used to indicate an assembly of baptized believers in Christ united together in a single location for worship, fellowship and ministry. Every congregation in the New Testament was a complete, autonomous "body of Christ" in their locale (1 Corinthians 12:27).

The Church is not Universal and Invisible

Earl D. Radmacher (1931-) describes in his book, *The Nature of the Church*, the development of the universal, invisible church doctrine. "*During the first four centuries there gradually developed a trend toward external unity.*" One of the reasons for this trend was "*the development of the ecumenical*

---

14   B. Gray Allison (1924-), *The Journal, Vol 4.,* Ecclesiology, 2017.

domination. It was inevitable that the bishops of the great cities should gain preeminence in influence and prestige because the churches in smaller towns and villages turned to them for advice. This resulted in the metropolitan bishop. Likewise, it was inevitable that bishops from the greatest and most ancient churches would have influence over the others. Thus, the pattern of an episcopacy for the whole (or universal) church was developing. Hand in hand with this growth of the episcopacy was the blossoming of the universal consciousness and practical disappearance of the concept of the local congregation as related to Christ." Man's doctrine of a universal church replaced God's doctrine of the local church. Of course, restructuring local churches into a universal hierarchy required that the smaller churches forsake their autonomy. Churches became dependent on notable bishops and churches and less dependent on the Holy Spirit for guidance. Jesus Christ was replaced as the head of local churches by the influential men (bishops) of the new universal church, and churches came under the governing control of men. Radmacher points out that eventually *"the local churches were no longer conceived of as separate units, but as part of the universal church. They were regarded as true churches as long as they were loyal to the Catholic church as a whole."*[15]

Bob Pearle (1953-) answers the questions, *"Why all the debate about the distinction between the universal and local church? Why spend so much time on the etymology of "ekklesia" and its uses in the New Testament? The reason is simple. Misunderstanding the New Testament concept of the church diminishes the importance of the local church to the individual believer. When the local church is trumped by the universal*

---

15   Earl D. Radmacher (1931-), *The Nature of the Church*, pp. 40, 123, 342, quoted from Patrick R. Briney (1956-), *The Local, Visible Church*, p. 14.

*church, personal accountability is minimized, Christian growth
is stunted, and practically, the local church vanishes. People
move from church to church to 'bless' each congregation with
their 'gifts' and insights only to become spiritual pygmies. The
work of God in this world is done primarily through the local
congregations. That is God's plan."*[16]

The famed pastor of Bellevue Baptist Church, in Memphis
TN, Dr. R. G. Lee (1886-1978), was once approached by a
woman who wanted to sing in the church's choir. When Dr.
Lee asked about her church membership she said she was a
member of the invisible church. The pastor replied, "Fine,
then go sing in their choir."

B. H. Carroll (1843-1914), founding President of the
Southwestern Baptist Theological Seminary, wrote, *"The
whole of the modern Baptist idea of a now existent 'universal,
invisible church' was borrowed from Pedo-baptist* (those who
advocate or practice infant sprinkling, jdl) *confessions of
faith in the Reformation times, and the Pedo-baptists devised it
to offset the equally erroneous idea of the Romanist 'universal
visible church'. We need to be well indoctrinated on this point,
because the error is not harmless. It is used to depreciate Christ's
earth-church, the pillar and ground of the truth."*[17]

The supposed invisibility of the church does not
harmonize with the metaphors used of the church: a flock, an
assembly, a building, a bride. These terms demand visibility
for understanding and meaning.

C.I. Scofield (1843-1921), in his well-used Reference
Bible, calls the universal-invisible church the *"true church."*[18]
Yet, in his notes on Matthew 16:18 he states that an accurate

16   Bob Pearle (1953-), *The Vanishing Church*, pp. 48-49.
17   B.H. Carroll (1843-1914), *An Interpretation of the English Bible,
     Colossians, Ephesians and Hebrews*, p. 164.
18   C.I. Scofield (1843-1921), *Scofield Reference* Bible, p. 1249.

definition of the word *ecclesia* is *"an assembly of called out ones. The word is used of an assembly; the word implies no more ... "*[19]

　　Willard A. Ramsey (1931-2011) points out in his book, *The Nature of the Church on Earth,* the confusion that is created when one splits the *one* church Christ established (Matthew 16:18) into *two* separate and distinct kinds of churches – the "universal/invisible" and the "local." It creates two diametrically opposed views of the nature of the church.

The Scriptural Church	*The Invisible Church*
1. Visible, definite, localized	1. Invisible, indefinite
2. Organized	2. No organization
3. Officers	3. No officers
4. Unity	4. Schism
5. Functional	5. Not functional
6. Commissioned	6. Not commissioned
7. Ordinances	7. No ordinances
8. Discipline	8. No discipline
9. Pillar and ground of the truth	9. Every wind of doctrine
10. Is an assembly	10. Has never assembled
11. Cares for and edifies saints	11. Saints drift without direction
12. Maintains sound doctrine	12. No doctrine-promotes ecumenicalism[20]

　　Protestant-influenced Bible teachers do spiritual gymnastics jumping between the universal-invisible church and the local-visible church when it suits their needs. On one hand, they will speak of the body of Christ in which all believers are united and then talk about being together in close, coordinated, conscious relationship with all other members. A universal, invisible body is a contradiction of terms.

19　Ibid, p. 1021.
20　Willard A. Ramsey (1931-2011), *The Nature of the Church on Earth,* pp. 14-15.

The Southern Baptist 1925 *Baptist Faith and Message,*
which is largely based on the *New Hampshire Confession
of Faith* written in 1833, does not even mention or
acknowledge a universal-invisible church. It was not until
1963 that the *Southern Baptist Confession of Faith* added "the
church is the body of Christ which includes all the redeemed
of all the ages." It's principle architect, Herschel H. Hobbs
(1907-1995), admitted this was *"the first new development
in ecclesiology among Southern Baptist since 1845."*[21] That
should not have been something of which to be proud. The
downward slide away from the historical position of Baptist
continued in the *2000 Baptist Faith and Message* when they
added, "The New Testament speaks also of the Church as
the Body of Christ which includes all the Redeemed of all
the ages, believers from every tribe, and tongue, and people,
and nations."[22]

The *2000 Baptist Faith and Message* is not the long-
held belief of Baptists as seen in the following. J. W. Jent
(1877-1941), past President of Southwest Baptist College,
Bolivar, Missouri, wrote, *"Ecclesia is 'a congregation of
baptized believers associated together in the fellowship of the
gospel' – that it is a spiritual democracy – visible and local or
particular; that it is a New Testament institution, designed by
Our Lord, historically instituted by Him; persisting from century
to century; conserving the characteristics of the New Testament
model; easily identified by the marks of its doctrinal integrity;
functioning true to the genius of its Holy Mission; justifying its
existence by its challenging achievements and its benevolent
blessing to sin-cursed humanity."*[23]

21   H.H. Hobbs (1907-1995), *The Baptist Faith and Message*, p. 146,
     footnote 2.

22   www.sbc.net/bfm/bfm2000.asp

23   Roy Mason (1894-1978), *The Church That Jesus Built.*

> A church is properly defined as *"a congregation
> of Christ's baptized disciples, acknowledging Him
> as their Head, relying on His atoning sacrifice for
> justification before God, depending on the Holy Spirit for
> sanctification, united in the belief of the Gospel, agreeing
> to maintain its ordinances and obey its precepts, meeting
> together for worship, and co-operating for the extension
> of Christ's kingdom in the world."*
> - J. B. Cranfill (1858-1942)[24]

It was curious to Baptist pastor and professor Wendell H. Rone (1913-2003) to think of an unassembled church. *"I always thought persons had to assemble or congregate before one could call it an assembly or congregation. But the new ecclesiological innovation now tells me that you can have an un-assembled assembly, an un-congregated congregation, and un-churched church – which has never met and never will meet on this earth in this gospel age."*[25]

The "local ecclesia (assembly) only" position is advantageous for many practical reasons.

(1) It advances the clear meaning of *ecclesia* as a "gathered assembly."

(2) It reinforces the compelling need for church membership after a believer's salvation.

(3) It exposes the subtle and obvious dangers of ecumenical and interdenominational cooperation.

(4) It underscores the local church's complete autonomy and dependence on Christ.

(5) It places the need to maintain doctrinal purity as each congregation's own responsibility.

---

24 J. B. Cranfill ((1858-1942), *Re-Thinking Baptist Doctrines*, p. 140.

25 Wendell H. Rone, Sr. (1913-2003), *What is the Church?* p. 10.

The Roots and Fruits of New Testament Churches are Historical, not Modern

For centuries Baptist-minded people have believed and taught they have historic roots back to the church Jesus started in Galilee; the one our Lord trained throughout His ministry in the Holy Land, commissioned before His ascension, empowered with His Spirit on the Day of Pentecost and codified through Paul's epistles to do His work.

"If by a Dissenter we are to understand, one who comes out of the English Protestant Church, then the Baptists, strictly speaking, are not Dissenters; for they existed before the Established Church; were never in the Established church; consequently they could not come out of the Established Church, and therefore not Dissenters. If a Protestant be one who comes out of the Papal Church, then the Baptists, strictly speaking, are not Protestants; they existed prior to the Popish Church; were never as a body in communion with the Popish Church; consequently could not come out of the Popish Church, and are therefore not Protestants. If it be asked, then, What are the Baptists? Our answer is, They are the Primitive Church… the Baptists are the original church, which has existed through all ages since the time of Christ down to the present day, and is properly denominated The Baptist Church." Joseph Foulkes Winks (1794-1860)[26]

"All earthly things go down through these dread gates, but Christ's church, for which he gave himself, will never cease to exist; there will always be Christians in the world. This was a bold prediction for a homeless teacher, with a handful of

---

26   Joseph Foulkes Winks (1794-1860) Editor, The Baptist Reporter and Missionary Intelligencer, *"The Baptist" His Name and Antiquity*, p. 6.

followers." John A. Broadus (1827-1895)[27]

"Those who oppose Baptist succession have no logical ground to stand on in organizing a church out of material furnished by other churches, and with those regular baptized by regularly ordained Baptist ministers." T.T. Eaton (1845-1907)[28]

"Succession among Baptists is not a linked chain of churches or ministers, uninterrupted and traceable at this distant day… The true and defensible doctrine is that baptized believers have existed in every age since John baptized in Jordan, and have met as a baptized congregation in covenant and fellowship where an opportunity permitted. " S. H. Ford, LLD (1819-1905)[29]

"The Baptists claim to have descended from the apostles. It is true that the line of descent cannot always be traced. Like a river, that now and then in its course is lost under the surface of the ground, and then makes its appearance again, the Baptists claim, that from the days of the apostles until the present time, there have not been wanting those persons, either separately or collected into churches, and known under different names, who, if now living, would be universally recognized as Baptists. The principles for which the Baptists contended were fiercely denounced as heresy and treason. Their existence and continuity can be traced down the ages by 'the stains of their martyr's blood, and the light of their martyr's fires.'" Clarence Larkin (1850-1924)[30]

"All that Baptists mean by 'church succession' or church perpetuity is: there has never been a day since the organization of the first New Testament church in which there was no genuine church of the New Testament existing on earth. " W. A. Jarrell,

---

27   John A. Broadus (1827-1895), *Commentary on the Gospel of Matthew, An American Commentary of the New Testament,* p. 360.

28   Quoted by D. B. Ray (1830-1922), *Baptist Succession,* p. 15.

29   W.A. Jarrel (1849-1927), *Baptist Church History,* Chapter 1.

30   Clarence Larkin (1850-1924), *Why I Am A Baptist,* pp. 8-9.

D.D. (1849-1927)[31]

"To be well born is to enter life with advantage. Baptists are justly proud of their parentage—the New Testament. They have an ancient and scriptural origin. Certain characters in history are named as founders of various denominations: The Disciples began with Alexander Campbell, the Methodists with John Wesley, the Presbyterians with John Calvin, the Lutherans with Martin Luther, and the Church of England with Henry VIII and Cranmer's Book of Common Prayer in the reign of Edward VI. Not so with the Baptists. There is no personality this side of Jesus Christ who is a satisfactory explanation of their origin. The New Testament churches were independent, self-governing, democratic bodies like the Baptist churches of to-day. We originated, not at the Reformation, nor in the Dark Ages, nor in any century after the Apostles, but our marching orders are the Commission, and the first Baptist church was the church at Jerusalem. Our principles are as old as Christianity, and we acknowledge no founder but Christ."[32]

"Baptist churches seek to follow the pattern of Christ's church in the New Testament. Baptists thus believe that their history began with Christ and the apostles." Joe T. Odle (1899-1980)[33]

In his 1939 Southern Baptist Convention Presidential address, the President of Southwestern Baptist Theological Seminary, L.R. Scarborough (1870-1945), began his address by saying, *"Without boast or pride but with joy and certainty, Baptists trace their lineage back to an ancient and honorable beginning – to the meeting of John the forerunner and Jesus in the holy baptizing scene in the Jordan River. Through the centuries, sometimes by indistinct lines, sometimes by definite groups and*

---

31   Quoted by Roy Mason (1894-1978), *The Church Jesus Built*, p. 16.
32   George W. McDaniel (1875-1927), *The People Called Baptists*, pp. 12-13.
33   Joe T. Odle (1899-1980), *Church Member's Handbook*, p. 13.

mighty doctrines, they profess love for and loyalty to teachings and principles which Christ gave to the apostolic group and are recorded in the New Testament."[34]

Baptist perpetuity is not about an unbroken chain of churches back to the church of Jerusalem or an unbroken chain of churches named "Baptist" back to Christ. It is a matter of doctrinal succession.

Distinctively Baptist principles have existed since the time of Christ because Baptist-like churches have existed throughout the ages following Christ until now. B.H. Carroll (1843-1913) said, *"When Baptists say that the New Testament is the only law for Christian institutions they part company, if not theoretically at least practically, with most of the Protestant world, as well as from the Greeks and Romanists."*[35]

True churches have existed in every age since the time of Christ. You have God's promise of that, whether it can be proven historically or not. Our faith doesn't rest in the potentially flawed history of men, but in the unfailing promises of God.

The modern view being postulated is that Baptist beginnings are linked to the English Separatists in 1641. William H. Whitsett (1841-1911), sometime after writing *A Question in Baptist History* (1896), lost his job as President of Southern Seminary, Louisville, KY, propounding this flawed view. While the name "Baptist" may not have come into general use until 1641, that was only because the prefix of "ana" was not yet dropped from those who were identified as "Anabaptist."

Many historians reluctantly agree that the principles of

34 Editors Ergun (1966-) and Emir Caner (1966-), *The Sacred Desk*, p. 134.

35 J.B. Cranfill (1858-1942), *Baptist and Their Doctrines*, 1913, pp. 10-11.)

sound Baptists have existed through the centuries. What they refuse to admit is that such principles do not exist in a vacuum. For principles to exist, they must be held by people who are willing to believe them, teach them, and, when necessary, die for them.

If down through the centuries genuine New Testament churches at some point ceased to exist, and later reemerged in 1641, then the only conclusion is that for centuries the Roman Catholic Church (with its Popes, Traditions, Apocrypha, Inquisitions, infant sprinkling, Mariology, etc.) was the pillar and ground of the truth! What other conclusion can be drawn?

Robert Baker (1910-1992), Southwestern Baptist Theological Seminary history professor for thirty-nine years, advanced this reasonable position. *"The rapid appearance of Anabaptists over a wide area lends confirmations to what reliable historians have asserted; small communities of pious Christians, rarely appearing in historical records but endeavoring to reproduce the New Testament in simple, anticlerical, nonsacramental purity, were interspersed throughout the length and breadth of Europe in the centuries before the Reformation. It would have been impossible for them to leap full-grown into the focus of history had this not been true."*[36] Yet, Professor Baker asserted the beginning of Baptists was during the Reformation.

The historical churches back to the New Testament were all Anabaptist in that they were openly opposed to "infant sprinkling or infant immersion" of Catholics and Protestants. There were groups who became churches that lived and died advocating that all believers in Christ were to be immersed as a personal confession of their personal faith.

---

36   Robert Baker (1910-1992), *The Baptist March in History*, p. 31).

The Importance of the New Testament Church is Essential, not Optional

After salvation, every professed believer in Jesus Christ should pursue membership in a New Testament church. Someone might respond, "How would you know what I need to do? You don't even know me and I do not know you." I say it because it is God's will for every Christian to be a functioning part of a congregation. New Testament Christianity is both Christ-centered and church-connected; you will not find any other kind.

If you want it a little straighter: every professed believer in Jesus Christ who is not a church member or is intentionally not pursuing their Christian life inside a church is out of God's will. "**Therefore to him that knoweth to do good, and doeth *it* not, to him it is sin**" (James 4:17).

In his book, *Authentic Faith*, Gary Thomas (1961-) says, *"This may sound shocking to some, but biblically, living for God means living for his church."*[37] What is shocking is that such a statement would be shocking to anyone who reads the New Testament.

In the first century...

- If you *assembled* with believers, it was with a church assembly.
- If you had *Christian fellowship*, it was church fellowship.
- If you had a *prayer meeting* with other believers, it was a church prayer meeting.
- If you had a *Bible study* with other believers, it was a church Bible study.
- If you were involved in *ministry*, it was a church

---

37   Gary Thomas (1961-), *Authentic Faith*, p. 11.

ministry.

- If you had a *spiritual gift*, it was exercised as a church gift.
- If you operated with *divine authority*, it was with church authority.
- If you *gave financially* to God's work, it was given to and for church work.
- If you were *doing God's work*, you were doing church work.
- If you were doing *missionary work*, you were doing missionary work out of a church.

"Christ loved the church and gave Himself for it" (Ephesians 5:25). Christ purchased the church "with His own blood" (Acts 20:28). After His resurrection, Christ was seen in the presence of seven of His churches (Revelation 2-3). It is by the church that God is to receive glory by Christ Jesus (Ephesians 3:21).

God established three vital institutions: the family, government and the church. God performed the first wedding ceremony in Genesis 2. The institution of marriage and the family was God's idea. Romans 13:1 informs us regarding human government, that "there is no power but of God: the powers that be are ordained of God." Even the Roman government that crucified Jesus had its power "from above" (John 19:10-11). Of God's three institutions, only the church is said in Scripture to be personally founded by Christ. The family and government are of a natural order, while the church of the living God is of a supernatural order.

Any valid work done in God's name in this age must be done God's way – through a New Testament church.

The story is told of a fictional wealthy Boston family

who was holding a christening party after the dedication of their new baby. Guests and friends swarmed into their palatial home. Soon the party was in full swing. People were having a wonderful time, enjoying one another, eating, drinking, and being merry. Somebody asked, "By the way, where's the baby?" Instantly the mother's heart shuddered! In questioning panic, she left the room and rushed into the master bedroom where she had left her baby asleep in the middle of their large bed. There on the bed she found a huge pile of the guests' coats. The mother rushed to them and began to fling them aside as she clawed down to the bottom of the pile. To her horror she found her baby...dead... smothered by the coats of her guests.

While this story is not based on fact, what is true is that under the heavy covers of Bible societies, student ministries, for-profit publishers, benevolent ministries, radio programs, prison ministries, camps and conference centers, recreational ministries, evangelistic ministries, missionary organizations, mission boards and clearing houses, the churches of the living God are being smothered. Nothing can take the place of the church of Jesus Christ.

It becomes more vital than ever that those who hold to historic Baptist beliefs prize them, preach them, practice them, protect them, preserve them, and propagate them.

CHAPTER 3

The Characteristics of New Testament Churches (Part 1)

Acts 2:41-47

Since we are investigating the nature and work of New Testament churches, we will need to become familiar with the book of Acts. It's author, Luke, says his gospel was a record of what Jesus "began to do and teach" (Luke 1:1). The implication in his second book, Acts, is the continuation of what Jesus *began* to do and teach – *His unfinished work.*

Modern church-planters are in hot pursuit for a perfect "model" to follow. Thousands of congregations are following the *seeker-sensitive* movement started by Bill Hybel. It has a pragmatic foundation. With certain parameters, they give people what they want. Bill Hybel started by surveying people, asking them what they liked and didn't like about churches, and created a church everyone would like. It reminds me of a sign on a west Texas dude ranch. It read, "We aim to please at this ranch. For big people we have big horses; for little people we have little horses; for people who want to ride fast we have fast horses; for people who want to ride slow we have slow horses; and for people who have never ridden a horse we have horses that have never been ridden." Ten years ago, in late 2007, the Hybels model sadly discovered while it had been effective for introducing Christ to those who were new to church, it had not been successful in turning "irreligious people into fully devoted followers of Christ." They have since moved to teaching their people to become "self-feeders."

Some church-planters have opted for the *purpose-driven* model by Rick Warren, a plan even adopted by Catholics and Protestants alike. Over 400,000 ministers and church leaders have attended Purpose-Driven Church seminars led by Warren and his associates checking out this modern method.

And amazingly, others are so desperate they have embraced the *positive-church* facsimile represented by Joel Osteen.

While discovering the *pattern* followed by the churches of the New Testament in the book of Acts, we are under divine obligation to *practice* that pattern in the way we do church. While Acts is easily divided by the ministries of Peter (chapters 1-12) and Paul (chapters 13-28), we must see it in the light of God's churches. Peter was one of the leaders of the *first* and only church at the time – the Jerusalem church. Like all churches of the New Testament, it was a local (identified by its city) and visible (made up of baptized believers) church. Paul was one of the leaders of the *furthest* church – the Antioch church.

The churches in Acts had "great power" (Acts 4:33), "great grace" (Acts 4:33), "great fear" (Acts 5:5, 11), "great persecution" (Acts 8:1), "great joy" (Acts 8:6, 8), and "great numbers believed and turned to the Lord" (Acts 11:21). Believers were first "added" to the churches, then disciples were "multiplied." The people of God planted, they watered, and God gave the increase (1 Corinthians 3:9). They saw all this accomplished without any buildings, without any technology, and without any professional staff.

So, what were the characteristics of the churches in Acts?

They were Empowered Churches

Jesus had already conveyed upon the apostles the Holy

Spirit after His resurrection. That is recorded in John 20:19-23. Just before Jesus' ascension He had promised the Holy Spirit would give power to be His witness, reaching to the ends of the earth. **"But ye shall receive power, after that the Holy Ghost is come upon you: and ye shall be witnesses unto me both in Jerusalem, and in all Judaea, and in Samaria, and unto the uttermost part of the earth"** (Acts 1:8). Jesus promised they would be "endued with power from on high" (Luke 24:49).

"And when the day of Pentecost was fully come, they were all with one accord in one place. And suddenly there came a sound from heaven as of a rushing mighty wind, and it filled all the house where they were sitting. And there appeared unto them cloven tongues like as of fire, and it sat upon each of them. And they were all filled with the Holy Ghost, and began to speak with other tongues, as the Spirit gave them utterance" (Acts 2:1-4).

Pastor Bob Pearle (1953-) says, *"The significance of Pentecost is the empowering of the church with the public inauguration of the ministry of the Holy Spirit. The Acts of the Apostles is really a chronicle of the Holy Spirit's ministry and work in the early church. Jesus had a public inauguration of His ministry as well. That occurred at His baptism by John the Baptist. Jesus began the church during His ministry. In Acts, the spreading of the church by the Holy Spirit is seen beginning on the day of Pentecost. What Jesus began in the Gospels, He continues in Acts."*[1]

God's empowering the church at Jerusalem with His presence follows the patterns of the Tabernacle and the Temples, God's houses of witness in the Old Testament. (Exodus 40:334-35; 1 Kings 8:10-13) And now, on the Day

---

1   Bob Pearle (1953-), *The Vanishing* Church, p. 72.

of Pentecost, God again moved into a new house, "the house of God, the church of the living God, the pillar and ground of the truth" (1 Timothy 3:15). This was not the *formation* of the church, but the *confirmation* of the church. New Testament churches would be "an habitation of God through the Spirit" (Ephesians 2:22). With this miraculous and visible demonstration, God authenticated His new house – the place where He would put His name. God would not fill this house with furniture, but with "living stone," built into "a spiritual house" (1 Peter 2:5).

They were Preaching Churches

"But Peter, standing up with the eleven, lifted up his voice, and said unto them, Ye men of Judaea, and all *ye* that dwell at Jerusalem, be this known unto you, and hearken to my words:" (Acts 2:14).

Peter learned his preaching from his time spent with the Master Preacher, Jesus Christ. From Peter's sermon on the Day of Pentecost we can say his preaching was Scripture-filled, hard-hitting, straight-forward, Christ-centered, Spirit-convicting, sinner-inviting and soul-saving.

As you read through of the book of Acts you see people preaching: Stephen (Acts 7), Philip (Acts 8:5, 35), Peter (Acts 10), Paul (Acts 9:20; 17:18; 24-26). On most of the occasions, some trouble resulted. Paul preached so long on one occasion a young man went to sleep and fell out of the window of a third story loft. Paul checked on him, declaring that the boy was okay and went back to preaching until morning (Acts 20:7-12).

Steven W. Smith (1968-) asks, *"Where does the pastor get the nerve to stand in the pulpit and tell others what they should or should not do? If he is not the most quick-witted or does not*

have the greatest leadership ability, is he not setting himself up?
The authority comes from nothing more or less than Scripture."[2]

The contemporary approach in churches today is to either play down or outright apologize for any form of preaching. One mega-church advertises on their website, *"Our pastors don't preach sermons as much as they simply teach the Bible. They will refer to it often – and even encourage you to mark it up as your life-textbook."*

When people go to an ice cream shop they expect to be offered some ice cream. When they attend a car show they expect to see automobiles. When people enter a church they should hear some preaching.

They were Soul-Winning Churches

"...ye shall be witnesses unto me both in Jerusalem, and in all Judaea, and in Samaria, and unto the uttermost part of the earth" (Acts 1:8). **"Then Peter said unto them, Repent, and be baptized every one of you in the name of Jesus Christ for the remission of sins, and ye shall receive the gift of the Holy Ghost"** (Acts 2:38).

After preaching a gospel message, Peter called on those who heard to respond by repenting. It was both a command and an invitation. In that day 3,000 people were added as believers (Acts 2:41). Acts 2:47 tells us **"And the Lord added to the church daily such as should be saved."** Acts 4:4 records that 5,000 men believed. In Acts 5:28 they are accused of filling Jerusalem with their doctrine. Then the spiritual math changed from addition to multiplication. **"And the word of God increased; and the number of the disciples multiplied in Jerusalem greatly; and a great company of the priests were obedient to the faith"** (Acts

---

2   Steven W. Smith (1968-), *Dying to Preach*, p. 131.

6:7). "**Then had the churches rest throughout all Judaea and Galilee and Samaria, and were edified; and ... were multiplied**" (Acts 9:31). By Acts 17:6 it was testified God's people, in their cities, had "turned the world upside down (really, right-side up)." When Paul later visited, the leaders of the church of Jerusalem declared "**how many thousands of Jews there are which believe**" (Acts 21:20).

Peter and John encountered a lame man who was healed and saved by the mighty name of Jesus (Acts 3-4). Stephen was a faithful witness who impacted the unsaved Saul. (Acts 7:58) Philip saw many in the city of Samaria turn to Christ, disavowed the profession of Simon and the Spirit directed him to an Ethiopian eunuch who trusted Christ (Acts 8). Peter changed his attitude about Gentiles and led Cornelius and all his household to Christ (Acts 10). Paul saw God "open the heart" of Lydia in Philippi and the jailer and his family turn to Christ (Acts 16). In Athens, a city full of idols, some mocked, some procrastinated, but some believed (Acts 17:32-34).

Jesus had commanded His church, "**Go ye therefore, and teach all nations...**" (Matthew 28:18). The Jerusalem church would eventually move beyond Jerusalem because of great persecution and be scattered throughout Judea and Samaria (Acts 8:1-4). The early Christians in and through their churches were about the business of making much of Jesus. Modern day churches need to see themselves as God's light in a dark world; as God's life in a dead world.

"Jesus designed His church for the very purpose of evangelism; therefore, nothing could be more important to evangelism than the understanding, preservation, and application of the biblical doctrine of the church."[3]

3   Willard A. Ramsey (1931-2011), *The House of God*, pp. 3-4.

They were Believers' Churches

"Then they that gladly received his word..." (Acts 2:41). **"And the Lord added to the church daily such as should be saved"** (Acts 2:47).

The Jerusalem church, and the churches that followed, were not simply a gathering of people. People often gathered at the temple. People gathered at the markets. People gathered at their courts. Churches were marked as gatherings of openly professing believers in Christ. A clear line was drawn between them and the world. These churches were made up of the redeemed of God. They were God's *ecclesia* – the "called out" ones.

Some dangerous trends mark church-life today. Churches have made much of their efforts to get unsaved people to church services. There is certainly nothing wrong with that. Many churches have family and friend days and other emphases to have their members reach those around them by bringing them to a special evangelistic service. 1 Corinthians 14:23-25 gives us an example of a potential church visitor who might observe our worship and be drawn to the Lord. However, sinners are never called to "come in," but believers are commanded to "go out."

The temptation is to create an atmosphere in church services where the lost feel comfortable, welcomed and unthreatened. So, churches today marginalize preaching and maximize drama, modern music, the latest technology, and great facilities to get people to attend church services. It is unlikely a hard-hitting message like Peter preached on the Day of Pentecost would be allowed because it might be considered too "exclusive" and "divisive."

The church is its membership of believers, gathered to worship and to be trained for the work of God. While unbelievers are encouraged to attend, they are there to observe.

Most churches would never consider having an unbeliever preach from their pulpit, yet it is not uncommon for large churches to have professional musicians contribute to their worship music. No one would consider having a lost person teach a Bible class for children. What kind of confused message that would be? Churches are blurring or removing reasonable and scriptural lines for the sake of expediency. When non-Christian are used in worship, it is implying that the *art* of worship is more important than the *heart* in worship. I am in full agreement with one man who wrote, *"If what we're engaged in is a media production, drawing a crowd, or a motivational event, then it's not as important who does what. But if we are the gathering of the church, the called-out ones, those whom Jesus Christ has redeemed by His blood, who have professed faith in His substitutionary sacrifice, and are seeking to live for His glory, then it matters."*[4]

Obviously, all people are welcome to attend church services, but the ministry and work of the church is to be carried out by believers.

They were Baptizing Churches

"Then they that gladly received his word were baptized: and the same day there were added *unto them* about three thousand souls" (Acts 2:41).

The order of these events is significant. They heard the gospel, were convicted by the Holy Spirit of their need for Christ's redemptive work in their behalf, they repented and were baptized. Those who believed were immediately

---

4   Bob Kauflin, *Non-Christians on the Worship Team?*, May 22, 2008, www.worshipmatters.com

led to be baptized as their profession of faith. Peter would later add in his first epistle that baptism is "the answer of a good conscience toward God" (1 Peter 3:21). John Phillips says, *"It was a bold step to be thus publicly baptized in the name of the Lord Jesus. For many a Jew it meant persecution, to be cut off from family and friends, and denied further place in the synagogue and in Jewish society. As it became increasingly clear that the church was not just another Jewish sect, and as official attitude toward the church hardened, so the cost of baptism increased. The price of this first step of obedience remains high in many countries and cultures even today."*[5]

The Jerusalem church, led by the apostles, was following the command Jesus had given them in the Great Commission. **"Go ye therefore, and teach all nations, baptizing them in the name of the Father, and of the Son, and of the Holy Ghost:"** (Matthew 28:18). While the mode of this baptism is not specified in the Acts 2 narrative, other passages in the gospels, Acts and the epistles define it as immersion (Matthew 3:16; Acts 8:38-39; Romans 6:4).

Those who might doubt the viability of 3,000 people being immersed on a single day in Jerusalem should become aware of the "mikvah" around the Temple Mount. The word "mikvah" (plural "mikva'ot") means "collection" and refers to a collection of water that was used by the Jews for ceremonial washing. They are ritual pools. The Jews would purify themselves before several activities or after certain events that made them ceremonially unclean. Conversion to Judaism requires submersion into a mikvah. A mikvah had to have a source of running water, such as a spring, or fresh water, such as rain. A mikvah had to be large enough to allow an average sized person to immerse his whole body.

---

5   John Phillips (1927-2010), *Exploring Acts, Vol. 1*, p. 63.)

Stairs would be used to descend into and ascend out of the mikvah. Often there was a wall separating the clean side from the unclean side. One source stated that there were over a hundred "mikva'ot" in use in Jerusalem by 70 A.D., forty-eight of which have been discovered by archeologists.

They were Faithful Churches

"And they continued stedfastly..." (Acts 2:41).

The immediate response of those who were added to the church of Jerusalem by baptism was to demonstrate a high level of devotion. When the Bible says, "they continued stedfast," it means they were "firm," "they persevered," they "remained faithful." The faithfulness of a follower of Jesus is possible because of God's faithfulness, which is "great" (Lamentations 3:23). Any measure of faithfulness on our part is because God is faithful to us. We can trust God because in every situation He is trustworthy.

- God is faithful to forgive those who honestly confess their sins (1 John 1:9).
- God is faithful to sustain us in our trials (1 Corinthians 10:13).
- God is faithful to guide us away from evil (2 Thessalonians 3:3).

The church where I have been a member in total for more than forty-five years was founded by my namesake, Jerry L. Davis, when he was seventy-four-years old. He and his wife were joined by only eighteen members. The total offering on the first Sunday they met in 1937 was $2; it was paid to their new pastor. Through the steadfastness of hundreds of people for eighty years the church remains strong.

There is one thing every believer can be, young or old,

without regard to their giftedness, without the assistance of anyone, without the forces that come against them – they can each be faithful to their Lord and Saviour.

Notice, again in Acts 2:41 that it was a *collective* faithfulness. "They" continued steadfastly. It is so much easier to be faithful when others are faithful.

Further, theirs was a *contagious* faithfulness. The influence of faithfulness on others is far-reaching.

> *Oh, may all who come behind us find us faithful.*
> *May the fire of our devotion light their way.*
> *May the footprints that we leave,*
> *Lead them to believe,*
> *And the lives we live inspire them to obey.*
> *Oh, may all who come behind us find us faithful.*
>
> Steve Green

These new believers demonstrated a *comprehensible* faithfulness. Years ago, on my first trip home from a tour of Israel we missed our connecting flight in New York at JFK Airport. Our flight home the next day was changed to LaGuardia, so they flew us that night by helicopter to a hotel nearby. On the quick trip the pilot circled the Statue of Liberty. It was dark and we were tired, but it was a special moment as we saw "America's Great Lady." She was dedicated October 28, 1886, well before anyone travelled by air. No one was ever expected to see the top. Yet, its creator, Frédéric Auguste Bartholdi, gave no less attention to small details on the top than to the other places people would more easily see. It is a testament to his faithfulness.

Notice what was connected to the faithfulness of these new believers who made up the Jerusalem church.

It wasn't limited to a few things but encompassed a long list of noble interests as Acts 2:42 goes on to say.

They were Learning Churches

"**And they continued stedfastly in the apostles' doctrine...**" (Acts 2:42).

Having believed and having been baptized, these new church members now began listening to and learning from the apostles, the eye-witnesses of the Lord Jesus' life, ministry and resurrection. The early churches at first depended on the spoken words of the apostles for their truth.

What was the "apostles' doctrine"? It was the third part of the Great Commission. Jesus said, "**Teaching them to observe all things whatsoever I have commanded you:...**" (Matthew 28:20) The apostles' teachings were the teachings of Christ. Christ had promised that the Holy Spirit would bring to the mind of the apostles what Jesus had taught them (John 14:26; 16:13).

These new Christians in the church at Jerusalem were hungry to learn more about their Saviour and Lord. We are to be always learning. The apostle Paul spoke about the wonder of the "unsearchable riches of Christ" (Ephesians 3:8).

A famous painter who was nearly seventy said, "If God spares me for another ten years I think I may learn how to paint."

It still amazing to me that people can gather regularly in church services and learn so little. Jesus calls us to "learn" of Him (Matthew 11:29). Paul called Timothy to "study" to be approved of God (2 Timothy 2:15). James implies we learn best by hearing that is combined with doing, "**But be ye doers of the word, and not hearers only, deceiving your own selves**" (James 1:22).

They were Unified Churches

"And they continued stedfastly in…fellowship… And all that believed were together…" (Acts 2:42, 44).

In an amazing and supernatural way, these 3,120 people found they had something significant in common; it was Christ and this new community called "the church."

"Fellowship" is the Greek word *koinonia* and it means "all together." When you consider the diversity in even a small church, it is an amazing work of God to be "all together" when it comes to the things of God. Genuine spiritual unity is a work of God in the hearts of those who are obedient. This was not man-made union or a forced uniformity, but the "unity of the Spirit in the bond of peace." (Ephesians 4:3).

The spiritual kinship we share in Christ is greater than that of a biological family, a military unit, an athletic team or a work force.

"A new commandment I give unto you, That ye love one another; as I have loved you, that ye also love one another. By this shall all *men* know that ye are my disciples, if ye have love one to another" (John 13:34-35). **"We know that we have passed from death unto life, because we love the brethren…"** (1 John 3:14). They were finding out what would later be clarified, that they were "members one of another…" (Romans 12:5). **"And whether one member suffer, all the members suffer with it; or one member be honoured, all the members rejoice with it. Now ye are the body of Christ, and members in particular"** (1 Corinthians 12:26-27).

They were Observant Churches

"And they continued stedfastly in…breaking of

bread…" (Acts 2:42).

It seems that this is a reference to the Lord's Supper, one of the two ordinances of the Lord's churches. Our Lord had commanded His apostles at the very first Supper, "this do in remembrance of me" (Luke 22:19). Paul later added, **"For as often as ye eat this bread, and drink this cup, ye do shew the Lord's death till he come"** (1 Corinthians 11:26). The frequency of the church's participating in this memorial is not specifically stated, but it is clearly implied it would be "often" instead of "infrequently."

There is something to be said about being regularly reminded of Jesus' death in our behalf, not only as individual believers (Galatians 2:20), but also as His gathered church (Acts 20:28; Ephesians 5:25).

They were Praying Churches

After the ascension of Jesus, **"Then returned they unto Jerusalem from the mount called Olivet, which is from Jerusalem a sabbath day's journey. And when they were come in, they went up into an upper room, where abode both Peter, and James, and John, and Andrew, Philip, and Thomas, Bartholomew, and Matthew, James *the son* of Alphaeus, and Simon Zelotes, and Judas *the brother* of James. These all continued with one accord in prayer and supplication, with the women, and Mary the mother of Jesus, and with his brethren… (the number of names together were about an hundred and twenty,)…"** (Acts 1:12-15).

And after the Day of Pentecost, **"…they continued stedfastly in…prayer…"** (Acts 2:42). What an absolutely unique privilege these believing Jews now had. They had instant and open access to the presence of God through

Christ's perfect work of redemption. At Jesus' death, the veil of the temple was torn from top to bottom opening the way to God. It was such a dramatic turn of events, that later "a great company of priests were obedient to the faith" (Acts 6:7).

The very next event after the explosion of thousands being saved was the apostles Peter and John "went up together into the temple at the hour of prayer…" (Acts 3:1). These leaders of the church at Jerusalem were not merely setting an example of prayer, they understood the privilege and responsibility of personal prayer.

Within days, the leaders and members of the Jerusalem church would come under threats, arrest and persecution. Once they were released, they "went to their own company" (the church), gathering specifically to pray (Acts 4:23-31). Later, the apostle James was killed and Peter was arrested, awaiting execution. **"Peter therefore was kept in prison: but prayer was made without ceasing of the church** (at Jerusalem) **unto God for him"** (Acts 12:5). Upon Peter's miraculous release, he made his way to where "many were gathered together praying" (Acts 12:12). The answer to their prayer was at the door where the prayer meeting was being held and they could not believe it!

The Temple in Jerusalem had been God's "house of prayer" (Matthew 21:13), but now God's churches would be His houses of prayer.

They were Giving Churches

"And all that believed were together, and had all things common; And sold their possessions and goods, and parted them to all *men,* **as every man had need."** (Acts 2:44-45) **"Neither was there any among them that**

lacked: for as many as were possessors of lands or houses sold them, and brought the prices of the things that were sold, And laid *them* down at the apostles' feet: and distribution was made unto every man according as he had need. And Joses, who by the apostles was surnamed Barnabas, (which is, being interpreted, The son of consolation,) a Levite, *and* of the country of Cyprus, Having land, sold *it*, and brought the money, and laid *it* at the apostles' feet"** (Acts 4:34-37).

Some have tried to say this was a foreshadowing of communism. Nothing is further from the truth. It hardly demands answering. These were believers, not atheists. This was voluntary, not forced. While it was spontaneous, it was organized. This was church-controlled, not state-controlled. It was a temporary expression of love, not a permanent demand. Communism says, "What's yours is mine, I am taking it." Christianity says, "What's mine is yours, I gladly give it."

This was not a church-welfare program. It was an expression of Christian love. **"Hereby perceive we the love *of God*, because he laid down his life for us: and we ought to lay down *our* lives for the brethren. But whoso hath this world's good, and seeth his brother have need, and shutteth up his bowels *of compassion* from him, how dwelleth the love of God in him?"** (1 John 3:16-17). Those in the church were given the opportunity to assist the poor (Romans 15:26; 1 Corinthians 16:1-2), widows (Acts 6:1; 1 Timothy 5:3-10, 16), and orphans (James 1:27). The expectation was that those who were able to provide for themselves were expected to do so (1 Timothy 5:8; 1 Thessalonians 4:9-12; 2 Thessalonians 3:10-15). Greediness is not a Christian virtue, but neither is laziness.

You know something real has happened in a person's heart when it gets in their pocketbook! Jesus had taught, **"For where your treasure is, there will your heart be also"** (Matthew 6:21). Our heart always follows what we treasure. These early Christians had a heart for other believers so it was natural that their treasure was transferred to meet their needs. God had their hearts, so their possessions were easy to reassign.

They were Reverent Churches

"And fear came upon every soul: and many wonders and signs were done by the apostles" (Acts 2:43).

The idea of the verb "came," according to the Greek scholar A.T. Robertson is it "kept on coming." A sense of awe kept coming on these new believers in Christ. It never got old to them. That sense of awe translated into a proper fear of diminishing or disgracing or defiling the holy gatherings before their great God.

Regardless of your political stance, if you were invited to the White House to personally meet the President of the United States of America I would hope you would be on your best behavior. The fact is, we live our lives in the presence of the King of kings, and Lord of lords. The apostle Paul wrote to young Timothy with concern, **"…that thou mayest know how thou oughtest to behave thyself in the house of God, which is the church of the living God, the pillar and ground of the truth"** (1 Timothy 3:15).

Later, after the sudden and unexpected deaths of Ananias and Sapphira, the church's first funerals, the record says, **"And great fear came upon all the church, and upon as many as heard these things"** (Acts 5:11). The believers of the church at Jerusalem were sobered to the core when

God took the lives of two of its members. They had already found out it was dangerous to follow Christ from their local government. Now, they are in greater reverence as they witnessed the hand of God's judgment on a couple of followers who were less than fully committed. This resulted in a temporary slow-down of people wanting to join their ranks. **"And of the rest durst no man join himself to them: but the people magnified them"** (Acts 5:13).

Churches will never have the respect they desire from those outside the church until they restore the reverence due to God inside the church. **"For the time *is come* that judgment must begin at the house of God: and if *it* first *begin* at us, what shall the end *be* of them that obey not the gospel of God?"** (1 Peter 4:17).

CHAPTER 4

The Characteristics of New Testament Churches (Part 2)

Acts 2:41-47

The best way to build a house is to meticulously follow the blueprint designed by the architect. Many projects have gone really wrong when they deviated from the designer's plan.

When it comes to "doing church" in our day, we need to go back to the One who promised to build His church, Jesus Christ, and stay with His plan. And, since this is Christ's church, we are not free to cut corners or put our personal touch on what represents Him.

By just visiting a few churches, it is easy to see that each church is so different. They have different sizes, different potentials, different resources, different influences…the list is endless. It might seem since each church is different that there is no single model for every church.

In fact, there is a model for every church, large or small, rural or urban, ethnically diverse or segregated. The "one size fits all" model is the one discovered in the beliefs and practices of the churches of the New Testament. There may need to be some *modest adaptation*, but not *extreme alterations*. Man-made models don't work across the board, but God's model works when it is followed for His glory.

So, what were the characteristics of the churches of the New Testament? We have seen they were empowered, preaching, soul-winning, believers' baptism, faithful, learning, united, observant, praying, giving, and reverent churches.

They were Worshipping Churches

"And they, continuing daily with one accord in the temple,.." (Acts 2:46).

The courtyard of the Temple at Jerusalem provided a large and central meeting place for these new baptized believers. *"The daily worship consisted of the offering of a burnt offering and incense in the morning and the afternoon; it was carried out by the priests, but there was a congregation of people who stood where they could see the priests going about their duties and entering the sanctuary; they took part in prayer, and they received a blessing from the priest."*[1]

Whether it was immediate or eventual, they would come to understand that the Temple was under the old covenant and now they would live under a new covenant. It is believed by some that Luke (the human author of Acts) was also the human agent of the book of Hebrews. It is in the book of Hebrews where the dots are connected from the old way of worship to the new way of worship.

- The old sacrifices of bulls and goats was a shadow of the sacrificial death of Jesus.
- The many offerings of the Old Testament were replaced by one offering by Jesus.
- The work of the many priests was replaced by one superior High Priest who would never die.
- The unfinished work of the priests was completed by Christ who is now seated.
- The Temple would be destroyed in 70 A.D. but God would receive glory in the church throughout all

---

1   J. Howard Marshall (1934-2015), *Acts, the Tyndale New Testament Commentary,* p. 85.

ages (Ephesians 3:21).

This shift away from the Temple is underscored in Acts when it says, **"And the word of God increased; and the number of the disciples multiplied in Jerusalem greatly; and a great company of the priests were obedient to the faith"** (Acts 6:7). Believers in Jesus Christ would no longer continue to worship at the Temple in Jerusalem, but would assemble with baptized believers. It would be hundreds of years before God's people would have buildings dedicated for their gatherings.

Another change for Christians and churches would be away from Sabbath worship to gatherings on the first day of the week – the day of the resurrection of the Saviour. **"And upon the first *day* of the week, when the disciples came together to break bread, Paul preached unto them, ready to depart on the morrow; and continued his speech until midnight"** (Acts 20:7). The Apostle Paul directed the church at Corinth, **"Now concerning the collection for the saints, as I have given order to the churches of Galatia, even so do ye. Upon the first *day* of the week let every one of you lay by him in store, as *God* hath prospered him, that there be no gatherings when I come"** (1 Corinthians 16:1-2). By the time of the writing of the last book of the New Testament, the Apostle John states he **"... was in the Spirit on the Lord's day, ..."** (Revelation 1:10). The Sabbath recognized God's work of creation; the first day of the week recognizes God's work of redemption. The Sabbath was a day people did not work; the first day of week is a day for God's people to worship in His churches.

The pilgrims braved the hardships of sixty-three stormy days across the Atlantic to find a new and safe place of worship in America. It was Saturday when they were within sight of their new homeland, but a strange thing happened. Suddenly a storm arose and drove them to the shore of Clark Island where they disembarked and made shelter for the night. The next day was Sunday. Instead of reloading their ships and sailing for Plymouth Rock, they spent that day in prayer, praise, thanksgiving, and worship of Almighty God. On Monday, December 11, 1620, the Pilgrims set sail and landed at Plymouth Rock. They had a deep conviction about the Lord's Day that they did not leave behind in England or Holland.

It is important that we get the place (the assembly of God's people) and the day (the first day of the week) correct and, having those things in place, that we worship the true and living God. In Spirit and in truth (John 4:24). The acts of worship by the church involve the very act of gathering itself (Hebrews 10:25), singing (Colossians 3:16), praying (Acts 4:31), giving (1 Corinthians 16:2), observing the Lord's Supper (1 Corinthians 11:26) and preaching (2 Timothy 4:1-2). *"The acts of worship without actual worship is a miserable, hypocritical experience. So, if worship wearies you, you aren't really worshipping."*[2]

They were Loving Churches

"…and breaking of bread from house to house…" (Acts 2:46).

One of the best ways to create an opportunity for genuine love is a share a meal in your home with your brothers and sisters in Christ. In days gone by, the family table was the center of life; now it is the TV trays. In Bible days, there was

---

2   Donald S. Whitney (1954-), *Spiritual Disciplines for the Christian Life*, p. 90.

no school and no meal outside the home.

There is nothing wrong with going out and having a meal in a restaurant. This has become so common there is usually nothing special about it to most people. A woman said to her husband, "Honey, let's go eat where we haven't been in a long time." The husband took her by the hand and walked her to their kitchen!

What a special thing it is to have a meal prepared by a host in their home. It shows others hands-on love. It may express humility. It can testify of God's abundant goodness to us. Around our table we can break "daily bread," talk about "daily problems," share "daily blessings," receive "daily encouragement," accept "daily correction," and hear "daily instructions."

There seems to be little separation from home-life and church-life. Our love for others in Christ is to equal that seen in a well-rounded family. We are to have "brotherly love" in our gatherings and fellowship (Romans 12:10; 1 Thessalonians 4:9; Hebrews 13:1; 1 Peter 1:22; 2 Peter 1:7). *"The Lord is training every local church to be a family, not merely a group of individuals, and the greatest quality of a family is love."*[3]

They were Joyous Churches

"...they did eat their meat with gladness and singleness of heart. Praising God, ..." (Acts 2:46-47).

The churches of the New Testament were made up of forgiven sinners, working through the daily process of becoming more like Christ, with the full assurance that when they died they would be in the presence of God eternally. How could they not be full of joy and praise?

3   Peter Masters (1940-), *Do We Have a Policy?* p. 77.

As Vance Havner (1901-1986) once lamented, "Too many church services start at eleven o'clock sharp and end at twelve o'clock dull." What a shame that is. There is no excuse for anything related to church-life being dull or boring.

The word "gladness" is translated from a word that speaks of exuberant joy. It sometimes refers to singing and dancing.

While many churches are about as joyful as an IRS audit and as pleasant as an emergency appendectomy, that was certainly not the case with the church of Jerusalem; nor should it be with ours. The assembling of God's people ought to be marked by the unique mixture of seriousness and smiles, weeping and laughter, sorrow and joy.

We should be able to say with the songwriter:

> *There's a sweet, sweet Spirit, in this place,*
> *And I know that it's the Spirit of the Lord,*
> *There are sweet expressions on each face,*
> *And I know that it's the presence of the Lord.*[4]

They were Growing Churches

"**And the Lord added to the church daily such as should be saved**" (Acts 2:47).

With sincere motive but misdirected zeal, some who have set out to grow a church need to discover that a large crowd is not the same as the Lord's church.

Baptized believers are called into God's work to partner in His ministry. "**Who then is Paul, and who *is* Apollos, but ministers by whom ye believed, even as the Lord gave to every man? I have planted, Apollos watered; but God gave the increase**" (1 Corinthians 3:5-6). "**Except the LORD build the house, they labour in vain that build**

---

4   Doris Akers (1923-1995)

it:..." (Psalm 127:1). It is God who grants favor and is keeping the real role of the saved in His churches.

In our day of celebrity preachers, we should all be reminded that great men have always been eventually replaced through the centuries of God's churches. No one is irreplaceable.

The pattern of growth in the Scriptures is not always churches getting bigger, but churches reaching further by planting other congregations. The relatively few megachurches overshadow the fact that the average church in America has an attendance of under one-hundred. In the Bible, it doesn't seem there were ever "missions" established out of churches, but other "churches" with full authority to baptize and minister in their location for their Lord. And some recognized churches were small enough to be assembled in someone's house (Romans 16:5; 1 Corinthians 16:19; Colossians 4:15; Philemon 2).

Every church should pray and plan for numeric growth. In Acts, there are actual and real numbers given to record God's work in His first (and only one at the time) church – the church at Jerusalem. Surprisingly, beyond that first church there is little or no biblical emphasis on numeral growth. In all the epistles to the churches -Rome, Corinth, Ephesus, Colossae, Philippi, and the churches of Asia - there is no push for attendance growth, no soul-winning counts, or financial campaigns. It was assumed if you grow in Christ you will be effective in reaching others with the gospel.

The numbers craze in our day has made its way into sound Baptist churches. It may not be a part of the modern conversation, but God has never depended on numbers to do His work. King Saul's son, Jonathan, encouraging his armorbearer to join him in a mission said, "**...Come, and** let us go over unto the garrison of these uncircumcised: it may be that the LORD will work for us: for *there is* no restraint to the LORD to save by many or by few" (1 Samuel 14:6). God used Noah's small family to do a very large and important job, wouldn't you say? Gideon's army got trimmed down to size so God would receive all the glory. Jesus started His church with only twelve and one of them dropped out. Jesus performed a huge miracle with the small lunch of a boy. Like the gospel songs says, "Little is much when God is in it."

Beyond the *growth* of a church numerically, there should be some consideration of its *health* spiritually. In most large Baptist churches congregational discipline is never exercised against openly immoral members. Why? While it would be good for the *health* of the church, it presumably would not be good for the *growth* of the church.

They were Persecuted Churches

"...What shall we do to these men? for that indeed a notable miracle hath been done by them *is* manifest to all them that dwell in Jerusalem; and we cannot deny *it*. But that it spread no further among the people, let us straitly threaten them, that they speak henceforth to no man in this name. And they called them, and commanded them not to speak at all nor teach in the name of Jesus. But Peter and John answered and said unto them, Whether it be right in the sight of God to hearken unto you more than unto God, judge ye. For we cannot but speak the things which we have seen and heard. So when they had further threatened them, they let them go, finding nothing how they might punish them, because of the people: for all *men* glorified God for that which was done" (Acts 4:16-21).

It is evident that the Jerusalem church became well-known within a matter of a few months, but they were not well-liked. While Acts 2:47 says they had the general "favour with all the people," the religious and governmental establishments were not among them.

The faithful members of the church at Jerusalem were persecuted and martyred by the Jews. At first, they were arrested and threatened (Acts 4:1-3, 16-20). Then, they were imprisoned but miraculously released (Acts 5:18-19). The deacon, Stephen, was stoned to death for his witness (Acts 7:58).

And what was the attitude of the believers who were mistreated merely because of their newfound faith in Christ? **"And they departed from the presence of the council, rejoicing that they were counted worthy to suffer shame for his name. And daily in the temple, and in every house, they ceased not to teach and preach Jesus Christ"** (Acts 5:41-42). As one person put it, *"The apostles were described as dignified by indignity."*[5]

Eventually, God would use persecution to move His people beyond Jerusalem into the regions beyond. **"... And at that time there was a great persecution against the church which was at Jerusalem; and they were all scattered abroad throughout the regions of Judaea and Samaria, except the apostles. As for Saul, he made havock of the church, entering into every house, and haling men and women committed *them* to prison. Therefore they that were scattered abroad went every where preaching the word"** (Acts 8:1, 3-4).

---

5   Marvin R. Vincent (1834-1922), *Vincent's Word Studies in the New Testament*, p. 472.

The Apostle James, likely the pastor of the church at Jerusalem, was executed by king Herod (Acts 12:1). Peter was arrested and miraculously freed (Acts 12:6-10). Later, Paul would be accused by the Jews and would be under house arrest for two years before being beheaded at Rome (Acts 28:30, 2 Timothy 4:6-8).

As witnesses for Christ, they knew what they knew, shared what they knew and were prepared to suffer for saying what they knew.

They were Courageous Churches

Early on that the leaders and members of the Jerusalem church were tested in their dedication to their Lord and Saviour. After healing a lame beggar at the gates of the temple, a crowd gathered to examine exhibit A. They were amazed that a forty-year-old man who was lame from birth was "walking, and leaping, and praising God" (Acts 3:8). No more a denier, Peter seized the opportunity and preached a gospel message. **"But ye denied the Holy One and the Just, and desired a murderer to be granted unto you; And killed the Prince of life, whom God hath raised from the dead; whereof we are witnesses. And his name through faith in his name hath made this man strong, whom ye see and know: yea, the faith which is by him hath given him this perfect soundness in the presence of you all. And now, brethren, I wot that through ignorance ye did _it_, as _did_ also your rulers. But those things, which God before had shewed by the mouth of all his prophets, that Christ should suffer, he hath so fulfilled. Repent ye therefore, and be converted, that your sins may be blotted out, when the times of refreshing shall come from the presence of the Lord;"** (Acts 3:14-19).

Peter's message went on for three hours - from three o'clock (Acts 3:1) until "eventide" (Acts 4:3). He actually never finished it. It was interrupted by the Temple police and Sadducees who arrested them and held them overnight (Acts 4:1-3). Despite this awkward situation, five thousand men believed (Acts 4:4). By the next morning, Peter and John, two Galilean fishermen, were brought before the highest level of Jewish religious law – the Sanhedrin. **"And it came to pass on the morrow, that their rulers, and elders, and scribes, And Annas the high priest, and Caiaphas, and John, and Alexander, and as many as were of the kindred of the high priest, were gathered together at Jerusalem. And when they had set them in the midst, they asked, By what power, or by what name, have ye done this? Then Peter, filled with the Holy Ghost, said unto them, Ye rulers of the people, and elders of Israel, If we this day be examined of the good deed done to the impotent man, by what means he is made whole; Be it known unto you all, and to all the people of Israel, that by the name of Jesus Christ of Nazareth, whom ye crucified, whom God raised from the dead,** *even* **by him doth this man stand here before you whole. This is the stone which was set at nought of you builders, which is become the head of the corner. Neither is there salvation in any other: for there is none other name under heaven given among men, whereby we must be saved"** (Acts 4:5-12). Just a few months before, these very people had attempted to get rid of Jesus. Now they were dealing with thousands of Jesus devotees that would be known as the church at Jerusalem.

"Now when they saw the boldness of Peter and John, and perceived that they were unlearned and ignorant men, they marvelled; and they took knowledge of them, that they had been with Jesus" (Acts 4:13). The skillfulness with which Peter expounded the Scriptures, combined with his unshakable boldness, left them in astonishment. These men had been with Jesus. It showed in the way they spoke.

And then, there was the lame man. "**And beholding the man which was healed standing with them, they could say nothing against it**" (Acts 4:14).

"**But when they had commanded them to go aside out of the council, they conferred among themselves, Saying, What shall we do to these men? for that indeed a notable miracle hath been done by them *is* manifest to all them that dwell in Jerusalem; and we cannot deny *it*. But that it spread no further among the people, let us straitly threaten them, that they speak henceforth to no man in this name. And they called them, and commanded them not to speak at all nor teach in the name of Jesus. But Peter and John answered and said unto them, Whether it be right in the sight of God to hearken unto you more than unto God, judge ye. For we cannot but speak the things which we have seen and heard**" (Acts 4:15-20).

This would be the first of countless attempts to silence the voice of God's churches, but to no avail. The kind of courage the early churches exhibited is the courage that comes from certainty; courage that comes from God; courage that is not impressed by the world; courage that is willing to suffer for their Saviour.

They were Overcoming Churches

The model of the churches of the New Testament might leave us with the false impression that everything was always wonderful – that they were perfect churches.

The Perfect Church
I think that I shall never see

A Church that's all it ought to be;
A Church that has no empty pews,
Whose Pastor never has the blues;
A Church whose Deacons always Deke
And none is proud but all are meek;
Where gossips never peddle lies
Or make complaints or criticize;
Where all are always sweet and kind
And all to other's faults are blind.
Such perfect churches there may be,
But none of them are known to me.

Author Unknown

In fact, the churches of the New Testament had plenty of problems. In the early chapters of Acts, the Jerusalem church faced problems from *without*. In Acts 5 and 6, they would face problems from *within*. John Philips says, *"Thus far the church triumphant had been marching forward in victory. Satan was unable to conquer it, so next tried to corrupt it."*[6]

They Overcame Deceit

In Acts 5, they overcame the problem of *deceit.* No one likes a hypocrite, especially in a church. We expect people who express a love for Jesus Christ to be honest and on the level. We want a person's word to be their bond. Hypocrisy is repulsive to God because He is holy and true.

New people flooded into the Jerusalem church by the hundreds. Acts 21:20 confirms the magnitude involved saying "many thousands of Jews there are which believe."

It is possible that among the *believers* there are a few *make-believers.* We can't be sure whether Ananias and

---

6   John Philips (1927-2010), *Exploring Acts*, p. 92.

Sapphira were saved, but what we can be sure of is they were not living like they were. You can have a saved soul, but an unsaved life.

Ananias and Sapphira got caught up in the spirit of generosity that many in the Jerusalem church had exhibited. Barnabas had sold some land and given the money to the church. So Ananias and Sapphira followed suit, but instead of giving all, they kept back part and claimed otherwise. It resulted in the first recorded funerals of the Jerusalem church.

One Bible commentator wrote this whole event off as "improbable" and only "legendary," suggesting that both husband and wife died of shock of being confronted with their hypocrisy.

It should be pointed out that these are the very thing many churches have lost – the seriousness of sin and a sober respect for the holiness of God. Like a stream at its beginning, in the first (and only) church there was a unique level of purity and holiness. The immediate burial of Ananias without ceremony or mourning sent a strong message to all the followers of Jesus and **"great fear came upon all the church, and upon as many as heard these things"** (Acts 5:11).

It is even true today that some church people want to take credit for making some sacrifice when there is so much they keep for themselves – money, time, energy.

This slowed down the surge of growth while he Jews kept away from the Christians and left them alone (Acts 5:12), yet **"...believers were the more added to the Lord, multitudes both of men and women"** (Acts 5:13).

They Overcame Division

In Acts 6 they overcame the problem of *division*. "**And in those days, when the number of the disciples was multiplied, there arose a murmuring of the Grecians against the Hebrews, because their widows were neglected in the daily ministration**" (Acts 6:1). The Jerusalem church had among their members two kinds of Jews: the local Jews who spoke Aramaic, the Hebrews, and Jews who lived beyond Palestine who spoke Greek. *"They spoke Greek because their native lands had been conquered centuries earlier by Alexander the Great. So the church consisted of Hebrew-Jewish Christians and Greek-Jewish Christians, and there was a language and cultural barrier between the two groups."*[7]

The charge was that the local Jewish widows were being taken care of, while the widows outside the Holy Land were being neglected. Originally, the apostles had looked after this matter (Acts 4:35), but it became a distraction to their primary ministry – prayer and the ministry of the word (Acts 6:4). The wisdom seen in the solution of this matter was that the ones appointed to this work were Greek-speaking Jews.

The solution to the fair distribution of goods to those in the Jerusalem church leads to another observation.

They were Local, Visible, Independent Churches

"**Then had the churches rest throughout all Judaea and Galilee and Samaria, and were edified; and walking in the fear of the Lord, and in the comfort of the Holy Ghost, were multiplied**" (Acts 9:31).

"**And Paul chose Silas, and departed, being recommended by the brethren unto the grace of God.**

And he went through Syria and Cilicia, confirming

---

7   Ray C. Steadman (1917-1992), *God's Unfinished Book*, p. 92.

the churches" (Acts 15:40-41).

"And so were the churches established in the faith, and increased in number daily" (Acts 16:5).

In the book of Acts through the book of Revelation you find only local, visible, independent churches. "The church" is not a New Testament term; it is not New Testament language. The New Testament term is "churches."

Churches were not under some centralized "mother church," ruled by bishops. The old Baptist theologian John L. Dagg (1794-1884) asserted, ministers *"have no authority from Christ to combine themselves into an ecclesiastical judicatory to exercise power in any manner."*[8]

In the New Testament, when a congregation was constituted as a church, it seems to have been done without any recorded form or ceremony. The gospel was preached, people repented and believed, they were baptized, then assembled as a church and were taught. They did not forward an official constitution to some ecclesiastical headquarters somewhere – their headquarters was in heaven.

They were Organized Churches

It might be assumed that since churches in the New Testament operated under the exclusive Headship of Jesus Christ, administered by the Holy Spirit, that they would just "go with the flow" and allow things to work themselves out.

To the contrary, the early churches were organized assemblies with real structure and order.

In Acts 6 **"the Twelve"** (apostles) gathered the **"multitude of the disciples"** (the church at Jerusalem) together to seek out **"seven men of honest report, full of the Holy Ghost and wisdom, whom we may appoint**

---

8   John L. Dagg (1794-1884), *Manual of Church Order*, p. 243.

over this business" (Acts 6:3). While the apostles had the Christ-given authority to make the decision on their own, they wisely involved the whole church which would mark the governance of God's churches that would follow.

The New Testament views every Christian as a minister of God. W. A. Criswell reminds us, *"The New Testament church is not a Broadway play for which one pays a price to be entertained by professionals. It is an army whose readiness and worthiness depend on well-trained, dedicated soldiers, all of whom perform specific and vital tasks under the able leadership of a commander."[9]*

Here are the officers of the early churches: the apostles (called elders, bishops, pastors) and the seven (known as deacons, servants) (Philippians 1:1; 1 Timothy 3:1-13).

- Elder... *presbuteros* (1 Timothy 5:17).
  Bishop... *episkopos* (1 Timothy 3:1).
  Pastor... *poimen* (Ephesians 4:11).
  Evangelist... *yuangelestas* (Ephesians 4:11; Acts 21:8; 2 Timothy 4:5... missionaries).
  Minister.. *laturgos* (1 Corinthians 3:5; 4:1; 2 Corinthians 3:6; 6:4; 11:3).
  Man of God... *anthropos theos* (1 Timothy 6:11).
  Preacher... *karuks* (1 Timothy 2:7).
- Deacons... *diakonos* (1 Timothy 3:8-13).

Peter was not the pope of the Jerusalem church. He says he was an "elder" (1 Peter 5:1). Others saw him, along with James and John as "pillars" in the church at Jerusalem (Galatians 2:9). The early churches did not have an autocratic form of leadership, where one person had supreme power. Neither did the church have an episcopacy system, ruled

---

9   W. A. Criswell (1909-2002), *The Doctrine of the Church*, p. 68.

by bishops. Nor were they ruled by a Presbyterian form of a group of elders who supervised and directed the decisions for the church. Rather, each church was self-governing. This was not a democratic "rule of the people," but a congregation operating under direction of God's Word and God's Spirit for the glory of God. While certain in the church had different ministries, they were equal in rank, privileges and opportunity. Any preference of the rich over the poor was seen for what it was – sinful prejudice (James 2:9). Any preference of the young over the older (Titus 2:1-8) or the older over the young was seen as disrespectful (1 Timothy 4:12). There was no distinction between the minister and the member, except in matters of honor (Hebrews 13:7, 17) and responsibility (2 Timothy 4:2).

It is never demonstrated that the authority of a congregation can be delegated. No committee, no deacon group or pastor has the God-given right to govern the church.

They were Disciple-Making Churches

"And when Saul was come to Jerusalem, he assayed to join himself to the disciples: but they were all afraid of him, and believed not that he was a disciple. But Barnabas took him, and brought *him* to the apostles, and declared unto them how he had seen the Lord in the way, and that he had spoken to him, and how he had preached boldly at Damascus in the name of Jesus. And he was with them coming in and going out at Jerusalem" (Acts 9:26-28).

Saul had only been recently saved. The dust of the Damascus road was still on his sandals. The baptismal water administered by Ananias had hardly dried (Acts 9:18). Without a single seminar, Saul was immediately out "preaching Christ in the synagogues, that he is the Son of God" (Acts 9:19). Saul had been a highly respected and seasoned Pharisee, but he was at the beginning a raw Christian.

For the sake of accuracy, we need to understand there was a parenthetical moment in Saul's life right after he was first saved and baptized. From Galatians 1:16-17 we know that Saul went to the desert of Arabia and was alone with the Lord for three years.

Back in Damascus, Saul's brethren rescued him from certain death at the hands of the Jews by letting him down by the wall in a basket (Acts 9:25); a real "basket case," you could say. Where would he go?

The natural place for Saul to go was Jerusalem, but everyone was suspicious of him. Rumors were Saul had been converted, but he had disappeared for three years. Where had he gone? Actually, God's people probably had some relief from persecution because of his absence. When he showed up at the doorstep of the Jerusalem church wanting their fellowship and encouragement, no one would have anything to do with him. And for good reason. Saul was had been their persecutor and a blasphemer; he had consented to Stephen's death; he still had the blood of believers fresh on his hands.

Saul was a social leper to everyone in Jerusalem. To help us see how awkward this situation was, it would be like a member of the Taliban walking in today saying he had recently trusted Christ and wanted our fellowship. We are often the most unbelieving believing people on this earth. We say the gospel is the power of God unto salvation. We say the Holy Spirit is able to save the lost. We say the church is open to all people. We "say" all of that, but, we don't always practice it. Every day we underestimate the greatness of God's grace. No one should ever be able to say truthfully that they came to church and were unwelcomed and unwanted. Oh, we are polite enough, but it may not be genuine.

Barnabas came alongside of Saul and broke the ice for Saul. "But Barnabas…" (Acts 9:27). It was not James, Jesus' brother, not Peter, not John the beloved, not Andrew, "But Barnabas."

Saul would eventually become the Apostle Paul, with favored status by the church of Jerusalem, believed and beloved of all. Everyone would want some time with *Paul,* but it was only Barnabas who extended his hand and heart to *Saul.*

New Testament churches were not about *getting quick decisions,* but were fully committed to *making life-long disciples.* God's churches are His principal discipling agency. Is it any wonder that those who become disciples outside the church often never find their way inside the church?

They were Missionary Churches

Acts 13 marks the second division of the book. Fifteen years passed since the events of Acts 2 and the great work of the church at Jerusalem. Now it is the church at Antioch in Syria that is highlighted.

"Now there were in the church that was at Antioch certain prophets and teachers; as Barnabas, and Simeon that was called Niger, and Lucius of Cyrene, and Manaen, which had been brought up with Herod the tetrarch, and Saul. As they ministered to the Lord, and fasted, the Holy Ghost said, Separate me Barnabas and Saul for the work whereunto I have called them. And when they had fasted and prayed, and laid *their* hands on them, they sent

***them* away. So they, being sent forth by the Holy Ghost, departed unto Seleucia; and from thence they sailed to Cyprus. And when they were at Salamis, they preached the word of God in the synagogues of the Jews: and they had also John to *their* minister**" (Acts 13:1-5).

The initial work in Antioch had been the result of the scattering of the saints of the church at Jerusalem (Acts 9:19). At first, they preached only to the Jews, but soon the good news could not be contained. God forced the gospel toward the Gentiles, with the results being a great number believing, and turning to the Lord (Acts 11:21). Barnabas was soon sent by the church at Jerusalem to encourage and assist this young church in their walk with God.

As Barnabas is working he thinks about Saul and says in his heart, "This is the kind of place that would be great for Saul and Saul would be great for them." Barnabas searched for Saul, found him, and escorted him to the church at Antioch. For what purpose? Together they "taught much people." Saul was discipled by Barnabas and now Saul disciples others. God never intended for us to feed on our pastor's messages each week and get fat and sassy. We are sought to seek others. We are graced to be gracious. We are taught to teach others. We are served to serve others. We are loved to love others.

Barnabas and Saul would receive an offering from the church at Antioch and take it to the people of the church at Jerusalem who were suffering because of a region-wide famine (Acts 11:27-29). Somewhere between this time and Acts 13, Barnabas and Saul made Antioch their home church and were quickly recognized as a part of their leadership team.

Acts 13 would provide the biblical model for missionary

work. How would the Antioch church send the gospel beyond their city?

- It would be done by the highest levels of church leadership (Acts 13:1).
- It would be done only after much church prayer (Acts 13:2).
- It would be done under the clear direction of the Holy Spirit (Acts 13:2)
- It would be done by congregational approval, authority and accountability (Acts 13:3-4; 14:26-28).
- It would be done as a training ministry for young ministers (Acts 13:5).

The method of doing all mission work directly through a local church is both scriptural and financially sensible. When a congregation, and not a mission board, administrates the finances of one of their own missionaries one-hundred percent of the monies given for mission work is received by the missionary on the field without any expenses removed for administration.

They were Diverse Churches

The early churches would become what one man called, a *"magnificent and intricate mosaic of mankind."* But this did not happen overnight. The cultures in which God's churches originally ministered were deeply divided. There were divisions between Jews and Gentiles, men and women, Romans and non-Romans, Greeks and non-Greeks, free and slaves, and educated and uneducated.

What the early churches discovered and declared was while there were great divisions in their culture there was level ground at the cross. That God **"will have all men to be saved, and to come unto the knowledge of the truth"** (1 Timothy 2:4), really meant "all men." "Whosoever will" really meant "Whosoever will." The God who was not "willing that any should perish" really meant that "all should come to repentance." (2 Peter 3:9)

New Testament churches were not country clubs requiring letters of recommendation or the promise of substantial financial support. God's churches were open to all.

At the beginning, the gospel went out "to the Jew first…" (Romans 1:16). The charter members of the church at Jerusalem were converted Jews. When persecution pushed the Jews out of Jerusalem, **"…they that were scattered abroad went every where preaching the word"** (Acts 8:4). The deacon, Philip, turned evangelist, went to Samaria and to an Ethiopian (Acts 8). Peter went to Caesarea and lead Cornelius and his household to Christ (Acts 10-11).

Later on there was a meeting of the churches at Antioch and Jerusalem about how Jewish the new Gentile believers had to be (Acts 15). Speaking of the Gentles, the Apostle Paul wrote, **"That at that time ye were without Christ, being aliens from the commonwealth of Israel, and strangers from the covenants of promise, having no hope, and without God in the world: But now in Christ Jesus ye who sometimes were far off are made nigh by the blood of Christ. For he is our peace, who hath made both one, and hath broken down the middle wall of partition** *between us;* **ordinances; for to make in himself of twain one new man,** *so* **making peace; And that he might reconcile both unto God in one body by the cross, having slain the enmity thereby: And came and preached peace** to you which were afar off, and to them that were nigh. For through him we both have access by one Spirit unto the Father. Now therefore ye are no more strangers and foreigners, but fellowcitizens with the saints, and of the household of God; And are built upon the foundation of the apostles and prophets, Jesus Christ himself being the chief corner *stone;* In whom all the building fitly framed together groweth unto an holy temple in the Lord: In whom ye also are builded together for an habitation of God through the Spirit" (Ephesians 2:12-22).

Churches today are basically homogenous. In America eight in ten (86 percent) have congregations with one predominant racial group.

One thing that may help restructure our thinking is that there are different "racial groups." In fact, there is only one race – the human race. It is the race that began with the creation of Adam (Acts 17:26). After the flood, the one race was divided by the children of the three sons of Noah. At the tower of Babel, the one race was divided by language. It will take the reign of Christ to bring the human family together.

It is the obvious divisions of cultures and languages within the one race where the problems exist.

They were Hope-Filled Churches

"Now the God of hope fill you with all joy and peace in believing, that ye may abound in hope, through the power of the Holy Ghost" (Romans 15:13).

The believers who were members of the churches of the New Testament abounded in hope because they loved one person, the "Lord Jesus Christ," and had but one message, "the gospel of Jesus Christ." "The gospel" is a noun meaning "good message." In the ancient Greek world, the word was used to "publish the good news from a battle."

When it comes to God's "good news," we must be faithful to God's entire message because "the good news" begins with "bad news." **"Wherefore as by one man sin entered the world, and death by sin…"** (Romans 5:12). **"The wages of sin is death…"** (Romans 6:23). **"For all have sinned, and come short of the glory of God"** (Romans 3:23). The "bad news" is what makes the "good news" great! God has provided "good news" for man's two biggest problems: sin and death.

Jesus Answered the Sin Problem

"Moreover, brethren, I declare unto you the gospel which I preached unto you, which also ye have received, and wherein ye stand; By which also ye are saved, if ye keep in memory what I preached unto you, unless ye have believed in vain. For I delivered unto you first of all that which I also received, how that Christ died for our sins according to the scriptures;" (1 Corinthians 15:1-3).

JESUS PAID FOR OUR SINS

Paul declared the gospel "first of all." The good news of Jesus is first in sequence and first in significance, **"how that Christ died for our sins according to the scriptures."** Jesus Christ fully paid our sin debt. He **"bare our sins in his own body on the tree"** (1 Peter 2:25).

JESUS PUT AWAY OUR SINS

The good news also declares Jesus put away our sins by His burial. **"And that he was buried, …"** Too often, the burial of Jesus goes unnoticed and unmentioned. It is actually one-third of the gospel message of Jesus Christ. The "burial" of Jesus proves that He really died. The tomb reminds us that through Jesus all our sins have been put out of God's sight. Our sins are forgiven and forgotten!

- "As far as the east is from the west, *so* far hath he removed our transgressions from us" (Psalm 103:12).
- "I, *even* I, *am* he that blotteth out thy transgressions for mine own sake, and will not remember thy sins" (Isaiah 45:25).
- "...for thou hast cast all my sins behind thy back" (Isaiah 38:17).
- "He will turn again, he will have compassion upon us; he will subdue our iniquities; and thou wilt cast all their sins into the depths of the sea" (Micah 7:19). And God puts up a "No Fishing" sign!

Jesus Answered the Death Problem

"...and that he rose again the third day according to the scriptures: And that he was seen of Cephas, then of the twelve: After that, he was seen of above five hundred brethren at once; of whom the greater part remain unto this present, but some are fallen asleep. After that, he was seen of James; then of all the apostles. And last of all he was seen of me also, as of one born out of due time" (1 Corinthians 15:4-8).

The literal, physical, bodily resurrection of Jesus Christ proves that His payment for our sins cleared the Bank of Heaven!

There were between ten and eleven resurrection appearances of Jesus recorded in the Bible. Some were one-on-one. Some were with the apostles. On at least one occasion five hundred were present to be with the risen Christ. After His ascension, Jesus appeared to Paul. **"And last of all he**

was seen of me also, as of one born out of due time" (1 Corinthians 15:8). The phrase "born out of due time" is one Greek word which means "a child born before its time, a stillborn child, an untimely birth, a miscarriage." Paul saw himself as "dead on arrival." His religion was no answer. His righteousness was no answer. His zeal was no answer.

If you were to take the time to read through the book of Acts you would discover their focus was entirely on Jesus Christ – who He was and what He did. Their hope was in an *Actual Jesus* (historical), an *Authentic Jesus* (messianic), an *Atoning Jesus* (crucified), an *Alive Jesus* (risen), and they were anticipating the *Advent of Jesus* (returning).

"...Christ in you, the hope of glory:" (Colossians 1:27).

"Looking for that blessed hope, and the glorious appearing of the great God and our Saviour Jesus Christ; Who gave himself for us, that he might redeem us from all iniquity, and purify unto himself a peculiar people, zealous of good works" (Titus 2:13-14).

Now let's pause, before going to the next chapter, for an application. During my fifty years of ministry as a pastor, I have had hundreds of people come through looking for a church home. Some had relocated to our community and were shopping for a new church. Some had come hoping to find an excellent ministry for their children. Some had fallen out with another church and were either the victims or the perpetrators. Some had encountered a life-shaking event and were looking for support. Some were just curious and had no idea what they wanted or needed.

The next time you find yourself in need of a church home you might want to look at the characteristics of the churches of the book of Acts and model your search using them.

- They were *Empowered* churches
- They were *Preaching* churches
- They were *Soul-Winning* churches
- They were *Believers'* churches
- They were *Baptizing* churches
- They were *Faithful* churches
- They were *Learning* churches
- They were *Unified* churches
- They were *Observant* churches
- They were *Praying* churches
- They were *Giving* churches
- They were *Reverent* churches
- They were *Worshipping* churches
- They were *Loving* churches
- They were *Joyous* churches
- They were *Growing* churches
- They were *Persecuted* churches
- They were *Courageous* churches
- They were *Overcoming* churches
- They were *Local, Visible, Independent* churches
- They were *Organized* churches
- They were *Disciple-Making* churches
- They were *Missionary* churches
- They were *Diverse* churches
- They were *Hope-Filled* churches

CHAPTER 5

The Blood-Bought History of Baptists

The landscape of world and American history has been dotted with great people who were neither angry nor ashamed to be known as Baptists. Among them were the famed author of *Pilgrim's Progress*, John Bunyan (1628-1688); Henry Dunster (1609-1659) the first president of Harvard who was fired for becoming a Baptist; George Washington (1732-1799) our nation's first president who was immersed by the Pastor John Gano (1727-1804) of the First Baptist Church of Newburgh, New York, a chaplain with General Washington in the Revolutionary War; the famed English pastor Charles H. Spurgeon (1834-1892) known as "The Prince of Preachers"; and Sam Houston (1793-1863), the father of the Republic of Texas, who was immersed on November 19, 1854 by Baptist minister Rufus Burleson in Little Rocky Creek. The preacher said to Houston, "Now Sam, your sins are all washed away." Houston replied, "God help all the fishes." Houston, noticing he had forgotten to remove his wallet before he was baptized, told Burleson, "Well, preacher, you've baptized my pocketbook."

So, who are these people called Baptists? What are their spiritual roots? Where did Baptists come from? There are several different theories.

- Some assert that Baptists had their origin with other Protestants during the Reformation as Anabaptists in the 16th century or the Separatists in the 17th century. In answer to the question, *"Did the Baptist church start before the Reformation,"* Albert Mohler (1959-), President of Southern Seminary, in Louisville, KY, said, *"We as Baptists are heirs of the Reformation,*

> *and we emerged there in 1644 in organized form as a separatist movement out of the Church of England that was a part of the Reformation...we shouldn't be embarrassed to acknowledge that we too are sons and daughters of the Reformation."*[1] Some go so far as declaring Baptists originated from the *"right wing of the Reformation."*[2]

- It is not uncommon that many among the ranks of Baptists believe that current Baptists are connected as an unbroken chain of Baptist-like churches from the time of Christ. This is often labeled a "Landmark" position, most notably promoted by Southern Baptist pastors J. R. Graves (1820-1894) and J. M. Pendleton (1811-1891).

- A modified position called "spiritual kinship" is that true Baptist churches have a connection in doctrine and polity with the church that Jesus founded during His earthly ministry, which by sovereign providence has been perpetuated through churches in every age.

Some view any study of church history as unnecessary. Their response might be, "We are who we are and where we are, so why look back to where we came from?" Many seem to think that because the doctrine of the church is not essential to the gospel that it is not important to the gospel. In fact, God's churches throughout the ages are the proof of the power of the gospel. Churches are God's agency for carrying the gospel to the unsaved world.

History is important and intriguing, yet it is amazing

---

1   Albert Mohler (1959-), October 31, 2005, broadcast www.albert-mohler.com.

2   Fisher Humphreys (1939-), http://www.baptisthistory.org/bap-tistorigins/baptiststheology.html.

that so few are informed about the developing history of Christianity and how different baptistic groups were God's witnesses from the time of Christ.

So, who were these people who were Baptists in name or in teaching?

Gregory A. Wills (1962-), Dean of the School of Theology at the Southern Baptist Theological Seminary, asked, *"Are Southern Baptists in danger of losing their identity? My response is, 'No, it is already gone.' Not entirely gone. Rather it is a withered relic of what it once was and what it should be."*[3]

When you refuse to be openly identified
as something, you will be closer to being
identified as nothing.

It is readily admitted that the churches of the New Testament were never called Baptist churches, but neither does a builder hang a sign on his newly built house that reads "Brick House." In doctrinal and practical essence, the church that Jesus built was in every way a Baptist church. It certainly had Baptist baptism and Baptist church polity.

"Christian history, in the First Century, was strictly and properly Baptist history, although the word "Baptist," as a distinctive appellation was not then known. How could it be? How was it possible to call any Christians Baptist Christians, when all were Baptists?" J. M. Cramp, D.D. (1796-1881)[4]

Were Catholics the Original Christians?

According to www.religionfacts.com, "For the first

3   Gregory Wills (1962-), *Southern Seminary*, Fall 2005, Volume 75, Number 2, p. 18.

4   www.reformedreader.org

1,500 years of Christianity there was no 'Catholicism' as it is known today, simply because there were no other forms of Christianity to distinguish it. There was only the 'one, holy, catholic church (catholic means 'universal'), which was the body of Christian believers all over the western world, united by common traditions, beliefs, church structure and worship. Before the Reformation (in the 1500s), if you were a Christian, you belonged to the Catholic Church. Any other form of Christianity was considered a heresy, not a Christian denomination." And everyone knows, if it is on the internet, it must be true.

The previous quote is the company line when it comes to the authentication of Catholicism.

There are two major problems. First, the Catholic system does not represent in the slightest the model of churches we read of in the New Testament. According to the new *Catechism of the Catholic Church*, they openly affirm (paragraph numbers are in parenthesis) that requirements for salvation include: baptism (1257), church membership (845), the sacraments (1129), obeying the commandments (2068), good works (1821), and the sacrifice of the mass (1405). The Catholic mass is the "sacrificial memorial in which the sacrifice of the cross is perpetuated" (1382) and that the sacrifice of Jesus must continue daily on its altars for the reparation of the sins of the living and the dead (1414). "Devotion of the Blessed Virgin is intrinsic to Christian worship" (971) because she was "preserved immune from all stain of original sin" (491), is "exalted as Queen over all things" (966) and "continues to bring us the gifts of eternal salvation" (969). The tradition of the Roman Catholic Church is of equal authority with the Holy Scriptures (82,

95).[5] The contrasts are vast and numerous between New Testament doctrine and Roman Catholicism.

Second, what eventually became Catholicism developed out of those who "left" the fellowship of sound churches or those who were "marked" because of their non-biblical teachings.

"Little children, it is the last time: and as ye have heard that antichrist shall come, even now are there many antichrists; whereby we know that it is the last time. They went out from us, but they were not of us; for if they had been of us, they would *no doubt* **have continued with us: but** *they went out,* **that they might be made manifest that they were not all of us"** (1 John 2:18-19).

"Now I beseech you, brethren, mark them which cause divisions and offences contrary to the doctrine which ye have learned; and avoid them. For they that are such serve not our Lord Jesus Christ, but their own belly; and by good words and fair speeches deceive the hearts of the simple" (Romans 16:17-18).

"Beloved, when I gave all diligence to write unto you of the common salvation, it was needful for me to write unto you, and exhort *you* **that ye should earnestly contend for the faith which was once delivered unto the saints. For there are certain men crept in unawares, who were before of old ordained to this condemnation, ungodly men, turning the grace of our God into lasciviousness, and denying the only Lord God, and our Lord Jesus Christ"** (Jude 3-4).

Baptists were Neither Catholic nor Protestant

The Catholic claim that they are the original Christians

5   Mike Gendron (1942-), *Preparing for Eternity.*

is seldom challenged. Their existence through the centuries is apparent by their elaborate buildings and cathedrals in the places they have invaded. But, what would eventually become the Catholic church in the fourth century had deviated well beyond the circle of scriptural New Testament churches.

Outwardly Catholicism appears in some ways to be Christian but has, over the centuries, embraced existing paganism wherever it has gone, modifying the Christian message to the extent that it is no longer mainstream, but heavily mixed with myths and magic. Superstitions were mingled with Scripture. Man-made church tradition has trumped God-given biblical truth.

The famed reformers, Luther, Calvin, Knox, and others, did not want to replace Catholicism, only reform it. So, Protestantism is only modified Catholicism. All the reformers died as baptized Roman Catholics having never received immersion upon a profession of their faith in Christ.

Baptists are not Protestants because they were never Catholics.

There is a dilemma for those Baptists who affirm that there had been doctrinal purity during the time of Christ and the apostles. Where was it through the centuries that followed? They must make one of two admissions. They must admit that their church's spiritual DNA is Catholicism, if Catholicism came from the apostles.

Or, they must sadly admit the apostolic roots died in the Catholic era of apostasy and were resurrected 1,200 years later during the Reformation period, leaving God without a sound witness for over a thousand years. One modern-day Baptist writer declared, *"True Christianity all but disappeared from the face of the earth. If the pure and simple faith of Jesus was alive during those years, it was underground, suppressed and hidden."*[6] What an amazing and unbiblical statement.

It was God's unfailing promise that He would receive glory in the church by Christ Jesus "throughout all ages" (Ephesians 3:21). Christ had promised "the gates of hell" would not prevail against His church (Matthew 16:18). To deny the certainty of this is to deny God's Word and Christ's promise. How would the call to "earnestly contend for the faith" (Jude 3) be possible if there were no saints, no churches, no faith existing after the pattern of the New Testament during those thousand years? Jesus had warned that the church at Ephesus could reach a certain level of unfaithfulness and have their "candlestick" (the source of their collective light) removed (Revelation 2:5). The light of any congregation is the presence of Jesus. If He leaves, turn out the light, the life of the church is gone. It may survive as a dead corpse for years, but without the life of Christ it is useless and dangerous.

A better confession is to understand that Catholicism was never *apostolic*, but *apostate* from the beginning.

New Testament churches had been repeatedly warned by the apostles about internal invasions that threatened the gospel.

"For if he that cometh preacheth another Jesus, whom we have not preached, or *if* ye receive another spirit, which ye have not received, or another gospel, which ye have not accepted, ye might well bear with him... For such *are* false apostles, deceitful workers, transforming themselves into the apostles of Christ. And

---

6   Paul Powell (1933-2016), *Basic Bible Sermons on Handling Conflict*, p. 120.

no marvel; for Satan himself is transformed into an angel of light. Therefore *it is* no great thing if his ministers also be transformed as the ministers of righteousness; whose end shall be according to their works" (2 Corinthians 11:4, 13-15).

"Take heed therefore unto yourselves, and to all the flock, over the which the Holy Ghost hath made you overseers, to feed the church of God, which he hath purchased with his own blood. For I know this, that after my departing shall grievous wolves enter in among you, not sparing the flock. Also of your own selves shall men arise, speaking perverse things, to draw away disciples after them" (Acts 20:28-30).

"I marvel that ye are so soon removed from him that called you into the grace of Christ unto another gospel: Which is not another; but there be some that trouble you, and would pervert the gospel of Christ. But though we, or an angel from heaven, preach any other gospel unto you than that which we have preached unto you, let him be accursed. As we said before, so say I now again, If any *man* preach any other gospel unto you than that ye have received, let him be accursed" (Galatians 1:6-9).

"Finally, brethren, pray for us, that the word of the Lord may have *free* course, and be glorified, even as *it is* with you: And that we may be delivered from unreasonable and wicked men: for all *men* have not faith. But the Lord is faithful, who shall stablish you, and keep *you* from evil" (2 Thessalonians 3:1-3).

"Whosoever transgresseth, and abideth not in the doctrine of Christ, hath not God. He that abideth in the doctrine of Christ, he hath both the Father and the Son. If there come any unto you, and bring not this doctrine,

receive him not into *your* house, neither bid him God speed: For he that biddeth him God speed is partaker of his evil deeds" (2 John 9-11).

Charles H. Spurgeon (1834-1892), famed English pastor known as "the Prince of Preachers," held to the following position regarding Baptists.

"We believe that the Baptists are the original Christians. We did not commence our existences at the reformation, we were reformers before Luther or Calvin were born; we never came from the Church of Rome, for we were never in it, but we have an unbroken line up to the Apostles themselves. We have always existed from the very days of Christ, and our principles, sometimes veiled and forgotten, like a river which may travel underground for a little season, have always had honest and holy adherents. Persecuted alike by Romanists and Protestants of almost every sect, yet there has never existed a government holding Baptist principles which persecuted others; nor, I believe, any body of Baptists ever held it to be right to put the consciences of others under the control of man. We have ever been ready to suffer, as our martyrologies will prove, but we are not ready to accept any help from the State, to prostitute the purity of the Bride of Christ to any alliance with Government, and we will never make the Church, although the Queen, the despot over the consciences of men."[7]

Spurgeon held an historic-Baptist position on the church. And a hundred years ago in America, the majority of Baptists believed what Spurgeon believed about the church. The influence of modernism, liberalism, neo-orthodoxy, new-evangelicalism, inter-denominationalism, ecumenicalism, and the modern church-growth movement

---

7   Charles H. Spurgeon (1834-1892), *Metropolitan Tabernacle Pulpit*, 1861, p. 225.

has left the past several generations with a distorted view of the true churches of Jesus Christ and the true doctrines of the New Testament.

Lester Hutson (1941-), in his book *A History of Churches*, makes a helpful contrast that had been established in just 300 years between the apostolic churches and the apostate churches in A.D. 325.

ORIGINAL CHURCHES	CHURCHES IN A.D. 325
Church and churches	Church visible and universal
Jesus the head of each church	Church headed by a system of priests
Each member equal; no hierachy	Members not equal; hierachy
The Bible the only rule of faith and practice	Tradition, the chief rule
Congregational government	Episcopalian government
Salvation by faith in Christ alone	Salvation thru rites and rituals
Membership of saved only	Membership of partakers of rituals
Members consisted of immersed believers	Membership by baptism, not belief
Only the saved eligible for baptism	Faith in Christ not a baptism prerequisite
Baptism only after a profession of faith	Infant baptism
Baptism by immersion	Baptism by sprinkling or pouring
Ordinances memorial	Ordinances redemptive
Permanent officers: pastors and deacons	Permanent officers: a system of priests
Freewill giving	Forced giving
Each church autonomous	State church
Spiritual warfare	Physical force[8]

Two Streams: One Pure, the Other Polluted

---

8   Lester Hutson (1941-), *A History of Churches*, p. 47.

All truth or heresy comes either from a pure stream or a polluted stream. Throughout history, these two sources have often run parallel to each other at the same times.

For more than thirty-five years I have enjoyed fly-fishing in the beautiful streams and high mountain lakes of Colorado. What I have personally discovered is that some streams are not what they seem. One year, only a few hundred yards downstream from where I was camping, a dead cow was floating in the middle of the stream. You would not want to drink from or fish in that stream. Everything downstream would have been affected by the contamination of the bloated cow.

There have been churches in every age, including our present day, which are in doctrine the offspring of Christ's original church and there are churches that are nothing more than man-made religious groups, founded hundreds of years after Christ and in many ways not conforming to the teachings of the New Testament. A church that has Jesus as its Founder, the Holy Spirit for its Administrator and the New Testament for its sole articles of faith and practice cannot be placed on the same footing as a church that was founded by a man and that teaches things contrary to the Bible. To say that all churches are alike is like saying all women are alike.

There are those who still strictly immerse believers with the authority of a sound local church and there are others who only perform merely "water ceremonies" after men's traditions.

Truth and error come from different sources, and when lived out, they follow two different courses and end up at two different destinations.

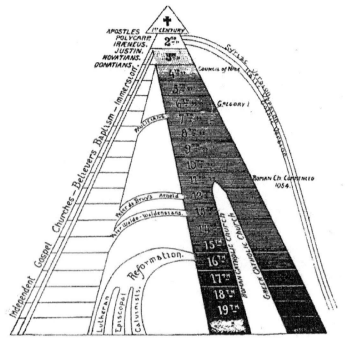

Chart by S. E. Ford (1819-1905)

"But the more I study the subject, the stronger are my convictions, that if all the facts in the case could be disclosed, a very good succession could be made out."

- David Benedict (1779-1874), *A General History of the Baptist Denomination in America and Other Parts of the World.*

"I now hasten to reply that it is not the teaching of the Southern Baptist Theological Seminary, through its Professor of History, that the origin of Baptists is to be traced to the Church of Rome in the sixteenth century... The Baptist churches, in my opinion, are of divine origin, and originated in the first century under the preaching and founding of the Apostles of our Lord."

- William Williams, D.D. (1836-1915) Professor of Church History in the Southern Baptist Theological Seminary, September 5, 1876.

"All well-informed Baptists are agreed in the belief that we, as a people, have continued from the time of Christ until the present."
- D. B. Ray (1830-1922), *Baptist Succession: Handbook of Baptist History,* 1871.

"All that Baptists mean by church "Succession," or Church Perpetuity, is: There has never been a day since the organization of the first New Testament church in which there was no genuine church of the New Testament existing on earth."
- W. A. Jarrel (1849-1927), *Baptist Church Perpetuity,* 1894.

"I have no question in my own mind that there has been a historical succession of Baptists from the days of Christ to the present time."
- John T. Christian (1854-1925), *A History of the Baptists Volume 1,* 1922, pp. 5-6.

Roman Catholicism taught a false gospel (the sprinkling of infants and the life-giving elements of the Lord's Supper) for over a thousand years before the reformation. All during that time there were still churches faithful to the Bible and the gospel. A Southern Baptist professor declared his appreciation for the Anabaptists who *"contended for the restoration of believer's baptism by immersion."*[9] In fact, neither the gospel nor the ordinances needed to be restored;

---

9   Barry McCarty (1953-), September 2015.

they only needed to be rediscovered. "Believers' baptism" by immersion has been in the world since it was first instituted by the first Baptist, John the Baptist.

Sound Churches Were Not Always "Baptist" in Name but Baptist in Principle

"… scattered, comparatively obscure, hunted and persecuted little churches, known by various names at different times and places – (were) churches of the New Testament type in doctrine and polity."[10]

While there were mild variation of doctrines through the years by our spiritual ancestors, they were in fact consistent in their major teachings. Baptist historian, Robert A. Baker (1910-1992) noted, *"Although sometimes tinged with errors of lesser or great magnitude, Christian groups holding to (their* individual relationship to God) … *were of sufficient numbers and strength to crowd even into the pages of the histories of their enemies. Considering the few histories written and the general bias of the ecclesiastical leaders who wrote, it is surprising that any record at all was made of religious dissent from the heavy-fisted, self-styles circle of orthodoxy."*[11]

It even took me a while to understand that when it comes to my Baptist family - you don't have to be *twins* to be *brothers*. Ancient Baptist identity has been defined by various separatist groups throughout church history. With regard to *form* and *function*, Baptists have historical connections with the following.

---

10   R. K. Maiden (1858-1939), quoted by Louis Entzminger, *The New Testament Church*, pp. 82-83.

11   Robert A. Baker (1910-1992), *The Baptist March in History*, p. 29.

- Montanists…150 A.D. Located in Asia Minor (modern-day Turkey).
- Novatians…150 A.D. Located in Armenia, Algeria, Spain, Phrygia, Constantinople, Alexandria, Carthage and Rome.
- Donatists…305 A.D. Located in Northern Africa.
- Paulicians…650 A.D. Located in Armenia.
- Albigenses…700 A.D. Located in Eastern Europe.
- Waldenses…1100 A.D. Located in Italy, France, Germany and South America.
- Anabaptists…1500 A.D. Located in Switzerland, England, Moravia, Germany, Western Europe.

"To obtain accurate information concerning these dissident groups as given in their own words is practically impossible. They were considered enemies of both the state and the established (Catholic…jdl) church; hence their writings were systematically destroyed. Most of the literature on which researchers must base their judgments was written by the groups' enemies… Considering that these people lived and labored in an era of abysmal spiritual darkness, a more sympathetic view of them may be warranted. It is a wonder that they possessed as much light as they did, as they had limited access to copies of the Bible and where hunted and hounded at every turn."[12]

In every aspect of doctrine, beliefs and practices they may not have always been thoroughly orthodox. While there may have been fanatics among these groups, they should not be defined by them. There is no denying it that these persecuted churches had their shortcomings – as do we.

The similarities of these various baptistic groups do not relate to an intentional attempt at succession, but

---

12   Earnest Pickering (1928-2000), *Biblical Separation*, p. 32-33.

came from their individual allegiance to New Testament ecclesiology. What caused their apparent commonality was their love for and obedience to the Scriptures. Baptists, and our ecclesiastical ancestors, were separatists, but not all separatists were Baptists.

Trail of Blood Chart, J.M. Carroll

While Baptists existed during the Reformation period, they did not originate in the Reformation. Anabaptists received their name from their Catholic and Protestant enemies because they insisted that infant sprinkling was not scriptural and maintained that only believers be immersed upon profession of their faith, thus they were denigrated as Anabaptists, re-baptizers.

"The Anabaptists did not initiate a new school of thought; they merely re-stated an ancient ideology – in the idiom of the sixteenth century to be sure, but ancient nevertheless. No one is credited with having invented the Anabaptism of the sixteenth century for the sufficient reason that no one did. Rebaptizing is as old as Constantinianism. There were Anabaptists, called by that name, in the fourth century. The Codes of Theodosius already prescribed very severe penalty, capital punishment, for anyone who was convicted of having rebaptized. In fact, the first Anabaptist martyrs of Reformation times were put to

death under the terms of these ancient Codes."[13]

Baptists Are Different from Other Christian Denominations

For a church to be a true, New Testament church it must have been started ...

- At the right time: 30 A.D.
- In the right place: Palestine.
- By the right person: Jesus Christ.
- With the right doctrine: the commandments of Jesus and the Apostles' doctrine.

From the first church founded by Christ, and expanded by the apostles, true churches have existed that hold the essential doctrines held by sound Baptists today. *"Churches which cannot meet these conditions can hardly be the churches the Lord established ... Even if historical records are not considered, the doctrinal test is enough. For example, how can churches which teach sprinkling for baptism or sprinkling of babies, neither of which is found in the New Testament, claim that they are true New Testament churches?"*[14]

One is often asked, "Where did all the Christian denominations begin and by whom?" The beginning of the various church denominations within Christianity can be historically chronicled.

---

13 Leonard Verduin (1897-1999), *The Reformers and Their* Stepchildren, p. 189-190.
14 Joe T. Odle (1899-1980), *Church Member's Handbook*, pp. 14, 16.

Denomination	Founder	Place	Date
Roman Catholic	Pope Leo I	Rome	440
Greek Orthodox	Patriarch Photius	Constantinople	869
Lutheran	Martin Luther	Germany	1517
Mennonites	Simon Menno	Switzerland	1525
Church of England	King Henry VIII	England	1534
Reformed	John Calvin	Switzerland	1534
Presbyterian	John Knox	Scotland	1560
Congregational	Robert Browne	England	1560
Quakers	George Fox	England	1650
Free Will Baptist	Paul Palmer	USA	1727
Seventh Day Baptist	John C Beissel	USA	1728
Methodist	John & Charles Wesley	England	1740
Unitarian	W. E. Channing	USA	1825
Church of Christ	Alexander Campbell	USA	1827
Disciples of Christ			
Evangelical	Jacob Albright	USA	1800
Primitive Baptist	Daniel Parker	USA	1831
Salvation Army	William Booth	England	1865
Church of God	Daniel S. Warner	USA	1880
Pentecostal	Charles Parham	USA	1901
Four Square	Amiee S. McPherson	USA	1914
Assemblies of God		USA	1914
Nazarenes	W. H. Hoople	USA	1919
Bible Churches	William McCarrell	USA	1930[15]

Missing among this list is the historical documentation as to when the original Baptist church was founded and by whom. *"No date can be cited, no place designated, and no founder named, with the positive assertion, 'This is where Baptist began!'"*[16]

"For hundreds of years Baptists had no problem regarding

---

15   Joe T. Odle 1899-1980), *Church Member's Handbook*, pp. 15-16; Robert J. Sargent (1948 -), *What? I Must be Re-baptized*, pp. 35-36; M. L. Moser, Sr (1899-1986), *Baptist Doctrine in One Year*, p. 237.

16   Joe. T. Odle (1899-1980), *Church Member's Handbook*, p. 14.

their relationship to other denominations. They were a persecuted, hunted people, fleeing from the power of tyrannical religion. Ancient Baptists carried the banner of Gospel truth even through the period of the Dark Ages, meeting secretly, but evangelizing with remarkable success. Since the rise of post-reformation denominationalism, Baptists have been faced with the problem of their relationship to other denominational groups. In the last fifty to seventy-five years the problem of interdenominational movements has been accentuated from fundamental Baptists in the United States. The growth of fundamental inter-denominationalism has been notable during this period and has produced a flood of mission boards, radio programs, schools, and other agencies. Its influence has extended into Baptist churches and affected the thinking of Baptist people. The spirit of the day is the spirit of 'togetherness,' a spirit which declares, 'Let us forget our differences so that we may all work together.'"[17]

Is one church as good as any other? Which church should you choose?

- A church founded by man or a church founded by Christ?
- A church that exists for man or a church that exists for God?
- A church that teaches heresy or a church that teaches truth?
- A church that teaches only part of the truth or a church that teaches all the truth?

At the present, everyone in America has religious liberty to practice their faith, whether they are right or wrong, but

---

17 Earnest D. Pickering (1928-2000), *Baptist Principles and Inter-denominationalism,* from *The Baptist Heritage Journal,* Volume 1, Number 1, 1991, p. 79.

that does not mean Baptist people are free to accept, approve or support false doctrine and practice.

God's People and Churches Have Been Persecuted and Martyred

In his Presidential address to the 1951 Southern Baptist Convention, the famed R. G. Lee (1886-1978) reminded his audience, *"Our Baptist forefathers wrote history in blood before they wrote it in ink. They suffered death – made jail bars, whipping posts, and torture racks blossom like Aaron's rod. As Baptists, traced through the centuries by a trail of blood, we should leave some bloody footprints as did our forefathers... "*[18]

In Jesus' inaugural public message, the Sermon on the Mount, He informed His disciples that they would be persecuted because they openly followed Him. **"Blessed are they which are persecuted for righteousness' sake: for theirs is the kingdom of heaven. Blessed are ye, when men shall revile you, and persecute *you*, and shall say all manner of evil against you falsely, for my sake. Rejoice, and be exceeding glad: for great *is* your reward in heaven: for so persecuted they the prophets which were before you"** (Matthew 5:10-12).

Baptist historian and original librarian at the New Orleans Baptist Theological Seminary, John T. Christian (1854-1925) said, *"The footsteps of the Baptists of the ages can more easily be traced by blood than by baptism. It is a lineage of suffering rather than a succession of Bishops: a martyrdom of principle, rather than a dogmatic decree of councils."*[19]

---

18   Ergun (1966-) & Emir Caner (1966-), Editors, *The Sacred Desk*, p. 166.

19   John T. Christian (1854-1925), *A History of the Baptists.*

Persecuted and Martyred by Jews

The faithful members of the church at Jerusalem were persecuted and martyred by the Jews. At first, they were arrested and threated (Acts 4:1-3), 16-20). They were imprisoned and miraculously released (Acts 5:18-19). The deacon, Stephen, was stoned to death for his witness (Acts 7:58). **"... And at that time there was a great persecution against the church which was at Jerusalem; and they were all scattered abroad throughout the regions of Judaea and Samaria, except the apostles. As for Saul, he made havock of the church, entering into every house, and haling men and women committed *them* to prison"** (Acts 8:1, 3).

Persecuted and Martyred by the Romans

The Apostle James, likely the pastor of the church at Jerusalem, was executed by king Herod (Acts 12:1). Peter was arrested and miraculously freed (Acts 12:6-10). Later, Paul would be accused by the Jews and placed under house arrest for two years before being beheaded by Rome (Acts 28:30, 2 Timothy 4:6-8).

When the great fire of the city of Rome occurred in A.D. 64, Emperor Nero blamed it on Christians.

Before the end of the first century the pastor of the church at Smyrna, Polycarp, a disciple of the Apostle John, gave his life for Christ. When given the opportunity to recant his faith in Christ, he said, *"Eighty-six years I have served him, and he never did me any wrong. How then can I blaspheme my king and Saviour?"* He was burned at the stake.

"In the early years of the second century, Ignatius, the pastor of the church at Antioch, was arrested for being a Christian and taken in chains to Rome to face the lion. Traveling overland through Asia Minor, he wrote seven letters to the churches he passed, using his authority as a martyr-in-waiting to encourage and instruct them. The three main themes of his letters were the problems that would preoccupy the church throughout the century: persecution and martyrdom, heresy and the authority of bishops."[20]

On and off for 350 years the Roman Empire prosecuted the threat posed by any professing Christian. Hostility toward Christians fluctuated throughout the empire due to local events or individual officials' actions. Christianity was punishable by death during this era, yet pardon was available to those willing to renounce their religion by offering sacrifice to the emperor or Roman gods. The offering of sacrifices became a particularly contentious issue and a kind of religious litmus test. Honoring Rome's gods and goddesses was considered a civic obligation and, at times, a law.

---

20   Stephen Tomkins (1968-), *A Short History of Christianity*, p. 26.

But many Christians refused to break with their faith. They were executed by the Romans and then honored by their fellow believers as martyrs.

During Emperor Decius's short reign (A.D. 249 to 251), all Christians were required not only to offer sacrifice, but also to acquire official certificates from witnesses to their offering.

Perhaps the most comprehensive of such anti-Christian hostilities were the early fourth century persecutions by the co-emperors Diocletian and Galerius. Fortunately for the Christian faithful, they were to be the last from the Roman state.

Persecuted and Martyred by the Catholics

In 313 A.D. the emperor Constantine I and Eastern Roman Emperor Licinius ratified the Edict of Milan which made Christianity a legal religion of the Roman Empire. Constantine's own conversion was a rare blend of compromised New Testament teaching, developing church tradition and raw paganism.

THE DARK AGES 426 AD - 1628 AD

With the establishment of the new Catholic temporal power, a bloody persecution began. Loyal Christians in New Testament churches, by whatever name they were called, were hunted and hounded to the utmost limit by this new Catholic power. The now government established Catholic Church began a war upon all who opposed her. During the bloody times of persecution, as Catholicism tried to exterminate the true churches, many of the false doctrines of the Catholic church of today began to be embraced and enforced.

J. M. Carroll (1852-1931), author of *The Trail of Blood*,
states, "*I again call your attention to those upon whom the hard
hand of persecution fell. If fifty million died of persecution during
the 1,200 years of what are called the 'Dark Ages,' as history
seems positively to teach — then they died faster than an average
of four million every one hundred years. That seems almost
beyond the limit of human conception. As before mentioned,
this iron hand, dripping with martyr blood, fell upon Paulicians,
Arnoldists, Henricians, Petro Brussians, Albigenses, Waldenses
and Ana-Baptists — of course much harder upon some than
others.*"[21]

Henry H. Halley (1874-1966), in his *Halley's Bible
Handbook*, wrote "*Anabaptists appeared through the Middle
Ages, in various European countries, under different names,
in independent groups, representing a variety of doctrines,
but usually strongly Anti-Clerical, rejecting Infant baptism,*

21   J.M. Carroll (1852-1931), *The Trail of Blood*, p. 26.

devoted to the Scriptures, and standing for absolute separation of Church and State.; very numerous in Germany, Holland, and Switzerland at the time of the Reformation, perpetuating ideas that had come down from preceding generations; as a rule, a quiet and genuinely pious people, but bitterly persecuted especially in the Netherlands."[22]

THE INQUISITION 1198 AD - 1700 AD

The Inquisition was instituted by Pope Innocent III and perfected under Pope Gregory IX. It was a "Church Court" established by the popes for the trying and punishing of "heretics"... a heretic being anyone who did not agree with Roman Catholicism. The Inquisition lasted for 500 years and was a time of indescribable horror. During all this persecution, Baptist churches continued to exist. More than ten thousand Baptists suffered death in the Netherlands alone, from 1566 to 1573, under the ferocious Duke of Alva.[23]

22   Henry H. Halley (1874-1966), *Halley's Bible Handbook*, p. 786.
23   *Encyclopedia Americana*, Anabaptists.

Persecuted by Protestants in Europe

While reformers Martin Luther (1483-1546) and John Calvin (1509-1564) are to be commended for standing against Roman Catholicism and fighting the free thinkers of their day, sadly, they battled the Anabaptists whom they labeled "fanatics," "libertines," "perverted," "malicious," "enthusiasts," people possessed of "insane pride," all quotes from John Calvin's *Institutes.* Other feared becoming Anabaptists because they were thought to be "insane hooligans."[24]

Unknown to many is the fact that John Calvin fought to maintain his own "state church" in Switzerland, including the ceremony of infant sprinkling he had learned from Catholicism. Geneva has been called the "Rome of Protestantism" and Calvin "the Pope of Geneva."

---

24   Stephen Tomkins (1968-), *A Short History of Christianity*, p. 164.

Beyond simply holding to his own positions and beliefs, Calvin led in the persecution of the Anabaptist who held exclusively to "believer's immersion." A section in Calvin's *Institute* is entitled, *Brief Instruction Arming All the Good Faithful Against the Errors of the Common Sect of the Anabaptists*, in *Treaties Against the Anabaptists and Against the Libertines*.[25] Such intolerance is inexcusable. Sadly, we must conclude Calvin's positions were not followed out of ignorance, but out of personal arrogance. The Anabaptists were God's witnesses to Catholics and to those who were leading the Reformation away from Catholicism. And, while it is true the Reformation leaders walked out the front door of the Roman Catholic church, all of them remained on its front porch. Ulrich Zwingli, Martin Luther, John Calvin, John Knox, all of them retained their Roman Catholic infant sprinkling and were never immersed as believers in New Testament fashion. They continued to retain and advocate infant sprinkling with no scriptural grounds.

In March of 1527, the Zwingli-influenced city council issued a strong edict against the Anabaptists, which was ratified in November: *"You know without doubt, and have heard from many that for a long time, some peculiar men, who imagine that they are learned, have come forward astonishingly, and without any evidence of the Holy Scriptures, given as a pretext by simple and pious men, have preached, and without the permission and consent of the church, have proclaimed that infant baptism did not proceed from God, but from the devil, and, therefore, ought not to be practiced. . . . We, therefore, ordain and require that hereafter all men, women, boys and girls forsake rebaptism, and shall not make use of it hereafter, and shall let infants be baptized; whoever shall act contrary to this*

25	Translated by B. W. Farley, 1982.

public edict shall be fined for every offense, one mark; and IF ANY BE DISOBEDIENT AND STUBBORN THEY SHALL BE TREATED WITH SEVERITY; for, the obedient we will protect; the disobedient we will punish according to his deserts, without fail; by this all are to conduct themselves. All this we confirm by this public document, stamped with the seal of our city, and given on St. Andrew's Day, A. D., 1525."[26]

Persecuted by the Protestants in England

Baptists were often arrested, fined and/or imprisoned as nonconformists in Great Britain.

The famed author of *Pilgrim's* Progress, John Bunyan (1628-1688) spent twelve years in prison for preaching without a government-approved license. He wrote, *"The Bedford jail was like all English jails of the day, and long after — a stink hole, foul and filthy almost beyond belief. The stench in the prisons was so nauseating and overpowering that those coming to visit doused their handkerchiefs with turpentine and held*

26   John T. Christian (1865-1925), *A History of the Baptists.*

them tight against the nose. There were no sanitation facilities except the most primitive. The only source of water was the hand pump in the prison yard. The food was meager, monotonous, unwholesome. Men and women prisoners were herded together, without privacy of any kind. All slept on straw, usually without a bedstead to keep it off the hard floor. Bedford prison had no fireplace so that it was freezing in winter. In summer, it was steaming hot because it had only a few small windows to let in a little light and air. Prisons were frequently swept by dread jail fever, which often carried off half the inmates. A long jail sentence at the time amounted, as often as not, to a death sentence. That Bunyan survived his long prison ordeal testifies to the health and strength of both his body and spirit — and to his good luck, too, though Bunyan ascribed his survival to the direct intervention of God."[27]

Years after his release, Bunyan recalled his possible demise by hanging as he sat in prison during the 1660s: *"Oft I was as if I was on the ladder, with the rope about my neck."* As his imprisonment wore on year after year, Bunyan sought a deeper meaning for the suffering that he was going through. He eventually came to the conviction that *"the church in the fire of persecution is like Esther in the perfuming chamber"*, being made *"fit for the presence of the king."* John Bunyan cared for his family by selling shoe laces until he was released. He died at age 60 after riding 40 miles on horseback in a driving rain to a preaching appointment.

Persecuted by Protestants in Colonial America

Clarence Larkin (1850-1924) wrote, *"The Pilgrims, or Puritans, did not come to this country to establish religious liberty; they came to establish their own faith, and to exclude all*

27   www.Cliffnotes.com

others from their colonies; and they were more intolerant in their colonial enactments against Dissenters than either England or Holland, whence they had fled from persecution."[28]

On a trip to Boston in July of 1651 pastors Dr. John Clarke (1609-1676) and Obadiah Holmes (1601-1682), with deacon Crandall, were arrested and committed to prison. What was their crime? They had held service at the William Witter home which resulted in converts being made and baptized. There was no prison in Lynn, so the alehouse was used. All were heavily fined, but Holmes refused to pay. He was taken to the Boston Commons and given thirty fierce strokes with a three-corded whip. This action was supported by the Congregational clergy that was the state church of Massachusetts. Holmes was left severely beaten

28   Clarence Larkin (1850-1924), *Why I Am a Baptist*, p. 10.

and bleeding. Two sympathizers who came to comfort him were immediately arrested and jailed also.

America was the home of the brave, long before it was the land of the free!

When the Great Awakening came to the American colonies, between 25,000 to 50,000 people turned to Christ. Since the population of the entire New England colonies at that time was no more than 340,000, this was an amazing move of God. It is a matter of record that from 1740 to 1760, 150 new Congregational churches were founded. Separatist churches multiplied, as did Baptist and Presbyterian bodies.

Isaac Backus (1724-1806) wrote that *"the great tragedy of the whole Awakening had been that many of its converts flocked into church 'very much blended with the world,' and did not see that infant baptism was the root of the evil which had deadened them in the first place."*[29] People who hold to Baptist beliefs have never been comfortable fellowshipping with other congregations who insist on holding positions that are clearly not scriptural.

John Leland (1754-1841), friend to James Madison and Thomas Jefferson, was an important figure in the struggle for religious freedom in America. Leland held strong Baptist beliefs. He wrote, *"John, the forerunner of Jesus, is called a Baptist fifteen times in the four Evangelists. Is it ignorance or ill will, that so often reproaches the Baptists with novelty? Is it not certain that the first preacher spoken of in the New Testament was a Baptist? Why should they be called a sect, when they can name their founders antecedent to the founders of any other society? Did not Jesus submit to therefore, a Baptist? These things are so. Baptism is no strange word in the New Testament. The*

---

29   C.C. Goen (1924-), *Revivalism and Separatism in New England: 1740-1800,* p. 208.

noun, with is relative verb and participle, occurs one hundred times.[30]

Baptists are More than Fundamentalists

The tide of liberalism came to the shores of Great Britain among the Baptists of the 1880s. The Baptist Union of Great Britain had been taken over by liberalism in most of their churches which led Charles H. Spurgeon and a few others to withdraw from its membership in 1887.

This is always the problem of joining unscriptural, man-made organizations; there is no real control over the slippery slope away from truth. The solution is that one will never need to withdraw from something they never joined in the first place.

Modernism and liberalism made their way to America in the early 1900's. The movement meant to offset this downward trend was labeled "Fundamentalism." It began in the 1920's focusing on the affirmation of five "fundamental" doctrines.

1. The inspiration and infallibility of Scripture.
2. The deity of Christ.
3. The virgin birth of Christ.
4. The substitutionary, atoning work of Christ on the cross.
5. The physical resurrection from the dead and the personal bodily return of Christ to the earth.

No Bible-believer would disagree regarding the importance of these core truths. These would be among the "first principles of the oracles of God" mentioned in

---

30   Miss L.F. Greene, *The Writings of Elder John Leland*, 1845 (1986 reprint), p. 79.

Hebrews 5:12. *"The Greek (word) refers to the basic elements in a system, or the elementary teachings. These are elementary in the sense that they are foundational."*[31]

The term "fundamentalist" has never seemed necessary or adequate to describe Baptists. Scriptural churches are called to **"earnestly contend for the faith which was once delivered unto the saints"** (Jude 3). We are to **"*be* ready always to *give* an answer to every man that asketh you** (and to those who don't) **a reason of the hope that is in you with meekness and fear:"** (1 Peter 3:15). Every sound Baptist affirms all the Bible to be God's Word which deserves our uncompromised allegiance, not just a small, select list of some teachings considered more principal than others. Jesus commissioned His church to teach believers to "observe (obey) all things" whatever He had commanded (Matthew 28:20), not just an abbreviated list of fundamentals, but the "counsel" of God (Acts 20:27).

From its very beginning, "fundamentalism" was a man-made Protestant movement which was intentionally and overwhelmingly interdenominational. The early leaders of fundamentalism came from all kinds of backgrounds: Congregationalist R.A. Torrey (1856-1928), Presbyterians B.B. Warfield (1851-1921), A.T. Pierson (1837-1911), and Donald Barnhouse (1895-1960), Methodist Bob Jones Sr. (1883-1968), Episcopalian J.C. Ryle (1816-1900), Baptist A.C. Dixon (1854-1925), and there were even Lutherans, and Wesleyan Holiness.

Fundamentalism was an ecumenical movement built on the false foundation of the universal-invisible church theory. This theory teaches that all believers at salvation are baptized by the Spirit into a universal/invisible body

---

31　Peter Masters (1940-), *Are We Fundamentalists?* p.7.

of Christ. It was called the "true Church" by C.I. Scofield.[32] Fundamentalism was at its very heart, interdenominational and took no position on the candidate or mode of baptism, the participants of the Lord's Supper, the form of government of the church, etc.

The fundamentalist movement was an attempt to reform Protestant churches, challenging them to retain biblical doctrine in the face of modernism. History records that their efforts ultimately failed. Just like the Protestant Reformation did not change Catholicism, fundamentalism did not remove the leaven of error in Protestant churches. Southern Baptist historian H. Leon McBeth (1932-2013) noted, *"A fact of far-reaching significance in American religious history is that while fundamentalism invaded most major denominations in the 1920's it captured none of them."*[33]

Many of the churches and schools that were started during the fundamentalism era are now moderate evangelicals at best, neo-evangelical at worse or no longer exist.

Kenneth T. Brooks (1951-) believes fundamentalism is now *"a dying patient on life support."* He further suggests, *"It is independent Baptists alone who are keeping it going. They should pull the plug."*[34]

Fundamentalism is a man-made movement.
Christ's church is a divine institution.

While true Baptists are fundamental in their beliefs, they do not seem to be benefited when they take to themselves the title "fundamentalists." We should treasure "the

---

32 C.I. Scofield (1843-1921), *Scofield Reference Bible*, p. 1249.
33 H. Leon McBeth (1932-2013), *The Baptist Heritage*, p. 578.)
34 Kenneth T. Brooks (1951-), *Why Cumbereth It the Ground*, p. 105.

whole counsel of God," not just things we might consider fundamental. It should be enough that we are known as Baptists. The major problem with fundamentalism is its tendency toward reductionism. The problem is not in what they affirm, but what they leave out.

Baptists are Less than Evangelicals

"The word 'evangelical' has been associated with the post-fundamentalist resurgence among Bible-believing Christians in North America. Significantly, the two most formative shapers of this movement are both Southern Baptist: Billy Graham and Carl F. H. Henry. While certain moderate Southern Baptists, reflecting an entrenched parochialism, have eschewed the label 'evangelical' as a 'Yankee word' unworthy for Southern Baptists to wear, more and more Southern Baptists are discovering that they have far more in common with conservative, Bible-believing Christians in other denominations than they do with left-leaning Baptists in their own denomination."[35]

And that is part of the problem. Too many current Southern Baptists view conservative Baptists as "right-leaning," when in fact they represent what Baptists have been for centuries.

While Baptists have always been orthodox in their doctrine and practice, Baptists have never been accepted as mainline and should not be in some important areas. We have always been marginalized by the majority of those who represent themselves as Christian.

Baptists are vastly different from the run-of-the-mill evangelical in their ecclesiology. Many evangelicals hold to infant sprinkling, while Baptists immerse believers only.

---

35   Timothy George (1950), *Southern Baptist Theology, Whence and Whither?* Founders Journal, Winter/Spring 1995.

Many evangelicals have open communion, Baptists keep the Lord's table for its members. Evangelicals have a variety of ways they order their congregations – bishops, elders, family owned and operated, while Baptists administrate their churches autonomously by congregational oversight.

It was true at least at one time, Baptists held to much stricter standards of separation in areas of gambling, the use of beverage alcohol and tobacco, dancing, music and modesty. Among many Evangelical churches or parachurch organizations you will find those who are openly pro-abortion, pro-LGBTQ (lesbian, homosexual, bisexual, transgender, questioning), pro-feminism, pro-drinking, pro-environment; the list is endless.

The problem of flying under the fundamentalists flag is minimalism, while flying under the evangelicalism flag is expansionism. Fundamentalists believe too little, while evangelicals affirm too much. For that reason, Baptists are less than evangelicals.

Baptists Are Not Pentecostals/Charismatics

Pentecostals take their name from the Acts 2 experience that occurred on the Day of Pentecost. As a movement, Pentecostalism coalesced in the early part of the twentieth century. The root of Pentecostalism, however, reached back into the nineteenth century with the holiness movement which was connected to the teaching of John Wesley and Methodism.

While Baptists and Pentecostals/Charismatics have some things in common – their belief in the inspiration of the Bible, the value of the death and bodily resurrection of Jesus Christ and worshipping on the first day of the week – there are vast differences that separate these Christians.

Baptists	Pentecostals/Charismatics
Once saved, always saved	Salvation can be lost
Salvation by grace is complete	Salvation is secured by good works
The Bible is God's final revelation	God still speaks through modern-day prophets or by the Spirit's direct revelation
The Spirit indwells every believer at salvation	The Spirit comes as a "second blessing"
Doctrinally-centered	Experience-centered
"Tongues" in the Bible were real language	"Tongues" is a heavenly/prayer language
"Men Only" called to be Preachers	"Women" may become Preachers
Divine healing	Divine healers by those who have "the gift"
"Sign gifts" discontinued when the Bible was completed and are now unnecessary	All "gifts" continue
Bible prosperity is spiritual	Bible prosperity is financial (name-it-claim-it)

While many in the Pentecostal/Charismatic movement could be considered brothers and sisters in Christ, there are plenty of indications of counterfeit leaders and followers who are "deceiving, and being deceived" (2 Timothy 3:13). The Charismatic preachers and evangelists on Christian television will one day be held accountable for taking advantage of the poor, the elderly, the sick, the suffering and the dying. The blatant materialism of these celebrity charlatans flies in the face of the values of our Saviour.

Baptists Are Not Ecumenical

While Baptist people are gracious to those from different denominations, most Baptist churches have "staunchly resisted most formal ecumenical involvement."[36] This is not because they are closed-minded, but because they have open Bibles. Baptists have never believed they are the only ones going to heaven, as they are often accused. It is not sectarian philosophy that separates Baptist churches from churches of other denominations; it is Bible truth and the failure to proclaim and practice it that separates Baptists from others. Those who do not join the ecumenical movement are charged with heresy hunting, causing division, rejecting diversity and spreading hate.

Christian coalitions made up of different denominations that have contradicting doctrinal beliefs and practices are conceived in naivety and birthed in confusion. The fact that Baptist churches are different is both positive and commendable.

W.A. Criswell (1909-2002) warned, "Ecumenicity is another name for death for our Baptist faith."[37]

What about many of our Christian brothers and sisters who are in churches that are not Scriptural and sound? How does God, who is not the author of confusion, (1 Corinthians 14:33), work with and bless those who are not entirely scriptural? J.I. Packer (1926-) says, *"God honors the tiny needle of truth hidden in whole haystacks of... error."*[38] Remember, God blessed the truth even when it was spoken by a donkey (Numbers 22:26) or a rooster (Matthew 26:74-75).

36 William H. Brackney (1948-), *Historical Dictionary of the Baptists*, p. 142.
37 W.A. Criswell (1909-2002), quoted by Joe T. Odle (1899-1980), *Why I Am a Baptist*, p. 89.
38 J. I. Packer (1926-), *Keep in Step with the Spirit*, 2nd ed, p. 21-22.

---

*"God honors the tiny needle of truth hidden in whole
haystacks of... error."*
- J.I. Packer (1926-)

Scripture is More Important Than History

One critic of Baptist perpetuity, Albert Henry Newman
(1852-1933), pressed, *"The claim of Baptists that in doctrine
and in polity they are in substantial accord with the precepts and
the example of Christ and his apostles would seem to make it
incumbent upon them to account for the early departure of the
great mass of Christians from the apostolic norm."*[39] In other
words, critics demand, "Show us the history."

Baptists do not need to rest their understanding of the
church's perpetuity on man's history, but on God's promises.
Louis Entzminger (1874-1958) wrote, *"I do not undervalue
church history, but far more important for me than fallible
human records of passing events is the New Testament forecast
of church history. The former may err – the latter never."*[40]

While we can appreciate those who have attempted
to preserve an accurate record of Baptist churches down
through history, we readily admit the following.

- Some history can be unintentionally flawed.
- Some history can be intentionally twisted.
- Some history is often purposefully omitted or
  carelessly overlooked.
- Some history was destroyed by its persecutors.

As one person noted, *"A lot of modern-day history books
record things that didn't happen by writers who were not there."*

---

39   Albert Henry Newman (1852-1933), *History of Anti-Pedobaptism*,
     1896.
40   Louis Entzminger (1874-1958), *The New Testament Church*, p. 58.

Buell H. Kazee (1900-1976) added, *"Our appeal is not to history, but to the Scriptures. History has had its good days and bad days, and that which has evolved through the councils and creeds of the last two thousand years is not the right basis of argument here. We go to the New Testament for our proper understanding of the church, and anything in history which does not agree with that is wrong."*[41]

Past president of the Southern Baptist Convention (1924-1926) and esteemed pastor of Richmond Virginia's First Baptist Church (1905-1927), George W. McDaniel (1875-1927), wrote, *"The first Baptist churches were the churches of the New Testament. It is not necessary to prove apostolic succession. It is of more importance to identify our churches today with those of the first century than it is to trace the history through the centuries when there was no recorded history... After the war, General Lee lost a beautiful mare, whether strayed or stolen he did not know. He advertised for her, describing her color and size in detail. Deacon William Campbell, of Essex County, Virginia, read the advertisement and saw near his home an animal that exactly answered the description. He wrote General Lee, who sent his son from Lexington to investigate. As soon as he saw the animal he said, 'That is father's mare.' It was not at all necessary to follow the tracks of that mare from Lexington to Essex. The main thing was to identify her with the one that was lost. The Baptist churches of the New Testament were local, independent, self-governing, democratic organizations. The Baptists of today answer precisely to that description and they are the only such in Christendom."*[42]

---

41   Buell H. Kazee (1900-1976), *The Church and the Ordinances*, p. 29.
42   George W. McDaniel (1875-1927), *The People Called Baptists*, pp. 138-139.

God Preserves What He Treasures

God Preserves His Creation

"**For by him were all things created, that are in heaven, and that are in earth, visible and invisible, whether** *they be* **thrones, or dominions, or principalities, or powers: all things were created by him, and for him: And he is before all things, and by him all things consist**" (Colossians 1:16-17).

While every creature in God's creation should be a good steward of the planet, we should not fall into the deep pit of pantheism with modern-day environmentalists. Everyone wants and needs clean air and water. It is doubtful that we have tapped all the resources the Creator made available for us. "This is our Father's world," as the song says, and He has done very well in keeping it together for us and to His glory.

God Preserves the Human Race

"**God that made the world and all things therein, seeing that he is Lord of heaven and earth, dwelleth not in temples made with hands;…And hath made of one blood all nations of men for to dwell on all the face of the earth, and hath determined the times before appointed, and the bounds of their habitation;…For in him we live, and move, and have our being;**" (Acts 17:24, 26, 28).

God created Adam and Eve as male and female to have the reproductive ability to extend and preserve the human race. The one-man-one-woman arrangement was God's means for perpetuating humanity. God's act of preservation applies to all people whether good or bad (Matthew 5:45).

God Preserves His Scriptures

"**The words of the LORD** *are* **pure words:** *as* **silver**

tried in a furnace of earth, purified seven times. Thou shalt keep them, O LORD, thou shalt preserve them from this generation for ever" (Psalm 12:6-7). We have God's Word in our possession today because the Almighty supernaturally inspired and sovereignly preserved it for us.

God Preserves His Ancient People – the Jews

In a conversation on religious questions, Fredric II, King of Prussia (1740-1786) asked Joachim von Zieten, General of the Husars, whom he esteemed highly as a Christian for his plain and uncompromised views, *"Give me proof for the truth of the Bible in two words!"* To which Zeiten replied, *"Your majesty, the Jews!"*

The preservation of the Jews must be one of the greatest miracles of history.

"If *it had not been* the LORD who was on our side, now may Israel say; If *it had not been* the LORD who was on our side, when men rose up against us: Then they had swallowed us up quick, when their wrath was kindled against us: Then the waters had overwhelmed us, the stream had gone over our soul: Then the proud waters had gone over our soul. Blessed *be* the LORD, who hath not given us *as* a prey to their teeth. Our soul is escaped as a bird out of the snare of the fowlers: the snare is broken, and we are escaped. Our help *is* in the name of the LORD, who made heaven and earth" (Psalm 124:1-8).

As one man asked, *"How probable is it that a tiny people, the children of Israel, known today as Jews, numbering less than a fifth of a per cent of the population of the world, would outlive every empire that sought its destruction?"* The fact that there are still Jewish people living in their promised homeland is a testament to God's power to save the nation through which He gave us the Scriptures and the Saviour.

God Preserves the Gospel

The word "gospel" means "good news." The apostle Paul clearly identified it as the message of Jesus' death, burial and resurrection. **"Moreover, brethren, I declare unto you the gospel which I preached unto you, which also ye have received, and wherein ye stand; By which also ye are saved, if ye keep in memory what I preached unto you, unless ye have believed in vain. For I delivered unto you first of all that which I also received, how that Christ died for our sins according to the scriptures; And that he was buried, and that he rose again the third day according to the scriptures:"** (1 Corinthians 15:1-4). Further, he said, **"...I am not ashamed of the gospel of Christ: for it is the power of God unto salvation to every one that believeth; to the Jew first, and also to the Greek"** (Romans 1:16).

"The Good News is the same for the teen with many years ahead as it is for the dying man with moments to spare. It's the message America with its plenty or Africa with its poverty most needs. It's the gospel for the world. The people to whom it is spoken or the place in which it is spoken change nothing."[43]

The gospel is called 'the everlasting gospel' (Revelation 14:6). Think about it. For the gospel to be everlasting it must remain precisely the same forever.

While many counterfeits have tried to replace it, the gospel has remained because God has preserved it by His power and by His providence.

---

43   R. Larry Moyer (1947-), *21 Things God Never Said*, p. 72.

God Preserves His Children – the Saved

Of the saved, 1 Peter 1:5 says, **"Who are kept by the power of God through faith unto salvation ready to be revealed in the last time."** Jude 24 affirms, **"Now unto him that is able to keep you from falling, and to present *you* faultless before the presence of his glory with exceeding joy, ..."** Jesus said, **"My sheep hear my voice, and I know them, and they follow me: And I give unto them eternal life; and they shall never perish, neither shall any *man* pluck them out of my hand. My Father, which gave *them* me, is greater than all; and no *man* is able to pluck *them* out of my Father's hand. I and *my* Father are one"** (John 10:27-30). Imagine Noah and his family precariously hanging on to eight huge pegs on the outside of the ark and God encouraging them, "Hold on." In fact, God called them into the ark and "shut the door" (Genesis 7:16). Noah may have fallen down many times on the inside of that ark, but he never once fell out of it! God has promised to never leave us nor forsake us (Hebrews 13:5). **"For the LORD will not forsake his people for his great name's sake: because it hath pleased the LORD to make you his people"** (1 Samuel 12:22).

God Preserves His Church

Is it reasonable that God would preserve His creation, the human race, the Scriptures, the Jews, the gospel, the saved ... and not preserve the church? Would Christ go to great effort to found a church to represent Him, and through whom He would do His work, love it, shed His blood for it, empower it by His Spirit and then not preserve the institution He had founded?

In fact, there are three promises the New Testament

records that guarantee the perpetuity of the church. Look them over carefully. Read them out loud. Turn them over in your mind.

- Matthew 16:18 "**...the gates of hell shall not prevail against it.**"
- Matthew 28:20 "**...lo, I am with you alway, even unto the end of the earth.**"
- Ephesians 3:21 "**To him be glory in the church by Christ Jesus, throughout all ages, world without end. Amen.**"

It is important to understand that the promises of perpetuity are not to an *individual church,* but to the *institution of the church.* The *institution* of the church has been perpetuated by *individual* churches.

For example, the first church, the church of Jerusalem no longer exists. According to F.F. Bruce (1910-1990), *"The first Jerusalem church lasted for some forty years. It left the city and went into dispersion not long before A.D.70, and although even in dispersion it continued...to call itself the church of Jerusalem, it had no more...direct association with the city. When Jerusalem was refounded as a Gentile city in A.D. 135 a new church of Jerusalem came into being, but this was a completely Gentile Christian church and had no continuity with the church of Jerusalem of apostolic days."*[44]

In fact, there is not a single present-day congregation from the New Testament era. The churches at Antioch, Ephesus, Laodicea, etc., did not survive. In the spring of 1812 Adoniram Judson (1788-1850), a Congregationalist missionary on his maiden voyage to India, became a Baptist

---

44   F.F. Bruce (1910-1990), *The Church of Jerusalem,* Christian Brethren Research Fellowship Journal 4 (April 1964): pp. 5-14.

after reading scriptures on baptism on that long trip. He stated, about the end of the apostolic age, that *"the truth is, that as soon as the spirit of inspiration withdrew from the earth, a multitude of errors and corruptions rushed in and deluged the church."*[45]

A former Episcopal layman, Clarence Larkin (1850-1924), who became a Baptist after a two-year study of the subject of New Testament baptism stated, *"The Baptists claim to have descended from the apostles. It is true that the line of descent cannot always be traced. Like a river, that now and then in its course is lost under the surface of the ground, and then makes its appearance again, the Baptists claim, that from the days of the apostles until the present time, there have not been wanting those persons, either separately or collected into churches, and known under different names, who, if now living, would be universally recognized as Baptists. The principles for which the Baptists contended were fiercely denounced as heresy and treason. Their existence and continuity can be traced down the ages by 'the strains of their martyr's blood, and the light of their martyr's fires.'"*[46]

Louis Entzminger (1874-1958) *"...could never understand why some Baptist rejoice to say there is no church-succession."*[47]

Perpetuity: The continuous existence of New Testament truth practiced by churches in every age from the time of Christ to the present.

The Apostle Paul tells the church at Ephesus that they were **"built upon the foundation of the apostles and**

45   Adoniram Judson (1788-1850), *Christian Baptism*, p. 90.
46   Clarence Larkin (1850-1924), *Why I Am A Baptist*, pp. 8-9.
47   Louis Entzminger (1875-1958), *The New Testament Church*, p. 56.

prophets, Jesus Christ himself being the chief corner stone; ... " (Ephesians 2:20). *"The succession which followed the setting of this foundation may not always have involved a person-to-person transmission, but there has been a succession of faithful teaching of the truth."*[48] And faithful teaching of the truth was carried on by "the church of the living God, the pillar and ground of the truth" (1 Timothy 3:15).

Roy Mason (1894-1978) adds this about Baptist continuity. *"There are some who insist that in order to adequately substantiate the continuity of Baptist churches through the centuries we would have to be able to establish a linked chain of such churches, without a break, from the very first one started by Jesus. I cannot agree with those who hold such a view, and indeed I consider it foolish. Let us remember what those dissenting groups were up against through the days of their awful persecution. Often they had to go into hiding, and if they wrote and published anything after printing came into vogue, it was usually seized and destroyed. Under the circumstances, it is remarkable that we have as much information about these groups as we have. Do I believe that there has been a linked chain of true churches through the centuries? I certainly do, but my belief in the continuity of Baptist churches does not depend upon being able to trace this unbroken chain. Rather IT DEPENDS UPON THE SACRED WORD OF PROMISE SPOKEN BY CHRIST OUR LORD. Since I have trusted my very soul to Christ, I can surely trust Him to keep His word to preserve His church. It is a pretty sorry Christian who says, 'I can't take the mere promise of Jesus - I must have some actual links hooked up in an unbroken chain from Christ until now, if I'm to believe in Baptist church continuity.'"*[49]

---

48 Mark Dever (1960-), *The Church-The Gospel Made Visible*, p. 19)

49 Roy Mason (1894-1978), *The Myth of the Universal Invisible Church Theory Exploded,* The Link Chain Bugaboo.

A.A. Davis (1900-1978), who preached the charge at my
father's ordination to the gospel ministry in 1943, devoted
a great deal of his life to preaching on Baptist doctrine and
church history. In his book *The Baptist Story... Sermons on
the Trail of Blood,* he offered an important insight.

*"Many facts relative to Divine Truth, some tangible, some
intangible, relate themselves to the great story of organized
Christianity. When God in the beginning created the human
family, He placed within them the power of reproduction and
commanded them to reproduce themselves. This, we believe has
been done continuously throughout all centuries, back to the
Garden of Eden. IF at any time in the journey the human family
had lost the power of reproduction or had refused to exercise it,
we believe the human family would have perished from the earth.
Then before the human family could have found its way down
to our day GOD would have been forced to another beginning,
another Eden, another creation of Man, and thus begin all
over again. In like manner, it appears to us that when Christ
established His Church on earth during his personal ministry He
placed within the* (institutional) *Church the Power to reproduce
itself (Matt. 28:19-20), and gave the Church the assurance of
His continual presence. This, we must believe, is exactly what
has happened. If the church lost that power to reproduce itself,
or refused to do so even though Christ was continually with
them, then TRUE Christianity would have perished from the
earth and Christ would have been forced to begin all over again.
Another Virgin Birth, another John The Baptist would have
been necessary to prepare a people for Him; in fact, if the Church
perished and no longer existed it meant Christ was unable to
prevent that disaster and the Gates of Hell did prevail against
the Church. We simply DO NOT believe this has occurred.
Therefore, we must reject the John Smythe (108) Se-Baptism*

movement as the origin of the Baptists, regardless of who teaches it. Also, the 1641 'New Discovery' incident cherished by Mr. Whitsett[50] back in the 1890's. We believe there is a dramatic story of a great people – today called Baptists."[51]

"Baptists need desperately to review their own Baptist history, rethink the Baptist position and rediscover the Baptist conscience."
- R. K. Maiden (1858-1939)[52]

---

50 William H. Whitsett (1841-1911), president of the Southern Baptist Theological Seminary in Louisville, Kentucky, taught that up to 1641 all Baptists employed sprinkling and pouring as the mode of baptism and that no case of immersion took place among American Baptists before the year 1644. Dr. D.B. Ray (1830-1922) believed, *"No man now living will see the end of the hurt Dr. Whitsitt has done the Baptists, no matter how often his position is disproved,"* *The Baptist Succession*, p. 53.

51 A.A. Davis (1900-1978), *Sermons on The Trail of Blood*, p. 9.

52 R. K. Maiden (1858-1939), *Re-Thinking Baptist Doctrines*, p. 166.

CHAPTER 6

What Do Baptists Believe?

Sherlock Holmes and Dr. Watson went on a camping trip. After a good meal and a short conversation, they lay down for the night and went to sleep.

Some hours later Holmes woke up. He nudged his faithful friend and said,

"Watson, I want you to look up and tell me what you see."

Watson said, "I see millions and millions of stars."

Sherlock said, "And what does that tell you?"

After a minute or so of pondering Watson said, "Astronomically, it tells me that there are millions of galaxies and potentially billions of planets. Astrologically, I observe that Saturn is in Leo. Horologically, I deduce that the time is approximately a quarter past three in the morning. Theologically, I can see that God is all powerful and that we are small and insignificant. Meteorologically, I suspect that we will have a beautiful day today. What does it tell you?"

Holmes was silent for about 30 seconds and said, "Watson, you idiot! Someone has stolen our tent!"

While Baptists were sleeping, someone has stolen our ecclesiology – right out from under our sight!

For one thing, the name "Baptist" is now missing. It hasn't just been removed; it's been discarded along with other items deemed useless or potentially harmful. Is the name "Baptist" still important? It has long been held that true churches are identified by their doctrine and practice, not just their name. But it seems that some churches, while dropping the Baptist name, have also softened what they are believing and practicing. Is it now necessary to fool people into attending a church by concealing its Baptist connections? The greater reality is they may not be that Baptist at all. This seems like a "bait and switch" marketing ploy which aggravates most consumers.

The Southern Baptist Convention set an example by removing "Baptist" from the names of their retreat centers (now simply Ridgecrest and Glorieta) and from their bookstores (now Lifeway), probably to have larger markets outside the traditional Baptist family. About 160 of the 253 Baptist churches in Minnesota and Iowa don't have the "Baptist" on their doors. Their previously named *Baptist General Conference* is now *Converge North Central.*[1]

Saying nothing seems to say everything!

Does posting a particular name matter less to God than what a church actually believes, stands for and practices?

There have been many good, Bible-believing churches throughout history that did not carry the name "Baptist," just as there are currently many liberal and unscriptural churches are Baptist in name and even still emphasize their Baptist name and heritage. According to Scripture, yes, God is concerned with what a church believes and practices. Doctrine, practice and philosophy of ministry do matter to God.

On the other hand, people looking for a Baptist church may avoid a "Fellowship Church" or a "Community Church," assuming it to be non-denominational or an inter-denominational group.

People have asked me, "What kind of Baptist are you?"

---

1   *Star Tribune,* Jean Hopfensperger, *What's in a Name? Churches Trade Old Names for New, Younger Members,* April 15, 2017.

I usually answer, "Do you know what Baptists were 200 years ago? That's what we still are." Sound, Scriptural Baptist churches have found no reason to move away from what they've always been.

Until recent years, if you openly held to the Baptist name you faithfully held to Baptist teaching.

Vance Havner (1901-1986), widely known Southern Baptist preacher and author, wrote, *"Some Baptists have departed so far from this position* (what Baptist once were) *that they would not be recognizable as Baptists to their forbearers. One old giant of my earlier days whom I came to know and admire used to say, 'When some of these Baptists get right they'll be with me for I'm where they used to be!'"*[2]

A.A. Davis (1900-1978), who for many years gave lengthy lectures on *The Trail of Blood*, affirmed, *"Pure doctrine, as it is found uncorrupted in the word of God is the only unbroken, though often disturbed, line of succession which can be traced throughout all the centuries."*[3]

We believe that Baptists originated, not in the reformation, not in the dark ages, nor in any century after the Apostles; that no person this side of Jesus Christ is a satisfactory explanation for their origin; that Baptist principles are as old as Christianity; and, that the likeness in doctrine and practice of sound Baptist churches to the churches in the days of the Apostles constitute them as churches of the Lord Jesus Christ.

In studying both the Bible and the history of Baptists, pouring over their writings and sermons, things becomes clear. As Joe T. Odle (1899-1980) wrote, *"There is no single distinctive doctrine which makes men Baptists. It is their position*

---

2   Joe T. Odle (1899-1980), *Why I Am a Baptist*, p. 24.

3   A.A. Davis (1900-1978), *Sermons on the Trail of Blood*, Foreword. p. 9.

*on a number of beliefs, which when taken together, make them a
distinctive people."*[4]

Baptists Believe in a Defined,
Declared and Defended Faith

George W. McDaniel (1875-1927), in his 1919 book,
The People Called Baptist, observed a sad state of affairs a
hundred years ago. *"In other decades Baptists were better
indoctrinated than they are today. The environment in which
they lived, sometimes inimicable* (unfriendly) *to them, was
conducive to the mastery of their principles. Of later years, a
tendency to depreciate doctrinal discussion is easily discernible,
and young converts particularly are not rooted and grounded in
the faith. Modern nonchalance acts as if it made little difference
what one believes. With cavalier air it belittles the man who has
the temerity* (nerve) *to make a denominational affirmation."*[5]

Baptist churches take seriously that they are **"the house
of God…the church of the living God, the pillar and
ground of the truth"** (1 Timothy 3:15). At least until recent
days, Baptists have held common theological convictions
which were typically found in most Baptist churches.

*"Baptists come in a variety of 'flavors.' They hold different
interpretations and views on certain issues, such as the
Second Coming of Christ, worship styles and denominational
organization. But all Baptists have the same basic ingredients.
There are certain ingredients that must be included, or the recipe
does not produce a Baptist. Leave the cornmeal out of cornbread
and substitute white flour, and you do not get cornbread.
Similarly, leave out a key ingredient of the Baptist recipe, and
you do not get a Baptist. What are these key ingredients in the*

4   Joe T. Odle (1899-1980), Why I Am a Baptist, p. 88.
5   George W. McDaniel (1875-1927), The People Called Baptists, p. 7.

Baptist recipe?"[6]

G. K. Chesterton (1874-1936) once said to keep a white fence looking white, you can't just leave it as it is. A white fence will eventually become a black fence. You must keep repainting it white repeatedly to keep it looking the same. If we are going to keep current Baptists believing the faith once delivered to the saints, we're going to have to keep repainting that fence in every generation. The point is that eternal vigilance is required to maintain doctrinal purity.

"Beloved, when I gave all diligence to write unto you of the common salvation, it was needful for me to write unto you, and exhort *you* that ye should earnestly contend for the faith which was once delivered unto the saints" (Jude 3). **"Preach the word; be instant in season, out of season; reprove, rebuke, exhort with all longsuffering and doctrine. For the time will come when they will not endure sound doctrine; but after their own lusts shall they heap to themselves teachers, having itching ears; And they shall turn away *their* ears from the truth, and shall be turned unto fables"** (2 Timothy 4:2-4).

"Baptists have not made their doctrines. We claim that they were handed down by a divine Lord through an inspired Bible and that it is not our duty to remake them or change them but our duty to know them, love them, live for them, proclaim them, and, if need be, die for them."[7]

The following are some of the major elements of Baptist faith.

---

6 William M. Pinson, Jr., www.baptistdistinctives.org/resources/articles/what-makes-a-baptist-a-baptist

7 Ergun (1966-) and Emir Caner (1966-), Editors, *The Sacred Desk*, p. 136.

Baptists Believe God's Word, the Bible, is their Sole and Final Authority

A man who became a Baptist from another denomination was asked how it happened. *"It was just plain carelessness,"* he said. *"Someone left a New Testament lying open and I read it."*

The Greek scholar, A. T. Robertson (1863-1934) said, *"Give a man an open Bible, an open mind, a conscience in good working order, and he will have a hard time to keep from being a Baptist."*[8]

Authentic

True churches have a high view of the Bible. **"All scripture *is* given by inspiration of God, and *is* profitable for doctrine, for reproof, for correction, for instruction in righteousness: That the man of God may be perfect, throughly furnished unto all good works"** (2 Timothy 3:16-17). **"For the prophecy came not in old time by the will of man: but holy men of God spake *as they were* moved by the Holy Ghost"** (2 Peter 1:21). All of the Holy Scriptures, not just certain parts, are divinely inspired, inerrant, infallible, imperishable, and preserved.

"The Old Testament in Hebrew and the New Testament in Greek, being immediately inspired by God, and by his singular care and providence kept pure in all ages, are therefore authentic; so in all controversies of religion, the Church is finally to appeal unto them."

- The Philadelphia Baptist Confession of 1742

---

8   Everett Gill (1869-1958), *Doctor Bob's Sayings,* p. 181.

God is true + God inspired the Scriptures = All Scripture is true
Romans 3:4   2 Timothy 3:16   *John 17:17*

Beyond a mere divine document, Baptists hold to the Bible as their sole authority. It has been simply said, "The Bible is the final authority of all matters of faith and practice."

Authoritative

Most Christians say they believe the Scripture to be God's word, but relatively few churches have submitted their beliefs and practices to its teachings. The Scriptures being a church's sole authority separates Baptists from Catholics, Protestants and Charismatics. Catholics recognize the Bible as a sacred book, but not their sole and final authority for truth and practice. Catholics add to the Bible (1) the requirement of someone in their church to interpret the Bible, (2) that the popes are infallible when speaking "ex cathedra" (from the authority of their office), (3) that their church's traditions have equal authority with the Bible, and (4) the addition of the apocryphal books which they declare are also inspired. In no sense is the Bible the sole and final authority of those who practice the Catholic faith.

It is little better among many Protestants. *"Both Luther and Calvin had real problems here. They properly interpreted the true teaching of Scripture in regard to baptism and other matters but would not submit to it. They defended the Scripture as God's word, but in many matters, would not obey it."*[9] While they both walked out the front door of the Catholic church, they stayed on the front porch, neither willing to renounce their infant sprinkling nor submit to believer's immersion. Their

---

9   Willard A. Ramsey (1931-2011), *The Nature of the New Testament Church on Earth*, p. 30.

intent was to reform the Catholic church, not renounce it.

While modern-day Charismatics openly and earnestly declare the authority of the Bible, their insistence on practicing the speaking gifts of the New Testament says differently. The Holy Spirit gave speaking gifts to the early churches until the written New Testament was completed. The speaking and sign gifts served as a confirmation to those who spoke as being God's men, giving God's word. When the full, written revelation was finished, those gifts naturally ceased (1 Corinthians 13:8-12). Most Charismatics base their life on the Bible *and* what they experience which never has to stand the test of the Bible.

Baptists are willing to hold up their beliefs to the pure and penetrating light of Scripture.

The problem with many modern-day Baptists is that their Bibles are unopened, unread, unknown, unbelieved and unlived.

Baptists Believe the Saving Gospel of Jesus Christ, Offered by Grace alone and Received by Faith alone, is the Exclusive Means of Eternal Salvation

One of my early mentors, Ray C. Morrow (1908-1991), taught there were two minimal essentials for a New Testament church: the right gospel and the right baptism.

"The right gospel is the gospel that we preach to every creature, Mark 16:15. It is the gospel that is the power of God unto salvation to everyone that believes, Romans 1:16. But what is the gospel? The word 'gospel' means 'good tidings' or 'good news.' Christ's gospel is the good news concerning what He has done to save everyone who believes on Him. 1 Corinthians 15:1-4 states very clearly that the gospel is His death, burial and resurrection for the complete payment for the believer's salvation.

This gospel tells us that Christ took our sins upon Himself and died in our stead to answer for the penalty of God's broken law; thus satisfying God's righteous demands, and offering the sinner a salvation completely paid for, Romans 4:25; 2 Corinthians 5:21; Galatians 3:10-13; 1 Peter 2:24; 1 Peter 3:18. Now Christ's gospel – the true gospel of the New Testament – does all of that. Which means that it is an eternal salvation that is offered, guaranteeing the believer that he shall never perish nor fall away and be lost again, John 5:24; John 10:27-29; Romans 8:29-39; Hebrews 6:4-6; Hebrews 10:14.

The true gospel of the New Testament presents Christ as the only Saviour, and the complete Saviour, Acts 4:12; John 14:6. When we by faith accept the finished product of grace, 'we are His workmanship, created in Christ Jesus unto good works,' Ephesians 2:8-10.”[10]

Unlike other churches that connect baptism or good works to receive or maintain salvation, Baptists believe the Bible teaches that eternal salvation is by grace alone through faith alone in Christ alone (Ephesians 2:8-9; 1 Timothy 2:3-6; Acts 4:12).

Some give credit to the Protestant Reformation for rediscovering *"the biblical truth of justification by faith alone [which] was a recovery of the biblical gospel.”*[11] Such a statement means that for hundreds of years the only message of salvation was in the Catholic church. God's message was never lost. Jesus promised, **"Heaven and earth shall pass away, but my words shall not pass away"** (Matthew 24:35). God has always had true witnesses in the earth. Since faith comes by hearing the Word of God (Romans 10:17), it requires that God's true word of salvation (apart

---

10   Ray C. Morrow (1908-1991), *What is a New Testament Church?*
11   Mark Dever (1960-), *The Church – The Gospel Made Visible*, p. 129.

from rituals and superstition) would be available in every age.

Baptist also believe in the eternal security of the believer. Salvation is not only a gift from God but also is sustained by the Lord. The Holy Spirit permanently indwells the believer at the point of faith and seals him in salvation for all eternity. Since salvation is wholly of the Lord, apart from the works of man, Baptists hold that the believer shall be kept by the power of God through faith unto eternal salvation (John 10:28; 14:16-17, 26; 1 Corinthians 2:9-14; Ephesians 1:13; 2:8-9; 1 Peter 1:5; Jude 24-25).

Baptists Believe Christ Founded the Church During His Personal, Earthly Ministry

Jesus declared, "…**That thou art Peter, and upon this rock I will build my church; and the gates of hell shall not prevail against it**" (Matthew 16:18). While some try to advance a Day of Pentecost birth for the church with the coming of the Spirit, Christ obviously promise He would built the church.

The initial formation of the church occurred on the day when He called the Twelve Apostles and ordained them (Mark 3:13-19; Luke 6:12-17). 1 Corinthians 12:28 says the apostles were the first to be set in the church by God. "**God hath set some in the church, first apostles…**"

The esteemed B.H. Carroll (1843-1914) affirmed, *"Christ alone founded his church. I mean that the church was established in the days of his sojourn in the flesh; that the work of its construction commenced with the reception of the material prepared by John the Baptist. That organization commenced with the appointment of the twelve apostles, and that by the close of his earthly ministry there existed at least one church as a model, the church at Jerusalem."*[12]

Baptists Believe in the Independency and Autonomy of their Congregations Under the Headship of Christ

Obviously, before the forming of Baptist associations and denominations, all Baptist churches were independent. All organized denominations, conventions, associations and fellowships with other churches are recent man-made organizations. The need to associate does not require that an association be created. Christian fellowship does not mandate that we form an organized fellowship. Independent is an adjective setting some Baptist Churchs apart from Baptist churches within organized denominations. The adherence to a church's independence does not come from a spirit of contention or an unwillingness to get along with other churches. It comes from a biblical understanding that the only scriptural institutions in the New Testament were independent churches, each of whom were fully equipped to do all of God's work.

Baptist historian, John T. Christian (1854-1925), said, *"The church, in the scriptural sense, is always an independent, local organization."*[13]

Baptist churches that are absolutely independent (without any denominational identity) are not *"off-brand," "split-off," "trouble-makers," "spurious"* but *"exactly like the churches of the New Testament."*[14]

Edward T. Hiscox (1814-1901), a respected Baptist

---

12 B.H. Carroll (1843-1914), *An Interpretation of the English Bible – the Four Gospels*, pp. 15-16.

13 John T. Christian (1854-1925), *History of the Baptists*, p. 14.

14 John C. Morgan (1930-2003), *Independent Baptist*, p. 29.

pastor and historian, wrote, *"As has been said, each particular and individual Church is actually and absolutely independent in the exercise of all its churchly rights, privileges, and prerogatives; independent of all other churches, individuals, and bodies of men whatever, and is under law to Christ alone. The will and law of the great Lawgiver are to be found in the New Testament, which is the only authoritative statute book for His people … A Church is not a legislative body, but administrative only … It cannot make laws, but it's the interpreter of the laws of Christ; the interpreter for itself, not for others. Nor can others interpret laws for it … There is no human tribunal to which they can be brought for trial and punishment, except that of public opinion."*[15]

The word "autonomous" means "self-governing." Each New Testament congregation was under the headship of Christ and conducted its own affairs under the supervision of the Holy Spirit. You can observe the autonomy of the Lord's churches in the following scriptures where they found solutions to the challenges within their own congregation (Acts 6), sent their own missionaries under their authority (Acts 13) and carried out church discipline on unrepentant members (1 Corinthians 5).

The ancient scriptural churches also stood for their independency against government control or intrusion into any of its affairs. The State-Church wedding that Constantine (274-337) performed in 313 A.D. brought together paganism and a corrupted form of Christianity. He made what would become the Catholic church the official church of the Roman Empire. The Donatists, and other of the likeminded Anabaptist in the centuries to come, wanted no part of it. The totalitarian state and church has wielded

---

15   Edward T. Hiscox (1814-1901), *Principles and Practices for Baptist Churches*, pp.145-146.

two swords to coerce people into false churches and kill those they branded heretics.

A current trend for modern mega-churches, Baptist and non-Baptist alike, is to have "satellite campuses." Modern-day Baptists expose their lack of understanding or appreciation of the pattern of the churches of the New Testament. I suppose they might dismissively shrug their shoulders and say, "That was then, this is now." Addressing this, Southern Baptist Seth Dunn warns, "*"Satellite ecclesiology is an accident waiting to happen. Church members who don't even know their own pastors are less likely to be doctrinally grounded or biblically discipled than those that do. Such church members are not in the care of any sort of biblical pastor but rather a 'campus pastor' in the employ of a self-styled CEO preacher who lives in another town. When I hear 'campus pastor' I don't hear 'poimén' (shepherd), I hear 'misthōtos' (which is translated into English as 'hireling'). When I hear 'multi-campus,' I don't hear 'Baptist,' I hear 'brand.'"*[16]

The first president of the Southern Baptist Convention, William B. Johnson (1782-1862), made this observation of what it means to be a church. *"The term church indicates one church, one body of the Lord's people, meeting together in one place, and not several congregations, forming one church."*[17]

There are no examples in the New Testament of a church having authority over churches in other locations. Churches that are under the authority of a mother-church organization follow the model of Catholic, Anglican, Episcopal and Presbyterian churches, not the New Testament model.

---

16   Seth Dunn, *Pulpit & Pen*, March 6, 2016, http://pulpitandpen. org/2016/03/06/recovering-the-satellites/

17   William B. Johnson (1782-1862), *The Gospel Defended*, quoted by Mark Dever, *Polity: Biblical Arguments on How to Conduct Church Life*, p. 171.

Before the current satellite campus trend, Baptist churches expanded by reaching out and planting new, independent churches.

It is recognized that while churches of the New Testament were independent, they also voluntarily assisted others churches as they carried the gospel or in areas of benevolence, but never at the expense of their own freedom to follow the Lord.

Christ alone is the Head of each congregation. **"And he is the head of the body, the church: ..."** (Colossians 1:18). **"And hath put all *things* under his feet, and gave him *to be* the head over all *things* to the church, Which is his body, the fulness of him that filleth all in all"** (Ephesians 1:22-23). **"But speaking the truth in love, may grow up into him in all things, which is the head, *even* Christ: From whom the whole body fitly joined together and compacted by that which every joint supplieth, according to the effectual working in the measure of every part, maketh increase of the body unto the edifying of itself in love"** (Ephesians 4:15-16). **"For the husband is the head of the wife, even as Christ is the head of the church: and he is the saviour of the body"** (Ephesians 5:23).

The analogy of the Headship of Christ is not one of an anatomical head (as though the body of Christ is headless and that Christ is a disembodied head), but an authoritative head (Christ being over the church at its Head). No human pope, bishops, elders or pastors preside as the head over Christ's churches. The omnipresent Christ alone is the Head of all His churches, as is clearly seen in Revelation 2-3.

John Huss (1369-1415) was burned at the stake by the Catholic church for declaring that Christ was the head of the church. He argued particularly that Christ alone is the head of the church and not the Pope, saying, *"who through ignorance and love of money is corrupt."* Even today in England, the Royal family is presumed to be the head of the Church of England.

God's churches have always recognized only one Head, Jesus Christ. (See more about the Headship of Christ in the next chapter.)

Here is a timely admonition made more than sixty years ago to the leaders and layman who are in rigid or loose Baptist denominations, associations or fellowships. *"Brethren who have been officials of a denomination have a paternal partiality about them which is so natural, and so sacred, that we have not the heart to censure it. Above all things, these prudent brethren feel bound to preserve the prestige of 'the body,' and the peace of the committee. Our Unions, Boards, and Associations are so justly dear to the fathers that quite unconsciously and innocently, they grow oblivious of evils which are as manifest as the sun in the heavens."*[18]

Baptists Believe in Two Church Ordinances Instituted by Christ

What is meant by the word "ordinance"? It means "order" or "command." Christ Himself ordained these two practices by example and teaching: baptism and the Lord's Supper.

CHURCH ORDINANCES, NOT MERELY CHRISTIAN ORDINANCES

The two ordinances are not merely Christian ordinances, but church ordinances, conducted with church authority, under church supervision and in church capacity. Sadly,

---

18   Willis B. Glover. Jr. (1917-2009), *Evangelical Nonconformists and Higher Criticism in the Nineteenth Century*, p. 170.

both baptism and the Lord's Supper have been turned into a sentimental soup, sometimes carried out without regard to the teaching of the Bible.

GOSPEL ORDINANCES

When New Testament churches faithfully practice baptism and the Lord's Supper, they are portraying the gospel - Christ's death and resurrection. Foot-washing is not a church ordinance among mainline Baptists. It is denied the same level as baptism and the Lord's Supper because it carries no picture of Christ's atoning work and was not practiced by the apostles as an order of the Lord. Foot-washing in John 13 was an "example" of Christian humility, but not a church ordinance.

RELATIONAL, NOT RITUAL

In the Old Testament, the lives of the ancient Jews were very much about rituals. Their annual feast days – the Day of Atonement, the Passover, and other feasts – were administered through priests. Their worship in the Tabernacle and in the Temple shadowed what Messiah would eventually do in their behalf.

On the other hand, the ordinances of the churches in the New Testament are relational – both with God and with other obedient believers. They would follow the exhortation of Jesus to "worship in Spirit and in truth." (John 4:24)

NOT SAVING, BUT NOT MERELY SYMBOLIC

Many non-Baptist churches attach "sacramental status" to the ordinances. Roman Catholicism teaches that through the sprinkling of an infant with water they are forgiven of original sin and at communion the bread becomes the literal body of Christ while the wine becomes the blood of Christ. They called it "transubstantiation." Protestant churches, like the Lutherans and Presbyterians, sprinkle infants to place them under the covenant relationship of their parents believing infant sprinkling is God's gracious means of conveying to human beings His saving grace. Most Protestant churches will accept any church's baptism "using water in any quantity and/or mode, together with the Trinitarian invocation instituted by Christ." Lutherans believe in something called "consubstantiation," that the substance of the bread and wine coexists with the body and blood of Christ in that moment. Both Catholics and Lutherans believe that baptism and the Lord's Supper are "sacraments" conveying God's grace to its participants.

The two ordinances of the church are symbolic, not saving. But they are more than empty symbols. They are repeated confessions within the assembly of their faith in a crucified, buried and risen Saviour and a testimony of their death to their old life and their resurrection to a new life in Christ.

BAPTISM ONCE, THE LORD'S SUPPER OFTEN

From the examples in the New Testament, baptism occurred after the time of conversion – and only once, while we are admonished to remember our Lord's sacrifice at His Table often until He returns.

Baptism

Baptism is the immersion in water of a believer to identify oneself with their Lord and Saviour by the authority of a New Testament church. This act of obedience is the initial step to becoming a member of one of the Lord's churches. Baptism is restricted for believers only, thus there is no infant sprinkling as a baptismal ceremony in the New Testament.

The sixth President of the United States of America, John Quincy Adams (1767-1848) wrote in his book, *Baptists, the Only Thorough Religious Reformers*, "*All who became members of the primitive churches were admitted by immersion; and as none were admitted but believers, none but believers were immersed.*"[19]

A.A. Davis (1900-1978) understood that "*Baptism has been the battleground of many hurtful religious heresies in the world today. That is where the religious world had its first argument. The waters of baptism. And significantly, the man who is wrong on the baptism question will invariably be wrong on the Lord's Supper question. Without a single exception.*"[20]

John A. Broadus (1827-1895) gives an insightful remark about the seriousness of baptism in his work, *The Duty of Baptists to Teach Their Distinctive Views*. "*Performing the ceremony in the name of the Lord Jesus, in the name of the Father and of the Son and of the Holy Ghost, makes it like an oath of allegiance, a vow of devotion, to Jesus Christ, to the Triune God. The early Roman Christians had a good word for this idea if only the word could have remained unchanged in use: they called it a 'sacramentum,' a military oath. As the Roman soldier in his oath bound himself to obey his general absolutely, so in baptism we solemnly vow devotion and obedience. But, alas! the word 'sacrament,' like many another word in Christian history has come to be employed in senses quite foreign to its original use.*"

The baptismal practice and position is where Baptists got their name, "Anabaptists." They did not receive the sprinkling of infants as scriptural. Our old Baptists friends called that simply "a water ceremony" and did not consider "moistened infants" as having been baptized. Further, they

---

19   John Quincy Adams (1767-1848), *Baptists, the Only Thorough Religious Reformers*, p. 152.

20   A.A. Davis (1900-1978), *Sermons on The Trail of Blood*, p. 23.

did not like the "Ana-Baptist" tag because they insisted they were not "re-baptizing" but performing genuine immersion of a believer after the pattern of the Bible.

There are several essentials that make baptism scriptural.

- Baptism is *not optional* for a believer. It is the first act of obedience for a believer and is the "answer of a good conscience toward God" (1 Peter 3:21).

- Baptism is for *believers only*. In the following Scriptures it is clear that baptism was always only for those who openly professed a personal trust in Jesus Christ for salvation (Acts 2:41; Acts 8:37-38).

- Baptism is by *immersion only*. John the Baptist baptized where there was "much water" (John 3:23). Scripture identified those being baptized as "going down" into the water and "coming up out" of the water (Acts 8:38-39). Romans 6:4 and Colossians 2:12 says baptism is a "burial."

- Baptism is *symbolic not saving*. Baptism does not procure salvation, but declares salvation. Baptism is a picture of the work of Jesus Christ in salvation – He was buried and raised from the dead. Believers are buried in water and raised out of the water in testimony of their faith in Christ and as a pledge to "walk in newness of life" (Romans 6:4).

- Baptism must have the *right authority*. Who has the authority to baptize? John the Baptist received his authority from heaven (John 1:6, Matthew 21:23-27). Initially, after Jesus was baptized by John the Baptist, He gave His divine authority to baptize only to His apostles (John 4:1-2). Then, before Christ returned to heaven, He clarified that the authority to do His work, which includes baptism, was in

His church (Matthew 28:19). The authority of the apostles to baptize was not as a special class of men, but as ministers of the first church. The apostles were the first to be set in the church (1 Corinthians 12:28). Apostles are not presently living on the earth to baptize believers, but churches of our Lord are here to carry out that work. Jesus' authority and presence has been extended "unto the end of the world" (Matthew 28:20), that is, to the end of this age.

- The authority is not individual, but congregational. If authority to baptize was given to individual believers, then little six-year-old "Billy" could dunk his buddy "Bobby" and that would be considered baptism. Except for the Ethiopian eunuch, every convert was added to a church by baptism. The Scripture is silent about the further story of the eunuch. Pastor Don McFarland (1937-) suggests, *"If Philip received authority to baptize the Samaritans from the Jerusalem church, and they became members of that church until they were organized, did not Philip have the same authority to baptize the eunuch? And, was he not also baptized into the Jerusalem church? It is unscriptural to baptize someone into nothing."*[21]

- The authority is not subjective, but objective. The issue of baptism isn't settled by how one "feels" about their baptism. Our personal feelings do not change the truth of the Bible

---

21 Don McFarland (1937-), Personal correspondence, April 25, 2017.

concerning scriptural baptism. The Bible is our final authority, not our personal opinions or feelings.

- The authority is not temporary, but permanent. Jesus declared in the Great Commission that His authority and presence has been extended "unto the end of the world" (Matthew 28:20).

• Baptism adds the obedient believer to a *church's membership* (Acts 2:41). Baptism is for a Christian, but it isn't simply a Christian ordinance. It is a church ordinance which places the believer in God's fellowship of believers, the church.

• Other forms of baptism ceremonies that fail to meet these requirements must be *rejected* (Acts 19:1-5).

Former pastor of the First Baptist Church, Jacksonville, Mississippi, Larry G. Rohrman (1938-2005) answers a question that is often asked, Why do Baptists not accept the baptisms of other churches? *"Although there are several answers to that question, the one that satisfied me most is that the person wishing to join a Baptist church must wish to do so badly enough to submit to the doctrinal beliefs of the church. If not, he should be a member of another church with which he can agree. If Baptists received members of any other church without asking them to be baptized, they would, of necessity, be forced to received members from all churches without baptism. Because of the divergence of belief about baptism they would create a theological state of confusion. One year the children in the church could be taught by a former member of the Church of Christ who would inform them that they have to be baptized to be saved and the next year they could be told by one who holds the Baptist position that they do not have to be baptized to be saved. Baptists are saying, 'If you wish to be a member of our church, you must submit totally to our theology.'"*[22]

While immersion is not entirely unique to Baptist churches, Baptist baptism is unique because our spiritual ancestors, the Anabaptists, gave their lives for their belief and for our privilege.

The blood of martyrs is in our baptismal waters.

- Felix Manz (1495-1527). His accusers planned to make a powerful mockery of his baptism by drowning him in the lake and thereby cruelly enforcing a recent edict that demanded death for those who resisted the powers on matters of baptism. It was the ultimate cost for Manz's convictions. Manz was executed by drowning in Zürich on the Limmat River. His alleged last words were, "Into thy hands, O God, I commend my spirit." Drowning an Anabaptist was a cruel lampoon of their practice of water baptism. This method was referred to as their "third baptism" by those who mocked and opposed immersion.

- Balthasar Hubmaier (1480-1528). Constantly hunted by imperial authorities, in 1527 Hübmaier was seized and taken to Vienna along with his wife. He was tried for heresy, convicted, and taken through the streets to the public square. As he was being prepared for the fire, his wife shouted exhortations to him to hold steadfast to his faith. Three days after his execution, his wife was taken to the River Danube and drowned with a large stone tied around her neck.

---

22   Larry G. Rohrman (1938-2005), quoted by Joe T. Odle, *Why I Am a Baptist*, p. 53.

Infant sprinkling has many defenders but no defense. When the Catholic Church split into the Roman and Greek branches in A.D. 1054, the Greek branch retained immersion (of infants) as its mode of baptism. Sprinkling did not become the official mode of the Roman Catholic Church until the 13th century. Although the Protestant reformers left the Catholic church, they took with them infant sprinkling.

Stephen F. Olford (1918-2004) points out that baptism by immersion is...

- Enjoined in the Gospels (Matthew 28:19; Mark 16:15).
- Exemplified in Acts (2:41; 8:36-38; 9:18; 19:47-48; 16:15, 33; 19:5).
- Explained in the Epistles (Romans 6:3-5; Ephesians 4:5; Galatians 3:27; 1 Peter 3:21).[23]

Russell D. Moore (1971-) reminds us, *"Our forefathers were drowned in European rivers, chained to the walls of English prisons and driven from the borders of New England colony towns, not because they saw baptism as a maker of ethnic identity, but because they believed that every word of Scripture (including the word 'baptizo') was breathed out by an infinitely holy God and thus carried with them the very authority of His majesty. They were willing to be indicted, convicted, horsewhipped and martyred because they believed that when Jesus said through His inerrant revelation, 'baptizing them in the name of the Father, the Son and the Holy Spirit,' He meant something specific."*[24]

---

23 Stephen F. Olford (1918-2004), *Committed to Christ and His Church*, pp. 84-85.
24 Russell D. Moore (1971-), *Southern Seminary*, Fall 2005, Volume 73, Number 2, p. 10.

The Lord's Supper

The Lord's Supper, Communion as it is sometimes called, is the memorial of the local congregation to remember their collective Saviour whose body was broken and whose blood was shed for them. The much-loved W. A. Criswell (1909-2002) wrote this about the Lord's Supper. *"When believers observe the Lord's Supper, they are to remember that Jesus gave Himself as a sacrifice for sin. Note the preposition 'for' in 1 Corinthians 11:24: 'This is my body, which is broken for you.' That preposition 'for' (hyper, Greek) means in behalf of. It means that Jesus has done something in our behalf that we could never do for ourselves. Only Jesus on the cross could have secured redemption for sin. The Lord's Supper is a perpetual reminder that it was the death of Jesus that secured atonement for sin. When the believer comes to the Lord's Table, he is to remember that Jesus died for him. As the Passover served as a remembrance of God's deliverance of the Israelites from the bondage of Egyptian slavery, the Lord's Supper, for the Christian, serves as a perpetual reminder of Christ's deliverance of unbelievers from sin."*[25]

The two elements used in observing of the Lord's Supper were taken from the Jewish Passover. They are unleavened bread, representing the pure, broken body of our Saviour and the fruit of the vine, representing the pure blood of Christ which was freely shed for the remission of our sins. These elements declare the redemptive work of Christ as the gathered church remembers their Saviour (1 Corinthians 11:24-25).

There are three common positions regarding those who are welcome at the Lord's Supper.

---

25   W. A. Criswell (1909-2002), *The Doctrine of the Church*, pp. 99-100.

OPEN COMMUNION...CHRISTIAN COMMUNION

Open communion is what D. B. Ray (1830-1922) called *"mixed communion"* or *"loose communion."*[26] This view teaches all who wish to partake may do so in any church, at any time. While not making any judgment about one's personal worthiness, such a position does not recognize the authority Christ gave His churches. To hold this view is to hold that all churches are equally sound in their view of salvation, the ordinances and doctrine.

CLOSE COMMUNION...BAPTIST COMMUNION

Baptists a hundred years ago used only the terms of "open" or "close" communion. John T. Christian's (1854-1925) 1892 booklet was entitled, *Close Communion.* The Preface says, *"The position of Baptists upon the Communion question is one of neutrality. We do not invite others to participate with us, and we not inviting others, we do not accept invitations...The brotherhood of the New Testament were one in fellowship and doctrines. Under those conditions open communion was impossible. This view is confirmed by all history. I have been unable to find an instance of open communion for the first sixteen hundred years after Christ."*

J. R. Graves (1820-1893) called allowing others who were not Baptist to take communion, *"intercommunion,"* declaring, *"now so generally practiced among Baptists, is not only unscriptural and inconsistent, but is working many and serious evils, and immense loss to our denomination."*[27]

In our day, close communion is considered the practice of allowing other Baptists to take communion in another

26   D.B. Ray (1830-1922), *Baptist Succession,* p.268.

27   J.R. Graves (1820-1893), *Intercommunion – Inconsistent, Unscriptural and Productive of Evil,* reproduced by www.baptisttheology. org.

Baptist church. Yet, the only church which could be able to know one's spiritual status is the one to which they belong as members. While we have regard and admiration for all people in Christ in other Baptist churches, our genuine and apparent relationship is with the church where we are members. The only authority a church exercises is among its own members.

For further clarification, another term has been introduced.

CLOSED COMMUNION...CONGREGATIONAL COMMUNION

Closed communion restricts the Lord's Supper to only those who are members in good standing of the church observing the Supper.

John T. Christian (1854-1925) said, "*Baptists are strict communionists, and are likely to remain such. We want to be as close as the Bible. If we have prospered as a people, it is because we have rigidly adhered to the Word of God. Whenever we turn aside from this well-trodden path for mere sentimentality or transient popularity, the day of our power and usefulness is gone. We are compelled to search for the old paths, and when we have found them to walk in them. Despite all criticisms and abuse we have prospered as strict communionists.*"[28]

Presbyterian J. L. Withrow (1888), speaking of Baptists, said, "*In their favor it is to be said, they have proved, beyond peradventure that narrow church doors and severe communion conditions do not bar people out of the Christian church.*"[29]

Dr. P. H. Mell (1814-1888), late Chancellor of the University of Georgia, said, "*There can be no scriptural*

---

28 John T. Christian (1854-1925), *Close Communion, or Baptism as a Prerequisite to the Lord's Supper*, p. 21.

29 Ibid, p. 22.

communion excepting as performed by a local gospel church; there can be no local gospel church excepting as composed of individual members; there can be no individual members excepting as they are received on a vote of the local church; none are eligible to be voted for as church members excepting such as have been baptized on a profession of their faith in Christ; nothing is scriptural baptism but immersion upon a profession of faith in Christ; therefore, there can be no scriptural communion which has not been preceded by that ordinance, scriptural immersion.[30]

Baptist giant, B. H. Carroll (1843-1914) believed, "*There is no more convincing argument against open communion of any kind. No open communion argument can stand before the declaration, 'It is the Lord's table'… No matter what anybody says, we should stick to the doctrine that Christ placed that table in his church, not for them to say who shall come, but for God to say who shall come. One has to be inside the church before he is entitled to sit at the Lord's Table.*"[31]

John A. Broadus (1827-1895) evidently believed in restricted communion. "*I once knew a lad of sixteen, well-educated for his years, whose father was a zealous and quite influential Baptist layman and his pastor an able and eloquent minister. The boy had been baptized, and with great joy and trembling had sat by his father's side and taken bread and wine in remembrance of Jesus. Some weeks later a Methodist preacher came through the country, a rare thing in that neighborhood, and after preaching he very tenderly invited all Christians to come to the Table of the Lord. The boy wanted to and knew of no reason why he should not, but thought he would wait till his older brother and sisters went forward; and, as they did not, he*

30   *Ford's Repos*, p. 251.
31   B.H. Carroll (1843-1914), *An Interpretation of the English Bible, Vol. VIII*, p. 180.

inquired on the way home why it was, and on reaching home asked his father about it. The argument was made plain enough, but it was all new to him. Pastors, parents, and all had never thought it necessary to explain that matter to anybody."[32]

Many modern-day Southern Baptist brethren have changed their position on the Lord Supper. One of its finest leaders at the beginning of the twenty-century was the pastor of the First Baptist Church of Dallas, Texas, George W. Truett (1867-1944). The following was his position on those who participate in the Lord's Supper.

"Since the Supper is an ordinance of the church, it must inevitably follow that whatever would debar a man from the church must also debar him from the Lord's table in that church. It is logically inconceivable that one should be deprived of membership in the church and yet not also be deprived of coming to the Lord's table in that church, since the first privilege is the source and foundation for the second.

That the local church is the custodian of this ordinance, and must judge the qualifications of those desiring to partake of it, is shown by the fact that the command to observe it was given, not to individuals, but to a company (Luke 22:29, 30). Manifestly, this table is inside and not outside the church. The church alone can, therefore, be charged with the responsibility of its government. The local church is the only body known to the Scriptures which has any competency or jurisdiction in the government of her two ordinances."[33]

J.R. Graves (1820-1893) saw the complete inconsistency of members of a church believing "they have equal rights in all Baptist churches as in his own, which is utterly subversive of the

---

32 John A. Broadus (1827-1895), *The Duty of Baptists to Teach Their Distinctive Views.*

33 George W. Truett (1867-1944), *The Supper of Our Lord*: A Sermon Preached at First Baptist Church, Dallas, TX, 1907, pp. 19, 20-21.

fundamental principles of Baptist Church independency, since it could neither administer its own government, or control its own ordinances."[34]

J. Clyde Turner (1879-1974), in his book, *The New Testament Doctrine of the Church*, states clearly the biblical position. *"If the Lord's Supper is an ordinance of the church, to be administered by the church, the natural inference is that it is to be administered only to those who are church members."*[35]

"The Lord's Supper ought to be one of the most meaningful services in the life of the local church. If it is not, the pastor and the people ought to work together to make it so."[36]

Baptists Believe in the Soul Competency and the Priesthood of the Believer

"From the Dark Ages on, the Roman Catholic Church taught (and still teaches) *that a person cannot directly approach God, but must go through a priest, much like the Old Testament system. This enslaves the individual to the Roman Catholic Church, and assures control over the individual. Baptists have always believed that each individual is a priest before God, and that there is no need for an intermediary. An individual has the right to pray directly to God, and the inalienable right to interpret Scripture, as the Holy Spirit guides him."*[37]

Soul competency, then, is the truth that each person (soul) is individually and personally accountable to God and "competent" to relate to God without mediation through

---

34 J.R. Graves (1820-1893), *Intercommunion – Inconsistent, Unscriptural and Productive of Evil*, Part II, p. 5.

35 J. Clyde Turner (1879-1974), *The New Testament Doctrine of the Church*, p. 75.

36 W.A. Criswell (1909-2002), *The Doctrine of the Church*, p. 106.

37 David A. West, Sr., Editor, *The Baptist Heritage Journal*, Premiere Edition, 1991, p. 15.

other humans or human institutions.

Let's be very clear about this. Soul competency was neither rugged individualism nor empty relativism. Baptists very well knew what they believed and they followed their belief with great conviction. Baptists were not doctrinal anarchists who were free to believe anything or nothing. They refused to join other religions like the Catholics, Protestants and Islamists who *forced* their beliefs on others with severe penalties for disobedience.

Baptist giant E. Y. Mullins (1860-1928) believed *"… the principle of the competency of the soul in religion under God is a distinctive Baptist contribution to the world's thought…"*[38]

Baptists Believe in Churches that are Led by Pastors, Served by Deacons and Governed by the Congregation

God's work in the church was designed to be carried out in a decent and orderly fashion (1 Corinthians 14:40). To accomplish this goal, God established two offices of ordination in His church: pastors (also called bishops and elders) and deacons (1 Timothy 3:1-13). Both offices have clearly defined requirements and roles in God's plan. Church leaders are not free to legislate. They are to carry out Christ's orders without adding or subtracting from them.

Baptist professor, Malcolm Yarnell III (1962-) says, *"The New Testament church is ruled by Jesus Christ, governed by the congregation, led by pastors, and served by deacons."*[39]

---

38   E. Y. Mullins (1860-1928) quoted in William M. Pinson Jr. and Doris A. Tinker, "Is Soul Competency the Baptist Distinctive," Jane and Noble Hurley Baptist Identity Fund, http://www. baptistdistinctives.org/article5_3_07_05.pdf

39   Malcolm Yarnell III. (1962-), www.BaptistTheology.org/questions.

Led by Pastors

In the New Testament, there is no distinction between "pastors," "elders" and "bishops" (Ephesians 4:11; Titus 1:5-7; Acts 20:17, 28; 1 Timothy 3:1-7; 1 Peter 5:1-4); these represent the same office and order. The term "elder" seems to refer to the pastor's office, while "bishop" refers to his work as overseer. Ideally, there should be a plurality of "elders" in every church, but as is seen in the seven churches of Revelation 2 and 3 there was just one pastor ("angel" – messenger) in each of the churches there (at least, only one was addressed).

REQUIREMENTS

The requirements for pastors is clearly laid out in the Bible – 1 Timothy 3:1-6 and Titus 1:5-9. Two areas that are now debated are the gender-specific nature of male-only church leaders and whether a man who has been divorced is qualified to serve in the capacity of a pastor.

Before the twenty-first century it was never considered that anyone but a man would serve as a pastor – even in non-Baptist denominations. That has been slowly abandoned. *"In 1924, the Methodist Episcopal church voted to ordain women. They were followed by the main body of the northern Presbyterians in 1956, and then the Episcopalians in 1976, and finally the main Lutheran body in 1979."*[40] Pentecostalism, which was started by Aimee Semple McPherson, has never had a problem with women preachers. Sadly, many liberal "Baptist" churches are joining them. In January 2017, a married lesbian couple were installed as co-pastors of the 155-year-old Calvary Baptist Church in downtown Washington D.C. A former Southern Baptist church, the

---

40   Mark Dever (1960-), *The Church – The Gospel Made Visible*, p. 157.

church is now affiliated with the American Baptist Churches USA.

The requirement that a pastor be "the husband of one wife" (1 Timothy 3:2) has also become a matter of debate. Is this the only pre-conversion requirement for an elder? Would we expect a prospective pastor before his conversion to have never committed adultery, never used alcohol, never was materialistic, or had always been patient? While all forgiven sinners can become members of a church, not every member is qualified for holding the office of the pastor. The fact that a potential pastor might have a previous wife or family would violate the general qualification of being "blameless" and having a "good report of them which are without." *"Another reason why the moral* (marriage) *qualification can reach back to the unsaved state is because this is God's standard for all society, not just for the church (Matthew 19:8)."*[41] As I have often said, "I determine the depth of my ministry; my wife determines the length."

RESPONSIBILITY

It is the pastor's primary responsibility to lead and feed the flock of God.

"But we will give ourselves continually to prayer, and to the ministry of the word" (Acts 6:4).

"Take heed therefore unto yourselves, and to all the flock, over the which the Holy Ghost hath made you overseers, to feed the church of God, which he hath purchased with his own blood" (Acts 20:28).

"The elders which are among you I exhort, who am also an elder, and a witness of the sufferings of Christ, and also a partaker of the glory that shall be revealed:

---

41   Homer A. Kent (1926-1981), *The Pastoral Epistles*, p. 130.

Feed the flock of God which is among you, taking the oversight *thereof,* not by constraint, but willingly; not for filthy lucre, but of a ready mind; Neither as being lords over *God's* heritage, but being ensamples to the flock" (1 Peter 5:1-3).

"**Remember them which have the rule over you, who have spoken unto you the word of God: whose faith follow, considering the end of *their* conversation … Obey them that have the rule over you, and submit yourselves: for they watch for your souls, as they that must give account, that they may do it with joy, and not with grief: for that *is* unprofitable for you … Salute all them that have the rule over you, and all the saints**" (Hebrews 13:7, 17, 24).

This role of a pastor "ruling over" a church seems to some an overstepping of their responsibility. In fact, for a pastor not to rule over a church would be an abdication of his scripturally stated responsibility.

"Obey" and "submit" are words that are consistently used for order in all organizational units.

- Citizens obey and submit to government (Romans 13:1-7).
- Employees obey and submit at work (Ephesians 6:5-9).
- Children obey and submit to their parents (Ephesians 6:1-4).
- Wives obey and submit to their husbands (Ephesians 5:22-24).
- Husbands obey and submit to Christ (1 Corinthians 11:3).
- Church members are to obey and submit to their pastors (Hebrews 13:7, 17).

- Pastors are to obey and submit to the Lord (James 3:1).

The "rule" of the pastor is clarified in 1 Timothy 3:4-5. This was the expectation of a pastor: **"One that ruleth well his own house, having his children in subjection with all gravity; (For if a man know not how to rule his own house, how shall he take care of the church of God?)"** The "ruling well" is equated as "taking care."

RESPECT

The God-given leadership of the pastor is not to be grudgingly accepted by the congregation as if he only fills a necessary position. What would a church be without a pastor?

"And we beseech you, brethren, to know them which labour among you, and are over you in the Lord, and admonish you; And to esteem them very highly in love for their work's sake. *And* be at peace among yourselves" (1 Thessalonians 5:12-13).

"Let the elders that rule well be counted worthy of double honour, especially they who labour in the word and doctrine" (1 Timothy 5:17).

REWARD

While the pastor does not serve for money (1 Peter 5:2), it is scriptural that he receive *financial remuneration* for his ministry to God's church. **"Even so hath the Lord ordained that they which preach the gospel should live of the gospel"** (1 Corinthians 9:14). The only recorded sin Paul confessed following his conversion to Christ was in not requiring the church at Corinth to be financially responsible for his care (2 Corinthians 11:7-8; 12:13). He considered them an "inferior" church because of it. This is the only time this word is used in the New Testament and it means "to rate lower, to be less."

Pastors will also receive *eternal recognition*. The people pastors have ministered to will become their "crown of rejoicing" at the Judgment Seat of Christ (1 Thessalonians 2:19-20).

An old pastor said to one of his ministerial students who had just been ordained to minister to a small congregation, *"I know the vanity of your heart, and that you will feel mortified that your congregation is very small, in comparison with those of your brethren around you; but assure yourself on the word of an old man, that when you come to give an account of them to the Lord Jesus Christ, at his judgment-seat, you will think you have had enough."*[42]

Served by Deacons

"Deacons" (doknos = servants) are the men selected by a congregation to give attention to the ministry of mercy (Philippians 1:1; Acts 6:1-6; 1 Timothy 3:8-13). Nowhere in the New Testament do deacons as individuals or as a group have ruling authority of the church. While all Christians are called to serve the church, deacons are the ordained servants of the congregation. Their ministry in the church is threefold: (1) To care for physical needs. (2) To protect the unity of the church. (3) To support the ministry of the church's leaders who are to give themselves to "prayer and the ministry of the Word" (Acts 6:4). The necessity and number of deacons would seem to be determined by a church's size.

Governed by the Congregation

By majority congregational consent, the church

---

42   Mark Dever (1960-), *The Church – The Gospel Made Visible*, p. 50.

meets together and moves forward. It is the whole church who formally approves those who serve and lead the congregation. Acts 20:28 says it is the Holy Spirit who appoints men as "overseers" of the church. It is the collective body of the church that recognizes and ratifies the direction of God's Spirit. There is no organization or ruling body above a church that determines its doctrine, its ministry or its membership. Under the Lordship of Christ, a church has the right and responsibility of self-determination.

Congregationalism is not adversarial in its final responsibility about its pastor and the church's direction. The congregation provides an opportunity to confirm the pastor's leadership when it is right and constrain it when it is not biblical or reasonable.

Baptist congregational governance is not a spiritualized form of secular democracy. It is based on the teachings of the Bible.

This is a good place for a word of warning and clarification. While having the God-given right of self-determination, we must confess all the decisions of a congregation are not always right. Sound churches have made the decision to become more liberal and tolerant and less scriptural. Churches fire pastors with regularity and with impunity. We must all remember we exercise our God-given authorities and privileges in a fallen world of sinners (of which we are one). Within certain scriptural parameters, a church can decide who will direct them, remembering that trustees or committees are not found in the New Testament. While there may be strong, influential advisers in the church, their voice cannot drown out the voice of the congregation. God is not honored by selfish leaders or stubborn members who try to be "lords over God's heritage." There may be those in every congregation who desire preeminence (3 John 9) that should be given to Christ alone.

Baptists Believe in a Regenerate, Recognized and Responsible Church Membership

Regenerate Membership

In Catholicism and in most Protestant churches you become part of their church by an act of your parents – through infant sprinkling. Infant sprinkling is not an innocent ceremony; it is powerfully evil. It professes to secure the salvation of the infant apart from personal faith in Christ.

In 1662, the Congregational churches in New England embraced a Half-Way Covenant to placate parents who did not have a clear experience of salvation themselves, but wanted their children sprinkled and received into their churches.

Jonathan Edwards (1703-1758) experienced the outcome of infant sprinkling in his Congregational church. In February 1727, Edwards was ordained to co-pastor with his grandfather, Solomon Stoddard, at the Congregational church at Northampton. Two years later, on February 11, 1729, Solomon Stoddard died, so Jonathan Edwards became the sole pastor of the most important congregation in western Massachusetts with over 600 members. Infant sprinkling had filled the church with unsaved hypocrites and ungodly men. He would faithfully minister for twenty-three years until he was eventually fired by his congregation. The flash-point was that Edwards came to refuse to the Lord's Table those who did not profess salvation. The vote to dismiss him was by a vote of two hundred to dismiss to less than 20 to keep him.

Had Jonathan Edwards found a Baptist group in a neighboring state, he would have found believers who agreed on that issue, plus the need to be immersed following a clear profession of faith in Christ.

New members are received for baptism by a Baptist church upon the public profession of their faith in Christ as their Saviour. An expression of that is found in Acts 2:41. **"Then they that gladly received his word were baptized: and the same day there were added *unto them* about three thousand souls."** Unlike Catholics and many Protestant groups who sprinkle infants, Baptists require persons to personally confess their faith in Christ before baptism. *"The doctrine of a visible church composed of only the baptized regenerate is the hallmark of Baptists."*[43]

Recognized Membership

It is both the duty and privilege of every saved person to unite with a church and join with its membership. From a simple reading of the New Testament it is apparent that the early churches were in specific places and were made up of professed believers in Jesus Christ. New Testament churches recognized those who had been baptized, had men who were their leaders that were to be respected (pastors), others who were servants (deacons), women who were known as "widows" (1 Timothy 5:9) and, at least at Corinth, someone who needed to be excluded from their congregation by other members in good standing (1 Corinthians 5).

"The New Testament knows nothing of Christian experience practiced independently and in isolation from other Christians… For the strengthening of our own experience, for our continuing instruction in the Christian way, for the contribution that we can

---

43   Ibid, p. 104.

make to the faith of other believers, for the privilege of fellowship in worship and witness, for the more effective influence of a united testimony, for obedience to the revealed will of Christ our Lord, it is required of Christians that they be church members."[44]

Membership in each New Testament church required a minimum of three things:

(1) A sincere profession of one's faith in Jesus Christ as Saviour and Lord.

(2) Proper immersion with church authority to testify of their faith.

(3) A proper walk to maintain church membership.

Responsible Membership

Church discipline is perceived by some as the mark of a false church, bringing to mind images of witch trials, scarlet letters, public humiliations, and damning excommunications, yet it is clearly taught in the New Testament.

Jerry Vines (1937-), former pastor of First Baptist Church of Jacksonville, Florida, says, *"At the turn of the century and as recently as thirty years ago, it was not uncommon in rural America for people to be dismissed from the fellowship of the church for a variety of reasons. The church took the biblical topic of discipline seriously. Today, we look back on those days and view them as relics of a puritanical past which don't apply to our enlightened day of tolerance and compromise. Yet, when we study the teachings of the New Testament, we discover that church discipline is taught consistently."*[45]

"Moreover if thy brother shall trespass against thee, go and tell him his fault between thee and him alone: if he shall hear thee, thou hast gained thy brother. But

---

44   Donald F. Ackland (1903-1994), *Joy in Church Membership*, pp. 4-5.

45   Jerry Vines (1937-), *The Corinthian Confusion*, pp. 99-100.

if he will not hear *thee, then* take with thee one or two more, that in the mouth of two or three witnesses every word may be established. And if he shall neglect to hear them, tell *it* unto the church: but if he neglect to hear the church, let him be unto thee as an heathen man and a publican" (Mathew 18:15-18).

John A. Broadus (1827-1895), in his work *The Duty of Baptists to Teach Their Distinctive Views* stated, *"Maintaining that none should be received as church members unless they give credible evidence of conversion, we also hold in theory that none should be retained in membership who do not lead a godly life; that if a man fails to show his faith by works, he should cease to make profession of faith. Some of our own people appear at times to forget that strict church discipline is a necessary part of the Baptist view as to church membership."*[46]

Baptist churches today seldom carry out discipline. It has been lost by default. If a church is forced to stand openly against false teaching or unrepentant immorality it usually does so apologetically.

It would seem if churches, who boast of membership in the thousands but have an attendance in the hundreds, required responsible expectations of membership their numbers would be greatly reduced, but their reputation would be greatly increased.

John L. Dagg (1794-1884) declared, *"When discipline leaves a church, Christ goes with it."*[47]

46   John A. Broadus (1827-1895), *The Duty of Baptists to Teach Their Distinctive Views.*

47   John L. Dagg (1794-1884), *A Treatise on Church Order,* p. 274.

Baptists Believe in Personal Evangelism, World Missions and Church Planting

Before Jesus ascended to heaven, He gave the church He had founded specific command to take His message to the ends of the earth. This command has been called "the Great Commission," which is clearly recorded in the four gospels and Acts: Matthew 28:16-20, Mark 16:15-16, Luke 24:46-47; John 20:21; Acts 1:8.

A respected Evangelical pastor made the following statement. Let's see if you can follow it. *"The Great Commission is the purpose of the universal church, lived out in the daily lives of the local church members."*[48] That kind of double-talk is common among those who assign a double meaning to the concept of "church." The only kind of church that has *ever* carried out the commission is a local church. That commission was not to Christians in general, but to His original church, and the churches that followed. The threefold work of the church is to *make disciples* through the gospel, *mark disciples* by immersion upon a profession of faith and to *mature disciples* by teaching them to be obedient to the commandments of Christ. The promised, "Lo, I am with you always, even unto the end of the world"[49] could not be to the apostles; they are not presently living. The promise is to Christ's church, as an institution, which has and will continue "unto the end of the world."

The churches of the New Testament were missionary. This missionary function of the church, which some say is "the heart of the church," is carried out collectively, universally, obediently, joyfully, sacrificially, and urgently. And we do it as Christ commanded.

---

48   Charles R. Swindoll (1934-), *The Church Awakening*, p. 107.
49   Matthew 28:20.

Some modern-day Baptist churches have voluntarily turned over their congregational responsibility to outside mission agencies, boards, and clearing houses which are both unscriptural and unnecessary.

The "Acts 13 Model" shows us all mission work is to be done directly under the authority of a sending, supporting, supervising church. After prayer, the church at Antioch sent Paul and Barnabas to evangelize, baptize and establish churches. When they finished their first missionary journey, they returned to the church at Antioch and reported to their congregation, "rehearsing all that God had done with them." (Acts 14:25-28) This is called "direct-missions," by which the missionary is directly accountable to the church and the church is directly responsible for the missionary.

Also, there is a monetary benefit of doing "direct-missions." When other churches voluntarily partner financially with the sending church, one-hundred percent of the money reaches the missionary without any deductions for administration. While the gospel remains free to all who believe, it still costs a great deal of money to get the gospel to people.

The extended ministry of the churches in the New Testament was in planting other churches. Churches were planting churches. Paul stated that he had taught the Corinthians the same doctrines "every where in every church" (1 Corinthians 4:17). When the gospel was preached and people believed, they were baptized and were soon constituted as a church. It all seemed to be done without much recorded form or ceremony (Acts 11:19-26).

Norman H. Wells (1918-1978) believed Baptists can cooperate around our mission – the Great Commission, our message – the gospel (Romans 1:16) and our method – the local church.[50]

When my son, Craig, was seven years old, I asked him, "Son, what is the most important thing a church needs to be doing? What is the number one purpose of the church?" After thinking a few moments, he said, "Get more people saved?" "How are we doing?" I asked. He responded, "Pretty good." Then I said, "Thanks for the help." And Craig asked me, "Dad, did *you* know what it was?"

Baptists Believe in the Ultimate Reign of Jesus Christ

The survival of God's churches is not ultimately based on human faithfulness, but on God's unchallenged sovereignty. Christ's own promise at the first mention of His church was that **"the gates of hell shall not prevail against it"** (Matthew 16:18).

Baptists never believed they had all the answers when it comes to the return and reign of Christ, but they consistently believed God will be the one who wraps up human history. Any disagreement among Baptists has been with the *timing*, not the *truth* of Christ's second coming. This we do know – the King is coming!

It should be exciting news to us that this generation of Christians may be the final chapter in God's eternal plan. **"... Even so, come, Lord Jesus..."** (Revelation 22:20).

---

50   Normal H. Wells (1918-1978), *The Church that Jesus Loved*, pp. 94-97.

*"If I thought it were wrong to be a Baptist, I should give
it up, and become what I believed to be right."*[51]
- Charles H. Spurgeon (1834-1892)

---

51   Charles H. Spurgeon (1834-1892), *C. H. Spurgeon's Autobiography*,
       p. 154.

CHAPTER 7

In Search of the Body of Christ

To simply write "The church is the body of Christ" is much more than a short, seven-word sentence. In our day, it either obscures or opens up a truth so few seem to understand. The misunderstanding seems to extend to the highest levels of biblical scholarship.

When God came to Earth He took a Physical Body

Jesus was miraculously conceived of the Holy Spirit in the womb of the virgin Mary (Luke 1:30-31, 35). Jesus was born into the human family with a real, physical body. In that body, He lived, walked, talked, worked and died.

The difference: Jesus was without sin (Hebrews 4:15; 1 Peter 2:22; 2 Corinthians 5:21; John 8:46).[1]

Jesus Christ was one person with two natures: a divine nature and a human nature. His person was not divided and his natures were not mixed. He was God as though He were not man. He was man as though he were not God. He was fully God and fully man, not half God and half man. Jesus Christ was the God man. Jesus was coeternal, coexistent with God the Father and God the Spirit. Jesus Christ became man without ceasing to be God. "**And without controversy great is the mystery of godliness: God was manifest in the flesh, ...**" (1 Timothy 3:16).

---

1   One of the heresies that found its way among Christians was advanced by the *Docetists,* also called the Gnostics. They taught that the divine Christ would never stoop to touch flesh, which is evil. Jesus only seemed (*dokeo,* in Greek) human and only appeared to die, for God cannot die. Or, in other versions, "Christ" left "Jesus" before the Crucifixion.

*"When Christ was on earth, He inhabited a body similar
to our physical bodies, and accordingly, knew something of our
physical limitations. But after His resurrection, He was free to
come again in the person of the Spirit and inhabit numerous
individuals who together, would become the means of His
continued activity on earth."*[2]

Before Jesus left the Earth, He left a Spiritual Body to Represent Him

Amazingly, many well-respected Christian writers
do not believe the body Jesus left is on the earth, but is in
heaven. While paying lip-service to the truth that Jesus
started a church, the church many people have assigned to
Him is invisible.

Charles R. Ryrie (1925-2016) identified the body of
Christ as *"that spiritual organism of which Christ is the Head,
and is composed of all regenerate people from Pentecost to the
rapture."*[3]

W. A. Criswell (1909-2002) says, *"The New Testament
speaks also of the church as the body of Christ which includes
all of the redeemed of all ages."*[4] Those who hold this view
have an interesting and substantial quandary. When were
the redeemed of the ages before Pentecost baptized into the
body of Christ? Was it retroactive?

Ray C. Stedman (1917-1992) believed, *"There is only one
church in all the world. All genuine Christians belong to it, and
it has nothing to do with denominations or church buildings or
church members. If you have been born of the Spirit, you are a
member of that one body Paul speaks of. Within that one body,*

2   D. Stuart Briscoe (1930-), *The Communicator's Commentary –
Romans*, p. 219.

3   Charles R. Ryrie (1925-2016), *Ryrie Study Bible*, p. 1843.

4   W. A. Criswell (1909-2002), *The Doctrine of the Church*, p. 11.

all of us who are born of the Spirit of God are members of one another – we belong to each other. There is one body, but many members."[5]

People might ask, "What do *you* think passages that refer to the body of Christ means?" Respectfully, it doesn't matter what *you* or *I* think. The intent of any word or verse or passage or book in the Bible is not what we think it means, but what the original writers, who were inspired by the Holy Spirit, meant.

The real question to be answered is what did *God* mean when the original men were divinely inspired to write it down? We must emphatically confess with conviction, the Bible can never mean what it never meant.

In the New Testament, there are 32 references to the church being the body of Christ. They are found in only four epistles written by the Apostle Paul: Romans (2), 1 Corinthians (18), Ephesians (8), and Colossians (4).[6] This is an amazingly few number of verses considering there are 7,957 in the New Testament.

When it comes to those who study the Bible, many seem to follow *the Law of Inversion* – the less that is said about a subject the more they want to add their opinions.

In fact, there is plenty of evidence from these few passages to gain a very clear understanding. Let's look into these "body" passages "in search of the Body of Christ." What do they say for themselves?

---

5   Ray C. Stedman (1917-1992), *Reason to Rejoice*, p. 252.

6   Romans 12:4-5; 1 Corinthians 12:12 (2), 13, 14, 15 (2), 16 (2), 17, 18, 19, 10, 11, 12, 14, 25, 27; Ephesians 1:23; 2:16; 3:6; 4:4, 12, 16; 5:23, 30; Colossians 1:18, 24; 2:19; 3:15.

The Misunderstandings of the Body of Christ

A search and rescue plan requires an intense and serious gathering of all available information. By investigating all of the "body" passages, we discover they are all in Paul's epistles to local churches – the church at Rome, the church at Corinth, the church at Ephesus, and the church at Colosse. We need to attempt to understand these passages as they were understood by their original readers. Overlooking, either intentionally or carelessly, that these are church letters allows for many unnecessary and unscriptural conclusions.

A thorough search for the body of Christ requires that we get a clear understanding of terms. As we have previously noted, the word translated "church" is from the Greek word *ecclesia* which denotes an assembly. The definition we have chosen is the "church (*ecclesia*) is an assembled body of baptized believers in a physical location who were carrying out God's work on the earth."

Part of the confusion around the concept of the church being the "body of Christ" is in not understanding that this is a metaphor. In the *Webster's New World Dictionary of the American Language* a metaphor is defined as *"a figure of speech in which one thing is likened to another, different thing by being spoken of as if it were that other; implied comparison, in which a word or phrase ordinarily and primarily used of one thing is applied to another."*[7] Charles L. Hunt (1954-) believes that failure to understand this metaphor inevitably leads to *"serious error and confusion."*[8]

In the New Testament there are four "bodies" attributed to Christ.

---

7   *Webster's New World Dictionary of the American Language*, p. 925
8   Charles L. Hunt (1954-), *The Body of Christ: Separating Myth from Metaphor*, p. 2.

(1) His physical body (Hebrews 10:5; 1 Peter 2:24; Hebrews 10:10).
(2) His resurrected/glorified body (John 20:17; Philippians 3:21).
(3) His symbolic body – the unleavened bread in the Lord's Supper (Luke 22:19).
(4) His institutional body – the church (1 Corinthians 12:27; Ephesians 4:4; Colossians 1:18; 3:15).

Many Misunderstand the Nature of the Body of Christ

If you read modern Christian authors or listen to preachers on Christian radio or television, the overwhelming majority will reference all believers as members of "the body of Christ" to the exclusion of any other concept.

In Lewis Sperry Chafer's (1871-1952) *Systematic Theology* his section of ecclesiology contains 263 pages. Amazingly, only 10 pages are devoted to what he calls the "gathered" church. Chafer wrote, *"The true church is not divided, nor could it be; yet the visible church is a broken and shattered attempt at the manifestation of the Scriptural ideal... the visible church, as such, is charged with no mission. The commission to evangelize the world is personal, and not corporate."*[9]

Charles R. Ryrie's (1925-2016) notes on Ephesians 1:22-23 regarding Christ being "the head over all things to the church, which is his body," state this is *"the universal Church to which every true believer belongs, regardless of local church affiliation. It is a spiritual organism entered by means of the baptism of the Spirit (1 Cor. 12:13). Christ is the risen Head of the Church and its members are subject to Him (Eph. 5:24). Local churches should be miniatures of the body of Christ,*

---

9   Lewis Sperry Chafer (1871-1952), *Systematic Theology*, p. 149.

*though it is possible to have unbelievers in local churches who are
not, therefore, members of the body of Christ."*[10]

Yet the Apostle Paul declares that the church at Corinth
was "the body of Christ, and members in particular" (1
Corinthians 12:27), not a miniature. By reading the entire
letter of the Apostle Paul to the church at Corinth it is very
clear he was referring to a local, visible assembly.

- "church of God ... at Corinth" (1:2)
- "take from among you" (5:2)
- "when ye gather together" (5:4)
- "Purge out ... the old leaven" (5:5)
- "not to company" (5:9)
- "not to keep company" (5:11)
- "judge them that are within" (5:12)
- "put away" (5:13)
- "come together in the church" (11:18) = the body
  of Christ
- "when ye come together" (11:20)
- "come together to eat" (11:33)
- "that ye come not together" (11:34)
- "whole church be come together" (14:23).
- "when ye come together" (14:26).
- "first day of the week ... lay ... in store" (16:2)[11]

The Apostle Paul states in 1 Corinthians 4:17 and 7:17
that he taught the same doctrines in every church. **"... as I
teach every where in every church ... And so ordain I
in all churches."** What he taught at Corinth he taught in
Ephesus, in Colosse, in Philippi, etc. – in all places and to all
churches.

---

10   Charles R. Ryrie (1925-2016), *The Ryrie Study* Bible, p. 1674.
11   Kenneth T. Brook (1951-), Aaron Strouse, *Why Cumbereth It the
     Ground*, pp. 209-210.

There is a much better, more consistent theological term to use in the place of the "universal-invisible" church. It would be "the family of God." All who are saved by God's grace through the atoning death and bodily resurrection of Jesus and regenerated and indwelt by the Holy Spirit are in the family of God (John 1:12-13). At salvation believers are placed in union with Christ and are immediately indwelt by the Spirit of God.

The "body of Christ" as a metaphor is only consistent when it is understood in a tangible and visible sense. *"The church is... described in the New Testament in figurative ways that emphasize differing aspects of her nature. Paul refers to Christians in the church at Corinth as God's fellow workers, God's field, God's building. The local church is referenced as the people of God, household of God, household of faith, bride of Christ, and body of Christ. These metaphors describe a local, particular assembly. To apply these metaphors to the universal church distorts the New Testament meaning."*[12]

The universal, invisible body of Christ is a Protestant explanation for all the vastly different Christian denominations. Saying there is unity in the universal, invisible body is a weak attempt to explain and excuse all the deep doctrinal disparity in the groups that make up Christendom. On a Baptist church's website, their statement of beliefs says, *"Each individual congregation is autonomous, yet part of the larger body of Christ with many expressions and locations. Believers achieve oneness in Christ that transcends all human limitations, including the differences that exist between denominations."*

How amazingly ridiculous to propose that different church denominations are united in spirit even though they

---

12   Bob Pearle (1953-), *The Vanishing Church*, p. 49.

are vastly divided in doctrine and practice.

Many Misunderstand the Head of the Body of Christ

Most would agree that Christ alone is the Head of the church. The Bible clearly states that He is. **"And he is the head of the body, the church:…"** (Colossians 1:18). **"And hath put all *things* under his feet, and gave him *to be* the head over all *things* to the church, Which is his body, the fulness of him that filleth all in all"** (Ephesians 1:22-23). **"But speaking the truth in love, may grow up into him in all things, which is the head, *even* Christ: From whom the whole body fitly joined together and compacted by that which every joint supplieth, according to the effectual working in the measure of every part, maketh increase of the body unto the edifying of itself in love"** (Ephesians 4:15-16). **"For the husband is the head of the wife, even as Christ is the head of the church: and he is the saviour of the body"** (Ephesians 5:23).

Many people misunderstand and misrepresent the Headship of Christ over the Body of Christ because they impose upon it a false narrative. Ray Stedman suggests the following. *"Stand in front of a full-length mirror and look at your body. What do you see? One body that divides into two major sections: the head; the torso with its limbs. The head is not large, compared with the rest of the body, but it is the control center of the body. The torso and limbs comprise the largest part of the body, but every part of this section of the body is under the command and control of the head. That is how the church, the body of Christ, is intended to function."*[13] Let's analyze that commonly held concept.

If a picture is worth a thousand words, possibly some

---

13   Ray Stedman (1919-1992), *Letters to a Troubled Church*, p. 175.

pictures below will help clarify how Christ is the Head of the Body, the church.

ANATOMIC HEAD... HEAD ON A BODY

Many see Christ as the organic Head and the church as the body coming together to form a whole. The idea postulated is the head (brain) is the command and control center of the human body, so the church receives life from its Head. Tony Evans (1944-) adds, *"If any part of your body ever disobeys the signals from your brain and starts acting independently, get yourself to a doctor right away because something is wrong."* And then he adds *"As Christ's body, the church is to move to His orders and make His presence visible as it was when Jesus was on earth Himself."*[14]

There is no challenge to the Biblical doctrine that the believer is brought into spiritual union with Christ at salvation.

"For as in Adam all die, even so in Christ shall all be made alive" (1 Corinthians 15:22). Adam, the head of the human family, sinned and his sin and its penalty was imputed to us (Romans 5:12). On the cross, our sin was imputed to Christ. **"For he hath made him *to be* sin for us, who knew no sin;..."** (2 Corinthians 5:21). Now, for those who place their faith in Christ and His work, His righteousness is imputed to us. **"...that we might be made the righteousness of God in him"** (2 Corinthians 5:21). **"Therefore if any man *be* in Christ, *he is* a new creature: old things are passed away; behold, all things are become new"** (2 Corinthians 5:17).

Augustus Hopkins Strong (1836-1921) says in his *Systematic Theology, "As Adam's sin was imputed to us, not*

---

14   Tony Evans (1944-), *God's Glorious Church*, p. 34.

because Adam is in us, but because we were in Adam; so Christ's righteousness is imputed to us, not because Christ is in us, but because we are in Christ – this is, joined by faith to one whose righteousness and life are infinitely greater than our power to appropriate or contain."[15]

When a person hears, understands and accepts the gospel record of Jesus' death for our sins, His burial, and His literal resurrection, they are at that very moment saved! At that moment the believer is taken…

- Out of the power of darkness and translated into the kingdom of God's dear Son (Colossians 1:13).
- Out of bondage into freedom (John 8:32).
- Out of death and into life (John 5:25).
- Out of Adam and placed into Christ (1 Corinthians 15:22).

Here is what is overlooked if one insists that Christ's headship over His body is organic. If the metaphor is meant to be understood that the life of the body comes from its head, then it must also mean that the head only survives with the body. To believe that Christ is not complete without the body is heresy. Jesus is not to be thought of as a disembodied head looking to hook up with a body to live. The Body is

---

15   Augustus Hopkins Strong (1836-1921), *Systematic Theology*, p. 862.

dependent on the Head, but the Head is dependent on nothing whatsoever. Further, the understanding of those in Bible days was that "the life of the flesh is in the blood" (Leviticus 17:11), not in the brain. In fact, *"amputation of the Head does mean death – death for the head as well as the body! One might react that you cannot press metaphors too far. This is true. You are not to press metaphors, similes and parables beyond the obvious. But is the conclusion that the head would die as well as the body if the body were severed from the head beyond the obvious? Is death to the head a minor detail that should just be overlooked for the greater cause of forcing this metaphor to teach the truth of a vital union with Jesus Christ? We think not."*[16] Jesus is infinite, eternal, sovereign and life.

AUTHORATIVE HEAD... HEAD OVER A BODY

It should be understood that Christ is the authoritative Head over all things in heaven and in earth (Ephesians 1:22-23). He is head over all principalities and powers (Colossians 2:10). He is King of kings and Lord of lords (Revelation 19:16). There is no higher authority in heaven or in earth (Matthew 28:18).

Jesus Christ

The Church

---

16 Charles, L. Hunt (1954-), *The Body of Christ: Separating Myth from Metaphor*, p. 7.

The baptized believers who made up the church at Corinth were taught to understand they were a complete body over whom Christ was their Head. **"Now ye are the body of Christ, and members in particular"** (1 Corinthians 12:27). **"And the eye cannot say unto the hand, I have no need of thee: nor again the head to the feet, I have no need of you"** (1 Corinthians 12:21). Notice, Paul saw the Corinthian church as having eyes, hands, feet and a head. It was this complete body over which Christ was their Head (Ephesians 1:22-23).

Previously, Paul had written in 1 Corinthians 11:3, **"But I would have you know, that the head of every man is Christ; and the head of the woman *is* the man; and the head of Christ *is* God."** Christ, man and God are considered heads. Christ is the head of every man. Husbands are the head of their wives. God was the head of Christ while He was on this earth.

When Henry Ford (1863-1947) was alive, he was the head of the vast Ford Motor Company. When Sam Walton (1918-1992) was alive, he was the head of every Walmart. When Conrad Hilton (1887-1979) was alive, he was the head of every one of his hotels the world over. This is how Christ can be the head of thousands of church bodies.

Christ's omnipresence allows Him to be the active and authoritative Head over every one of His churches. We should not just see that Christ is Head over the church as an institution, but He is also Head over every individual church that He claims as His own.

Jesus Christ

Churches

Many Misunderstand the Entrance into the Body of Christ
SPIRIT BAPTISM INTO A UNIVERSAL-INVISIBLE BODY

The single verse used by the advocates of the universal-invisible "body of Christ" is 1 Corinthians 12:13. It should not be overlooked that it was written to Christians who were members of a local-visible church. **"For by one Spirit are we all baptized into one body, whether** *we be* **Jews or Gentiles, whether** *we be* **bond or free; and have been all made to drink into one Spirit."** Here is a clear statement of how one becomes a member of a New Testament church. For the Corinthians, it would have been a flashback to their salvation and baptism. The phrase "by one Spirit" reminds us that salvation is a work of God. God the Spirit uses the hearing of the Word of God to bring conviction and regeneration to the believing sinner. So, to be members of one of the Lord's churches, a body of Christ, you must be saved and know it. In the phrase "are we all baptized" one identifies the way a person gains entrance into one of the Lord's churches. We are added to the church by water baptism (Acts 2:41). The "into one body" phrase would have been clearly understood by the Corinthian believers to be referring to their church – the church at Corinth. If they happened to overlook it, Paul would add in verse 27, **"Now ye are the body of Christ, and**

members in particular." The phrase "... whether *we be* Jews or Gentiles, whether *we be* bond or free; and have been all made to drink into one Spirit" would have been understood by those in the Corinthian church that there was equality in their membership. In the verses that followed through the end of the chapter there would be an emphasis placed on diversity.

There is no universal-invisible church that a believer becomes a member of at salvation. We are joined to the person of Christ by His work of redemption through the regenerating work of the Holy Spirit and become a member of God's family.

WATER BAPTISM IN A LOCAL-VISIBLE BODY

When 1 Corinthians 12:13 is understood considering it was written to a local church we realize *"the Holy Spirit leads those who are saved to a particular assembly to be baptized in water and become a functioning member of a body of Christ... Verse 13 teaches that a believer is led by the Spirit to be baptized in water to be identified with Christ. This ordinance is obviously used as an entrance into the body because he is dependent on the body for the first time. The church body must administer baptism because only it has the authority to do so."*[17]

Water baptism is the first step in the life-long process of sanctification that is fostered in the local-visible church. A life-time of obedience begins with the first step of obedience in baptism.

"Catholics believe water baptism actually places you into Christ. Protestants believe the Spirit baptizes you into the universal invisible body of Christ. Baptists believe that believers, already in Christ by a work of God's salvation, are baptized in

17   Ibid, *The Body of Christ: Separating Myth from Metaphor*, pp. 23, 38.

water representing the death, burial, and resurrection of Jesus Christ and are thereby brought into membership of a body of Christ." [18]

Galatians 3: 27 and 28 says, **"For as many of you as have been baptized into Christ have put on Christ. There is neither Jew nor Greek, there is neither bond nor free, there is neither male nor female: for ye are all one in Christ Jesus."**

The full, earthly sanctification of a believer cannot be attained outside the local church. Those in the *ecclesia*, the church, the body of Christ, are the called-out ones who are "set apart" to God, from sin, for service.

The church is God's means for instruction in righteousness (2 Timothy 3:17-4:2), for protection from false teachers (Acts 20:28-29), for correction from carnal behavior (1 Corinthians 3:1-3) and for participation in Christian ministry (John 17:17).

The Members of the Body of Christ

There are 19 references to those who are "members" of the Body of Christ. These are found in only 3 epistles: Romans, 1 Corinthians, Ephesians. [19] It should be observed that these "members" were already recognized as "members" of a visible, local church. The Greek word is *melos* which refers to our physical limbs – hands, arms, legs, feet.

Understanding the members in a body of Christ is very practical and important because the consumer mentality that drives our culture has made its way into the church. Modern believers very often go about seeking a church with

---

18　Ibid, p. 72.
19　Romans 12:4, 5; 1 Corinthians 6:15 (3); 12:12 (2), 18, 20, 22, 23, 25, 26 (2), 27; Ephesians 4:25; 5:30.

an unashamed "what can you do for me and my family" attitude. Reflect on the following questions:

1. Do I think that a church should present me with a menu of choices in the form of various programs?
2. Is my decision about where I attend church based on my personal tastes and preferences?
3. Do I see myself as primarily an individual who comes to worship God, but should not be expected to form intimate relationships with others in the body of believers?
4. Do I operate from the assumption that the church is completing its mission when it meets my felt needs?
5. Do I see the church as providing a product or a service: good religious feelings, self-help programs, children's activities, practical advice for living successfully, sports leagues, etc.?
6. Do I operate under the notion that I will leave when I don't feel like I am getting my money's worth or proper service?
7. Is my loyalty to the local church like my loyalty to a business?[20]

What a contrast this is to Paul's affirmations in this "body-members" passage. **"But now hath God set the members every one of them in the body, as it hath pleased him"** (1 Corinthians 12:18). Notice, in this verse *the placement of God*. "But now hath God set the members every one of them in the body..." The word "set" means "to put in place." The Greek scholar A.T. Robertson (1863-1934) says the tense of

---

20   Butch Smith, Living Hope Baptist Church, www.lhbc.net.

this verb[21] means "God did it and of himself."[22] The same truth of placement is mentioned in 1 Corinthians 12:28, **"And God hath set some in the church, first apostles,..."** God added the apostles to the church Jesus built. God set the members in the church at Corinth. When it comes to joining a church, we should be certain that God is the one who is adding us to that local body.

Also note the statement made here about *the pleasure of God*. "...as it hath pleased him." While there are personal benefits and enjoyments from being in a church, it should be of greater concern that we are where we are for God's pleasure.

Identity

God wanted this congregation to know who they were and where they should place their loyalties. They were "... the church of God which is at Corinth..." (1 Corinthians 1:2). They were the temple of God (1 Corinthians 3:17). They were the body of Christ (1 Corinthians 12:27).

Several years ago, I received a letter inviting me to join other churches and pastors which represented about 72 denominations whose goal was to bring a new wave of evangelism and spiritual renewal to America and the world. One of its honorary Chairmen, the founder of a well-known international parachurch organization, did not hesitate to lay out the conditions for the success of this event. In his words, *"If enough of us really take seriously the prayer of the Lord Jesus – that we may be as one – and if enough of us are willing to lose our identity and let Christ he honored and praised, the miracle will happen."* The assumption was you cannot honor Christ

---

21   Second aorist middle indicative.

22   A.T. Robertson (1863-1934), *Words Pictures of the New Testament, Vol IV*, p. 173.

and keep your identity. You must drop your identity, take up
their non-identity, which was their identity!

The truth is, if we lose our identity, we will lose God's
purpose and power.

Unity

While each church has many members, they make up
one body that operates in functional unity. From the early
chapters of 1 Corinthians we understand Paul was clearly
writing to a disunited, dysfunctional local church. It is each
church member's responsibility to endeavor "to keep the
unity of the Spirit in the bond of peace" (Ephesians 4:3).

Take time to look at all "unity" passages in the New
Testament and you will come to this conclusion – they are
writing to local churches. Genuine unity can only be lived
out in a local church setting. You cannot be in genuine unity
with people unless you are around them, know them, and
work together. The real power of a church, the body of Christ,
is the indwelling of the Holy Spirit who binds individual
members into a unified, spiritual whole.

*"Our bond as believers in Christ is much more than
something to keep us from fussing and fighting among ourselves.
It is a testimony to the world that the Lord and the faith we
preach are real."*[23]

**"Behold, how good and how pleasant *it is* for
brethren to dwell together in unity! *It is* like the precious
ointment upon the head, that ran down upon the beard,
even Aaron's beard: that went down to the skirts of his
garments; As the dew of Hermon, *and as the dew* that
descended upon the mountains of Zion: for there the**

---

23   Tony Evans (1944-), *God's Glorious Church*, p. 195.

LORD commanded the blessing, *even* life for evermore"
(Psalm 133:1-3).

Diversity
    **"For the body is not one member, but many. If the
foot shall say, Because I am not the hand, I am not of the
body; is it therefore not of the body? And if the ear shall
say, Because I am not the eye, I am not of the body; is it
therefore not of the body? If the whole body *were* an eye,
where *were* the hearing? If the whole *were* hearing, where
were the smelling?"** (1 Corinthians 12:14-17).

    The goal in many churches is for their members to all be
alike. That is *impossible.* Every believer God places in each
church is unique. And, further, it is *impractical* to presume
members could or should be alike. If two people are exactly
alike in the church, one of them is unnecessary.

    Picture how grotesque a body would be if it were just
one giant "eye" or one big "ear."

    God places in each body those who have different gifts
to accomplish His work. When each member of the body
is doing what he or she was gifted to do, there is health and
usefulness.

Dependency
    **"And the eye cannot say unto the hand, I have no
need of thee: nor again the head to the feet, I have no
need of you. Nay, much more those members of the
body, which seem to be more feeble, are necessary:
And those *members* of the body, which we think to be
less honourable, upon these we bestow more abundant
honour; and our uncomely *parts* have more abundant
comeliness. For our comely *parts* have no need: but**

God hath tempered the body together, having given more abundant honour to that *part* which lacked:" (1 Corinthians 12:21-24).

If you have ever been injured, you know how dependent a person is on other parts of their body. For example, those of you who have recovered from shoulder surgery know you were greatly challenged just to keep yourself clean, to eat or to dress yourself.

Two of your physical body's most important members are usually not fully appreciated – your big toe on each of your feet. Without your big toes you cannot stand or walk well. Your big toes have the ability to sense when you are leaning forward too much; they compensate all the time so you don't fall flat on your face.

So it is in the body of Christ. Alone there are many things that we are not able to do in the church, but when we work together we are able to do the job!

Before computers, people often used mechanical typewriters. A typewriter that functioned well had to have all its keys working properly. Someone once wrote the following:

My typxwritxr works quitx wxll xxcxpt for onx of thx kxys. Our Church is somxwhat likx that! Not all thx kxy pxoplx arx working propxrly. You may say, "Wxll, I am only onx pxrson. I won't makx or brxak thx Church." But, it doxs makx a diffxrxncx, bxcausx to bx xffxctivx a Church nxxds thx activx participation of XVXRY pxrson! DO YOU GXT THX MXSSAGX?

Harmony

"That there should be no schism in the body; but *that* the members should have the same care one for another"

(1 Corinthians 12:25). Each member of the body of Christ is to work in coordination for the good of the whole body. The idea of the word "schism" is "division."

Lucy walked into the room where Linus was watching television and demanded, "Okay, switch the channel." Linus responded, "Are you kidding? What makes you think you can come right in here and take over!" Lucy held out her hand and said, "These five fingers individually are nothing. But when I curl them together into a single unit they become a fighting force terrible to behold." Linus asked, "Which channel do you want?" Then looking down at his own little hand he mumbled, "Why can't you guys get organized like that?"[24]

The whole point of identity, unity, diversity and dependency in the body of Christ is to create genuine harmony in our coordinated effort to live together for the glory of God.

Sympathy

Christ cares for the members of His body, and so should we. **"For no man ever yet hated his own flesh; but nourisheth and cherisheth it, even as the Lord the church: For we are members of his body, of his flesh, and of his bones"** (Ephesians 5:29-30).

When a body is healthy there is something natural about caring for its members. **"And whether one member suffer, all the members suffer with it; or one member be honoured, all the members rejoice with it"** (1 Corinthians 12:26).

If you carelessly crush your finger, your whole body goes into action to show its sympathy. Your eyes fill up with tears.

---

24   Clark Gesner, *You're a Good Man, Charlie* Brown, 1967.

Your face contorts in pain. Your mouth opens. Your voice could raise the dead. Your whole body reacts to the incident.

When your body contracts an infection, parts of your body step up and immediately act. The immune system that is made up of a network of cells, tissues, and organs works together to protect the body. If you have a fever, your sweat glands go into action to cool you down.

The concept of a caring, supporting, sympathizing response to those who hurt or to those who are honored can only be genuinely experienced in the context of a church body. While we are emotionally touched by tragedies reported in the media, its distance from our lives insulates us from participating in helping to meet those needs. When they happens in a church, the pain is deep or the joy is unspeakable.

In the New Testament letters to various churches you will notice a long list of "one another" statements.[25] These provide a wonderful working plan to demonstrate mutual care and love for those in a church body.

Maturity

"**But speaking the truth in love, may grow up into him in all things, which is the head, *even* Christ: From whom the whole body fitly joined together and compacted by that which every joint supplieth, according to the effectual working in the measure of every part, maketh increase of the body unto the edifying of itself in love**" (Ephesians 4:15-16).

Growing up to maturity is God's goal for every Christian

---

25   Romans 12:10, 16; 14:13, 19; 15:7, 14; 1 Corinthians 12:25; Galatians 5:13; Ephesians 4:2, 32; 5:21; Philippians 2:3; Colossians 3:13; 1 Thessalonians 4:12, 5:11, 13, 15; Hebrews 3:13; James 5:16; 1 Peter 4:9;, 10;5:5; 1 John 3:11.

and every church.

During the days of the American Civil War a man happened on a young boy plowing behind a mule. The stranger asked the boy why he was doing a man's work. "Well, you see, sir," said the lad, "father's fighting, mama's praying, and I'm working. We're all doing what we can!"

That's maturity – doing what you can because you can.

The Ministry of the Body of Christ

"It's become fashionable lately to make fun of the church. I understand that the church has major flaws and deficiencies. It's been said that the church of Jesus Christ is like Noah's ark. The stench inside would be unbearable if it weren't for the storm outside! But my question to those who want to leave it is this: where else will you be able to submit to loving authority? Where else will God sanctify you? The church, for all its failures, is where we love one another, bear with one another, and stir up each other's affections for good deeds... The church exists primarily for God's glory, but it also exists for our good." [26]

The Inward Ministry of the Body of Christ: Edification

"And he (God) **gave some, apostles; and some, prophets; and some, evangelists; and some, pastors and teachers; For the perfecting of the saints, for the work of the ministry, for the edifying of the body of Christ:"** (Ephesians 4:11-12). The current-day ministry of pastors and teachers is to "perfect" (mature) the saints, so the matured saints can do the work of ministry, so the church body can be "edified" (built up, strengthened).

"But speaking the truth in love, may grow up into him in all things, which is the head, *even* Christ: From whom

---

26   Trevin Wax, *Counterfeit Gospels,* pp. 168-169.

the whole body fitly joined together and compacted
by that which every joint supplieth, according to the
effectual working in the measure of every part, maketh
increase of the body unto the edifying of itself in love"
(Ephesians 4:15-16).

The Greek term for the word "edifying" (or edification)
in Ephesians 4:16 is *oikodome*, defined by Thayer as: "(1)
(the act of) building, building up, (2) metaph. edifying,
edification, (2a) the act of one who promotes another's
growth in Christian wisdom, piety, happiness, holiness."

Robert Murray M'Cheyne (1813-1843) wrote about
two lepers who were once seen sowing peas in a field.
The one had no hands, the other had no feet-these bodily
members had wasted away because of the disease. The
one who lacked hands was carrying the other who lacked
feet upon his back, and the man riding on his friend's back
carried in his hands the bag of seed, and dropped a pea every
now and then, which the other pressed into the ground with
his foot; and so they managed the work of one man between
the two. Each of these men could not do certain things, but
together they could do the job.

The Outward Ministry of the Body of Christ: Evangelization

"A church that is busy ministering to itself, building itself up,
edifying itself, and reaches no farther than its own four walls is
self-centered. Training, edification and equipping of the saints is
not an end itself, but is a means to an end. God's goal is that the
church be built up so that it can effectively function in the world
and carry out Christ's will on earth."[27]

The outward ministry of the church is to reach others all

---

27   J. Delany, *The Purpose of the Church.*

over the world with the gospel.

This is very important to understand. The primary strategy in the New Testament for evangelism is to plant churches.

The Upward Ministry of the Body of Christ: Glorification

While there are many good and important ministries of the churches of Jesus Christ, the most obvious and overriding of all ministries is to bring glory to their great God and Saviour. Churches of Jesus Christ, His bodies on this earth, exist for His glory. "**Unto him *be* glory in the church by Christ Jesus throughout all ages, world without end. Amen**" (Ephesians 3:21). This verse does not say that the church is where we will experience the *manifestation* of God's glory. Rather, this is telling us the *means* God has ordained to receive glory. Those within a church are to be and live in such a way that individually and corporately they bring glory to God. Our first and foremost responsibility as a church is to God. Paul had previously admonished these believers in the church at Corinth, "**Whether therefore ye eat, or drink, or whatsoever ye do, do all to the glory of God**" (1 Corinthians 10:31).

In our culture of individualism (usually nothing less than raw rebellion), we want to be what we want to be and do what we want to do. That attention to self is crucified in Christ and now our desire is to glorify the One who saved us. And the good news is, what we do really matters. Our lives, devoted to Christ and His church, can and do bring glory to God.

"God established the church as a display of His glory. When the church is marked off from the world through the faithful practice of church membership and discipline, and led by godly,

qualified men who teach the Word and equip all the saints for works of service, the church's corporate character proclaims the glory of God through the power of the Gospel. But when a church fails to draw a bright line between itself and the world, its members live just like the world, its leaders fail to meet biblical qualifications, and that church will broadcast lies about God and His Gospel to the world."[28]

Conclusion

"The teaching of 1 Corinthians 12:12-28 may be summed up in this manner: The church here is the local church at Corinth, to which this passage addresses. It is a church in which all members have submitted, in a spirit of oneness, to the ordinance of water baptism, which was taught and practiced by Paul when he founded the church, Acts 18:1-8. This church can now be thought of as a closely-knit body of believers, bound together with the close ties of sympathy and interdependence. All of the members of this body are in one place and time, having intimate knowledge of each other, and sharing the benefits of the spiritually gifted persons that God has placed in their midst."[29]

---

28   Mark Dever (1960-), SBC Life, Winter 2016.
29   Thomas Williamson, The Universal Church Theory, Global Baptist Times, December 2007.

CHAPTER 8

Why Is the Church Still Important?

We are living in the days of "less." Laws are senseless. Communications are wireless. Surgeries are stitch-less. Coffee is caffeine-less. Oranges are seedless. Diets are fatless. Lawns are weed-less. Cigarettes are tobacco-less. Tans are sunless. Cars are driverless. And too many professed Christians are churchless.

When it comes to settling the issue of the importance of the church in our day there are those you could call *debaters*. They casually say, *"I can't come to a satisfactory conclusion about whether the church is valid or not."* Call off the debate. Jesus settled that long ago. He founded the church during His earthly ministry. Jesus loved the church and gave Himself for it. He purchased the church with His own blood. He is the Head of the church.

There are *deniers* who confess, *"I believe in Christ… I just don't believe in church. Forget the church. Follow Jesus."* Sorry, you can't have it both ways. Christ has bound Himself inseparably to His church. It is His body. It is His bride. *"In the UK, it was normal to go to church back in the 1950s—25% of British adults were in a service on a Sunday. Today, it's 5%. It's likely that more people will be in your local supermarket at 11 a.m. this Sunday than in your local church. In the US, that trend, though less far on, is nevertheless heading in the same direction."*[1]

Some are just plain *drifters*. *"I can't find the right church."* So, people drift from church to church blessing them with their overstated insights. These are the modern-day "hobos"

---

1   Sam Allberry, *Why Bother with Church?* p. 8.

of days past who jumped on a train, rode free, and then jumped off at their next site complaining about the ride and hoping for a free meal without any sense of personal obligation. What a life (or non-life).

Others say they have been *damaged* by the church. They say, *"I was forced to go to church when I was young and that was enough for me."* I personally don't get it. I am a PK – a preacher's kid. I am supposed to hate the whole church scene because I was forced to go to church every time the doors were open. Actually, we were the ones who opened the doors. Thinking back on my childhood, I was often forced to take a bath and amazingly I didn't turn out hating water. I was taken to school on the days that I didn't want to go, but it didn't turn me against education. My two brothers and I were encouraged to sing gospel music from an early age and we were pretty good. We got a second audition in 1955 on *The Original Amateur Hour* hosted by Ted Mack (check out the shows on YouTube). Amazingly, it didn't make us hate gospel music. For those who seem entirely disillusioned with the idea of church I must remind you, you don't have another choice if you are serious about Jesus Christ and serving Him. The only one who agrees with your decision to pull out of church is the enemy of your soul and you need to quit listening to him.

Then, there are *discoverers* who say, *"I can't find a church I like. The ones I have been going to seem to have a few problems."* People who are looking for a perfect church need to get real. There are no perfect churches because there are no perfect people. We are all flawed; the whole world is flawed. We will have to wait for Jesus' return for that to change.

Then, there is the *delinquent* crowd. There are far too many who used to go to church, who know they ought to go to church, but just are not doing it. If they believe church is important, their actions do not prove it.

In spite of all the naysayers, there are still the *dedicated* who testify, *"I've seen what life is like without the church. I am in the church, all in, and I am staying in the church."*

In the church-world, some are predicting the immediate or eventual demise of churches as we know them today. George Barna (1955-), who founded and heads a market research firm specializing in studying the religious beliefs and behavior of Americans, has given up on the church. *"If the local church is the hope of the world, then the world has no hope."*[2] Such an idea is misguided, but sincerely held by some.

That's not to say God's churches are without their problems. *"The apostles never suggested that the early churches were little colonies of heaven on earth. The New Testament letters speak about problems of sexual misconduct, legal wranglings, doctrinal errors, division over personalities, exaggerated claims about spiritual experiences, selfishness, lack of compassion, legalism, authoritarianism, pride, manipulative leaders, abuse of power and misappropriation of funds. The list is depressing, but the honesty is refreshing... If we follow the example of the apostles, we will have an appropriate humility when we speak about the church. God sees its failures and so does the world, and it does little good to pretend that they don't exist. It will be difficult for unbelieving people to take us seriously if we can't see what is obvious to them."*[3]

The depreciation of the local, visible church is the natural result of the false idea of the universal, invisible church seen as the "true church," to quote C. I. Scofield, author of

---

2   George Barna (1955-), *Revolution,* p. 36.
3   Colin S. Smith (1958-), *Unlocking the Bible Story Vol. 4,* pp. 122-123.

the famed reference Bible.[4] The local church is relegated to a secondary status, only being a representation or a manifestation of the real church. If all believers, at salvation, were automatically placed in the "true church," which is universal and invisible, of what real importance then is the local, visible church?

The idea of the irrelevance of churches is also because of a current emphasis on the "kingdom of God" which dismisses any important role for churches. Joseph Mattera, bishop of Christ Covenant Coalition in New York city says, *"There is a growing tendency in the body of Christ among practitioners in kingdom societal transformation to bypass the local church in order for the reformation of society to take place."* He went on to say, *"This is due to the frustration of many marketplace leaders with the slow pace, bureaucracy, myopic local view and lack of high-level leadership found in many of this nation's congregations."* He declared he had more of a kingdom mindset, than a church mindset, but warned of leaving out the church.

One of the first truths I learned in Ecclesiology 101 was to distinguish between the family of God, the kingdom of God, and the churches of God. This was illustrated by three ovals in diminishing sizes.

The *Family of God* includes all the children of God in heaven and in earth (Ephesians 3:15). A person is born into the family of God by personal faith in the Son of God (Galatians 3:26; John 1:12; 1 Peter 1:23).

---

4   C.I. Scofield (1843-1921), *Scofield reference Bible*, p. 1249.

The Family of God

The Kingdom of God

The Churches of God

The *Kingdom* (*basileia*) *of God* (or heaven) is the rule of God over all things and includes all the saved living on the earth at a given time (Matthew 11:11). In the present sense, the kingdom of God is in the hearts of those who are saved (Luke 17:29-21). Believers are delivered **"from the power of darkness, and** (God) **hath translated *us* into the kingdom of his dear Son:"** (Colossians 1:13). In the future sense, the kingdom will be God's rule on this earth for a thousand years following Christ's return (Revelation 20:4). We are taught by Jesus to pray daily, "Thy kingdom come..." (Matthew 6:10).

The *Churches* (*ecclesia*) *of God* is never used of any people or institution, except baptized believers meeting at a given location for worship, growth and ministry (1 Corinthians 1:2). The churches of God work within and for promoting and extending the kingdom of God (Acts 19:8; 20:25; Colossians 4:11; 1 Thessalonians 2:12; 2 Thessalonians 1:4-5).

All of God's children who make up the Kingdom of God are not in the Church of God. In many of the parables, Jesus pointed out that the kingdom on earth would have a mixture of saved and unsaved (e.g. wheat and tares, different kinds of fish, wise and foolish virgins). All believers are *in* the kingdom of God. The parables in Matthew 13 let us know the unsaved are *among* those in the kingdom and will be gathered *out from* its citizens (Matthew 13:41, 49). The church operates inside the family and kingdom of God.

We are *born* into the family of God.
We *enter* or *inherit* the kingdom of God.
We are *added to* a church of God.

It is unlikely in our day of "churchless Christianity" that one can overemphasize the importance of the local church.

Louis Entzminger (1874-1958), the chief assistant for J. Frank Norris at First Baptist Church of Fort Worth, wrote, *"Nine of the epistles written by the Apostle Paul in the New Testament were written to churches in a specific locality. Three of the other of his epistles were written to preachers who were acting in the capacity of pastors of such churches at the time he wrote them. God has no other kind of church on earth today."*[5]

So, why is the church still important?

Longtime Southern Baptist evangelist, Bailey Smith (1939-), reminded us, *"Christ did not create a group to be known as 'Christians Anonymous.' He wants every Christian to be a church member. A baptized, faithful, loyal, witnessing, working, tithing church member."*[6]

When you refuse to be openly identified as something (in particular), you will be closer to being identified as nothing (in general).

Beyond being concerned for the church's *existence*, we would do better to be concerned with why the church *exists*. Everything that is created has a purpose. Automobiles are created for transportation. Computers are created for

---

5   Louis Entzminger (1874-1958), *The New Testament Church*, p. 76.
6   Bailey Smith (1939-), *Real Evangelism*, p. 125.

information. Cell phones are created for connectivity.

So, why does the church exist? And what makes the church so important? Why does the church still matter?

The Exaltation of God Almighty

While churches have many horizontal benefits, their foremost purpose is vertical. Churches exists to exalt our God, our Creator, our Saviour and our Lord. "**Unto him *be* glory in the church by Christ Jesus throughout all ages, world without end. Amen**" (Ephesians 3:21).

The word "glory" comes from the Greek word "doxa," from which we get the word "doxology," meaning "that which is praise worthy."

God's glory has two aspects. First, God has *intrinsic glory.* We don't give God glory – it is His by virtue of who He is. Warren W. Wiersbe (1929-)says, *"The glory of the Lord means the sum of all God's attributes. He is glorious in wisdom, glorious in power, glorious in grace, glorious in mercy. God's glory means all that He is and all that He does, and He is unique. There is no one who has glory as God has glory."*[7] Glory is as essential to God as light is to the sun, wet is to water and words are to language. God is glorious. God has always been glorious (John 17:5). God is presently glorious. God will forever be glorious.

When God has been pleased to reveal Himself in time, the one word that expressed that revelation and manifestation was "glory."

- Jehovah is called, "The glory of glory" (Psalm 29:3) and "the Father of glory" (Ephesians 1:17).
- Jesus is called, "The Lord of glory" (1 Corinthians 2:8) and "the King of glory" (Psalm 24:8).

---

7   Warren W. Wiersbe (1929-), *From Worry to Worship*, p. 51.

- The Holy Spirit is called, "the Spirit of glory" (1 Peter 4:14).

We cannot add to the glory of God. Whatever God is it is glorious. And whatever God does is glorious. In creation, we see the glory of God (Psalm 19:1). In the Christian, it is "Christ in you, the hope of glory" (Colossians 1:27). In the church, God is to receive glory (Ephesians 3:21).

Beyond God's intrinsic glory, there is *ascribed glory*. We are called to do the obvious – give glory to our glorious God (1 Chronicles 16:23-29). We are urged to recognize God's inherent glory and acknowledge it, praise it, and submit to it. We cannot add to the glory of God, but we can give glory to the God of glory.

Worship is God-centered and Christ-centered. It is not about entertaining Christians with flashy displays or presentations, but about expressing our love by worshiping our Creator and Saviour. We are to praise and glorify God in worship. This involves…

- Joint Worship with the Lord's people.
- Weekly Worship on the Lord's Day.
- Reverential Worship in honoring the Lord's name.
- Joyous Worship in expressing the Lord's praise.
- Humble Worship in praying before the Lord's throne.
- Financial Worship in bringing the Lord's tithes.
- Memorial Worship in commemorating the Lord's ordinances -Baptism and the Lord's Supper.
- Proclaimed Worship by the preaching of the Lord's Word.

Churches exist for the glory of God.

The Edification of Believers

"**And he gave some, apostles; and some, prophets; and some, evangelists; and some, pastors and teachers; For the perfecting of the saints, for the work of the ministry, for the edifying of the body of Christ: Till we all come in the unity of the faith, and of the knowledge of the Son of God, unto a perfect man, unto the measure of the stature of the fulness of Christ: That we *henceforth* be no more children, tossed to and fro, and carried about with every wind of doctrine, by the sleight of men, *and* cunning craftiness, whereby they lie in wait to deceive; But speaking the truth in love, may grow up into him in all things, which is the head, *even* Christ: From whom the whole body fitly joined together and compacted by that which every joint supplieth, according to the effectual working in the measure of every part, maketh increase of the body unto the edifying of itself in love**" (Ephesians 4:11-16).

Beyond glorifying God, it is also a responsibility of a church to equip and edify (build up) believers in their faith and obedience, helping them to become mature in their walk with God. God's original support-group was His churches.

By pastoral training through teaching and preaching, believers are built up in their faith, prepared for ministry and assisted in discovering, developing and deploying their spiritual gift(s). It is very easy to connect spiritual gifts to church-life because they are never discussed outside the church. Jack MacGorman says, "Not only are the gifts *functional*, but they are also *congregational*."

> Spiritual gifts are special abilities granted by
> the Holy Spirit at salvation to every believer
> to empower him (or her) to serve within the
> framework of a New Testament church (Romans
> 12:3-8; 1 Peter 4:10-11).

It seems that every believer receives his spiritual gifts at the time of his salvation, but the application, authority and accountability for those gifts is always within a congregation's ministry.

The Evangelization of Our Jerusalem and Beyond

Jesus commissioned His church before his ascension with a promise and a purpose. The promise was, **"But ye shall receive power, after that the Holy Ghost is come upon you: ..."** The purpose was, **"and ye shall be witnesses unto me both in Jerusalem, and in all Judaea, and in Samaria, and unto the uttermost part of the earth"** (Acts 1:8).

Jesus means for us to reach out to a lost world with the Good News about Jesus, beginning where we live – our Jerusalem. We must be responsible for our own community – Jerusalem. *"The field is the world – of course – but the world begins in our own backyard, or across the street."*[8]

Evangelism is done through preaching (Acts 2:14-36) and personal witnessing (Acts 8:1, 4). Since people often have questions or doubts about Christ and Christianity, knowing the truth and being able to defend it (apologetics) is also part of the role of the church (1 Peter 3:15).

And beyond sharing the gospel with those around us, each church is to have a global view by sending and

8   Gene A. Getz (1932-), *Sharpening the Focus of the Church*, p. 40.

supporting those who are taking the news of Christ to the regions beyond (Acts 13:1-4). In a very real sense, global evangelism can only be done in and through Christ's churches.

The Establishment of Biblical Doctrine

The days in which we live are marked by Christians who are needlessly "tossed to and fro, and carried about with every wind of doctrine" (Ephesians 4:14.) The church is "the pillar and ground of the truth" (1 Timothy 3:15). One of the great benefits of being in a Scripturally sound church is the opportunity to be taught "sound doctrine." The pastors of churches are charged to **"Preach the word; be instant in season, out of season; reprove, rebuke, exhort with all longsuffering and doctrine. For the time will come when they will not endure sound doctrine; but after their own lusts shall they heap to themselves teachers, having itching ears; And they shall turn away *their* ears from the truth, and shall be turned unto fables"** (2 Timothy 4:2-4).

Paul enjoined a young pastor, **"But speak thou the things which become sound doctrine:"** (Titus 2:1). Pastors "labour in word and doctrine" (1 Timothy 5:17) and give themselves "continually to prayer, and to the ministry of the word" (Acts 6:4).

Every person, every couple, every family needs a Bible-teaching pastor. Ignorance is not bliss when it comes to the Bible. The very essence of the meaning of "disciple" is "learner."

The Enjoyment of the Godly Fellowship

"It is not good that man should be alone…" (Genesis 2:18). **"Two *are* better than one; because they have a**

good reward for their labour. For if they fall, the one will lift up his fellow: but woe to him *that is* alone when he falleth; for *he hath* not another to help him up. Again, if two lie together, then they have heat: but how can one be warm *alone*? And if one prevail against him, two shall withstand him; and a threefold cord is not quickly broken" (Ecclesiastes 4:9-12).

The world is full of discouragements and dangers—spiritual, emotional, physical, financial. We need the company of other children of God to assist us in our way. No one is meant to travel the road to heaven alone. We are all made for relationships.

The Bible plainly speaks of what other believers will do "together."

- Assemble together for worship (Hebrews 10:25).
- Dwell together in unity (Psalm 133:1-3)
- Pray together in faith (Acts 3:1).
- Planted together in baptism (Romans 6:5).
- Walk together in agreement (Amos 3:3).
- Labor together with God (1 Corinthians 3:9).
- Heirs together of the grace of life (1 Peter 3:9).
- Rejoice together in soul-winning (John 4:36).
- Knit together in love (Colossians 2:2).
- Joined together in marriage (Matthew 19:6).
- Strive together for the gospel (Philippians 1:27).
- Caught up together in the rapture (1 Thessalonians 4:17).
- Live together in eternity (1 Thessalonians 5:10).

Charles Wesley, lesser known than his brother, John who founded Methodism, was a gifted hymn writer, writing an amazing 8,989 hymns during his lifetime, that's ten poetic lines every day for 50 years. Charles wrote a love letter for his wife, Sally, as he thought of Ecclesiastes 4.

Two are better far than one
For counsel or for fight;
How can one be warm alone,
Or serve his God aright?
Join we then our hearts and hands,
Each to love provoke his friend;
Run the way of his commands
And keep it to the end
Woe to him whose spirits droop,
To Him who falls alone!
He has none to lift him up,
To help his weakness on:
Happier we each other keep
We each other's burdens bear;
Never need our footsteps slip,
Upheld by mutual prayer.

The Engagement in Spiritual Warfare

Churches and Christians are involved in a cosmic conflict. The Christian life isn't a playground, but a battleground. The evil forces who stand against us are powerful and invisible. **"For we wrestle not against flesh and blood, but against principalities, against powers, against the rulers of the darkness of this world, against spiritual wickedness in high *places*"** (Ephesians 6:12).

- We fight an enemy within us – the flesh (Romans 7:18).
- We fight an enemy around us – the world (1 John 5:19).

- We fight an enemy above us – the devil (1 Peter 5:8).

The weakness of the flesh to consistently do good, the influence of the world that tries to conform us to its way, and the wickedness of the evil one and his angels are formidable. You could call these the "unholy trinity."

To counteract these sinister influences, God has a "holy trinity" of resources that are available to Christians to fight the good fight of faith: (1) the Word,[9] (2) the indwelling Holy Spirit[10] and (3) the church of the living God. The very first mention of the church in the New Testament made by Jesus Christ Himself says "the gates of hell shall not prevail" against the church (Matthew 16:18). That means the church is to be on the attack, invading enemy territory, taking the saving gospel to those who are under Satan's influence and control.

When Christians become victims in this warfare, those who are spiritual in the church are to restore them in a spirit of meekness.[11]

The Exposure of False Teachers

The idea that a church is obligated to be nice to everyone and keep silent when churches and pastors promote error is not what you see in the New Testament.

While the church's founder and Head was on the earth, He exposed the false religious leaders for who they were: "hypocrites" (Matthew 15:7), "blind leaders of the blind" (Matthew 15:14), "blind guides" (Matthew 23:24). After Jesus was resurrected and glorified His last messages to some

---

9   Matthew 4:4, 7, 10; Ephesians 6:17.
10   1 John 4:4.
11   Galatians 6:1.

of His churches were pretty scorching (Revelation 2-3).

The apostle Paul assigned the elders of the church at Ephesus the unpleasant task of exposing those who were false teachers. "**Take heed therefore unto yourselves, and to all the flock, over the which the Holy Ghost hath made you overseers, to feed the church of God, which he hath purchased with his own blood. For I know this, that after my departing shall grievous wolves enter in among you, not sparing the flock. Also of your own selves shall men arise, speaking perverse things, to draw away disciples after them. Therefore watch, and remember, that by the space of three years I ceased not to warn every one night and day with tears**" (Acts 20:28-31).

There were also impostors in the church at Corinth. "**For such *are* false apostles, deceitful workers, transforming themselves into the apostles of Christ. And no marvel; for Satan himself is transformed into an angel of light**" (2 Corinthians 11:13-14).

The apostle John wrote of those who did not remain faithful to God's word and God's churches. "**They went out from us, but they were not of us; for if they had been of us, they would *no doubt* have continued with us: but *they went out*, that they might be made manifest that they were not all of us**" (1 John 2:19).

The apostle Peter was not bashful to say some harsh things about people who were false teachers. "**But there were false prophets also among the people, even as there shall be false teachers among you, who privily shall bring in damnable heresies, even denying the Lord that bought them, and bring upon themselves swift destruction**" (2 Peter 2:1).

One of the benefits of being in a Bible-centered church

is the knowledge of truth. For many churches, flirting with error is not in what they say, but what they choose not to say. The absence of theology (the study of God), the Bible, sin, hell, and the saving gospel of Jesus Christ or any in-depth Bible teaching by pastors, is tantamount to a doctor withholding life-saving treatment from dying patients.

The Expectation of Heaven and Eternity

A final reason the church is still important is that it may be the last place on earth that tells people to get their eyes off this world and on the next. When the church gathers, it helps keep them focused on the life ahead – heaven and eternity. The problem is, you must die to enjoy them.

Facing our Mortality

It is by living in community with other believers that we can honestly face our mortality. People you know and love in your congregation have accidents, get sick and die.

While making my rounds as a volunteer chaplain in a local hospital, I checked in on a 95-year-old man who was dying. His seventy-plus-year-old children said they were "surprised" by this event and it caught them unprepared. Are you kidding? If I am alive at 95, expect me to die at any moment! Death should not surprise any of us at any age. We all have an expiration date.

The Bible commentator, Matthew Henry (1662-1714), said, *"It ought to be the business of every day to prepare for our last day."* He went on to say, *"By going to our beds as to our grave, we shall make death familiar to us, and it will become as easy to close our eyes in peace and die, as it used to be to close our eyes in peace and sleep."*[12]

The only way to realistically face death is to know Christ is the one who has "abolished death, and hath brought life and immortality to light through the gospel."[13] It is Jesus Christ who has destroyed the power of death and gives us victory over death, hell and the grave.[14] *"Rather than being master, death is now the servant who opens the door to our eternal home, and closes the door on sin and suffering."*[15]

One old man was worried about *not* dying soon. He said, "If I don't die pretty soon all my friends in heaven are going to think that I wasn't really saved!"

Foreseeing Our Eternity

What is the hope of believers? A better job? A bigger home? A newer car? The "blessed hope" of believers is the second coming of Jesus Christ. You are probably a lot like me; there is nothing in my life that the rapture would not fix! Amen!

God helps us keep our eyes on the prize when we are connected to a solid church.

Some might be afraid of becoming "so heavenly minded that you're no earthly good." Most of the people I know can remove that from their list of concerns. The truth is, most people are so earthly minded that they are of no heavenly *or* earthly good.

Conclusion

I hope I have at least come close to making the case that

12 Matthews Henry (1662-1714), *The Miscellaneous Works of the Rev. Matthew Henry – Vol. 1*, p. 464.
13 2 Timothy 1:10.
14 Hebrews 2:14-15; 1 Corinthians 15:54-57.
15 J. Oswald Sanders (1902-1992), *Enjoying Your Best Years*, p. 145.

the church is still important two thousand years after its founding. My advice, based on my knowledge of Scripture and from fifty-plus years of being a serious Christian, is that if you are a believer in Jesus Christ, you need a solid church home. This means you need to seek and find God's direction about which Baptist church to join.

A little girl said there were three ways to become a Baptist: by baptism, by letter, or by accident! Well, at least the little girl had the first two right.

Attend by Providence

By the mysterious workings of God, you may have found yourself attending a Baptist church. This should be seen as something much more than fate or an accident. For me, it was initially my family's connection to a Baptist church that brought me to the people called Baptists. For you, it might have been a friend or neighbor who invited you to attend a Baptist church.

Added by Baptism

After a person is saved, they should present themselves to a sound Baptist church for baptism. This is known as "believer's baptism." This means you must give a credible profession of your personal faith in Jesus Christ *before* you are baptized. By "baptism" we mean full immersion. It is possible you had some water ceremony when you were a baby, but that does not qualify as New Testament baptism.

Affirm By Transfer of Membership or Statement of your Salvation and Baptism

It may be that you have been saved, scripturally baptized and held membership in another sound Baptist Church in the past. You can present yourself to the church God is leading you to join and request membership based on your past membership or your statement of faith.

Active by Conviction

This final element is very important. Becoming a member of a church is more than getting wet or doing some paper work. 1 Corinthians 12:18 says it is God who sets the members in a church. Acts 2:47 says the Lord adds people to a church. As a matter of conviction, you should know that God is leading you to the congregation where you seek membership.

CHAPTER 9

Calling God's Churches to Revival

There are an amazing 650 prayers in the Bible. Among them is a prayer recorded in the Epistle of Paul the Apostle to the Ephesians, chapter 3:14-19. This prayer serves as a model for all Christians and all churches. "**For this cause I bow my knees unto the Father of our Lord Jesus Christ, Of whom the whole family in heaven and earth is named, That he would grant you, according to the riches of his glory, to be strengthened with might by his Spirit in the inner man; That Christ may dwell in your hearts by faith; that ye, being rooted and grounded in love, May be able to comprehend with all saints what *is* the breadth, and length, and depth, and height; And to know the love of Christ, which passeth knowledge, that ye might be filled with all the fulness of God.**" Herein are four "that" statements defining the petitions.

- Petition 1: That the Spirit of God would strengthen us, vv. 14-16.
- Petition 2: That the Son of God would be at home in us, v. 17a.
- Petition 3: That the love of God would overwhelm us, vv. 17-19a.
- Petition 4: That the fullness of God would fill us, v. 19b.

At the end of this prayer there is a *praiseful doxology* in verse 20. This is how all these petitions are possible. "**Now unto him that is able to do exceeding abundantly above all that we ask or think, according to the power that** worketh in us,..."

The prayer concludes with a *pointed benediction* in verse 21. "**Unto him** *be* **glory in the church by Christ Jesus throughout all ages, world without end. Amen.**" We seem to want the *manifestation* of God's presence among us (which this verse does not address) while ignoring the *means* by which God receives glory. Look again at what it says in Ephesians 3:21.

- *Praise*..."Unto Him (God) be glory..." The theme of Ephesians chapter 1 is the glory of God.
- *People*..."In the church..." Glory is not given *to* the church but glory is to issue *from* the church.
- *Person*..."By Christ Jesus..." "Christ (Messiah) Jesus (Saviour)." God's Son is the person by which God's receives glory. Christ always and alone is the occasion of God's glory. There is only one star in the church—the Bright and Morning Star—Christ Jesus!
- *Plan*..."Throughout all ages..." that's history; "world without end..." that's all the way into eternity. "Amen."

What God's people need in the twenty-first century is revival...God-ordained...old-fashioned...Christ-center... Bible-based...sin-hating...devil-chasing...hell-hot... heaven-sweet...judgment-certain...soul-stirring...heart-breaking...sinner-saving...saint-surrendering...family-changing...nation-shaking...Spirit-sent revival!

Norman Grubb (1895-1993), who saw revival take East Central Africa for sixteen years, said, *"Revival is the Reviver in action."*[1]

---

1   Norman Grubb (1895-1993), *Continuous* Revival, p. 7.

"Christians in revival are accordingly found living in God's presence, attending to His Word, feeling acute concern about sin and righteousness, rejoicing in the assurance of Christ's love and their own salvation, spontaneously constant in worship, and tirelessly active in witness and service, fueling these activities by praise and prayer."[2]

There is something missing even from that long "revival" list. It didn't say it all. We need a *church-connected revival.*

Most honest people would admit churches are not what they have been or that they ought to be. Churches need revival. The reason churches need revival is that Christians are not what they have been or what they ought to be. Christians need revival.

How can we see revival come to God's churches? Where is it found? These are not trick questions. Most people will affirm the following.

- Christians and churches need revival!
- God is more than willing and able to send revival!
- God does not tantalize His people by setting vague requirements for revival that defy measurement. Revival isn't the carrot dangled in front of the donkey.

The hesitation usually comes when we look at the price tag for revival.

Would you be willing to do whatever it takes for your church to reach a place where God could get glory to Himself by sending your church revival?

If you said, "Yes," you don't need to move one inch from where you are right now!

Here is my simple conclusion after fifty-three years in

---

2   J.I. Packer (1926-), *Marks of Revival*, v. 1, n. 1.

the Christian ministry, fifty years as a Baptist pastor, and unmeasured hours of studying God's Word.

The Key to Revival is the Gathered Church

If that isn't dramatic enough, get over it and keep reading. What would happen if *all* the members of a church gathered… *every Sunday… to every service… every member participating at least on some level… every member praying before and during the gathering… every member bringing to the gathering at least a tithe… every member singing… every member with a Bible… every member with a specific burden for some lost person… every gathered member responding to God's message… every member leaving the gathering on mission to share the gospel.*

Now that would be amazing! The community around where you gather for church would begin to pay attention to you and take you seriously. If your church would ever get on fire, the world will come watch you burn!

The Gathered Church is our Doctrine

The New Testament word for "church" translated in our King James Bible is from the Greek word *ecclesia*. This is a two-part word - *ek*, the preposition "from" or "out" and *kaelo*, to call. The churches of the New Testament were the local, visible, called-out assemblies of baptized believers who gathered for worship and worked together to carry out God's work on the earth.

- God's people are called out *by* God – that's *salvation*. While the doctrine of salvation is vast and deep, when it is reduced to its simplest, it is hearing and obeying the call of God to salvation.
- God's people are also called out *to* God – that's

sanctification. God has set us apart to Himself. We
have been bought with a price and we belong entirely
to Him. We are in the world, but not of the world.

- Eventually, God's people will be called out to be *with*
God eternally – that's *glorification.*

Part of the process of sanctification is that God calls us
to be together with other believers.

There are all kinds of gatherings. Go to Walmart and
there will be a gathering. I like to go there just to see what no
one should go out looking like in public. There are gatherings
at Krispy Kream. That will put a smile on our face and inches
on your waist. There are gatherings at the local bars. There
are gatherings at 24-Hour Fitness. The doctor said I needed
to spend thirty minutes, three times a day on a treadmill.
That was okay for the first week and then someone turned it
on … and nearly threw me back into last week!

Believers gather as the church of the living God!
Christ founded the church with us in mind. Christ loved
the church and gave Himself for it.[3] Christ purchased the
church with His own blood.[4] Christ commissioned His
church to evangelize, baptize and train believers.[5] Christ
has perpetuated His churches for two-thousand years.[6]
Christ's church is the pillar and ground of the truth.[7]

The Gathered Church is in our DNA

Saved people gather with other saved people. "**We
know that we have passed from death unto life, because**

3   Ephesians 5:25.
4   Acts 20:28.
5   Matthew 28:18-20.
6   Ephesians 3:21.
7   1 Timothy 3:15.

we love the brethren…" (1 John 3:14).

Do your own personal survey. Ask people who are saved where Christ found them and where they found Christ. The majority will tell you they were saved in a church gathering.

Baptists have always believed and taught the requirement of a "regenerate" membership. Yet, here is a strange contradiction – many who were saved in church are not still in church. The greatest mission field in many churches is among a church's own membership. Every church has a staggering and embarrassing number of non-gathering professed members. In the average church only a third to half of its members attend on any given Sunday. Houston, we have a problem!

My daddy used to say, "Many problems in churches would be solved with some church people being saved… or a few good funerals" (I added that).

Personally, I would be more than a little concerned about a salvation that didn't take you to church while your living but was supposed to take you to heaven when you die!

The Gathered Church follows a Decision

If you are a person God has saved, then you are compelled by Scripture to get in one of God's churches (not the church of your choice).

For some people, it means they should profess their faith in a church and submit to being baptized. Baptism is how believers make their public profession of faith in Christ (the only exception was the thief on the cross and he had a legitimate hang-up). Baptism is God's means of adding you to one of His churches.[8] If you are saved and not baptized you are out of God's will. 1 Peter 3:21 says baptism it is "the

---

8   Acts 2:41.

answer of a good conscience toward God." Baptism is the first step of obedience in a life-time of obedience. When the baptismal waters are regularly stirred revival breaks out in church.

Others who are saved and scripturally baptized should seek membership in a church of like faith and practice in their community. Some saved, baptized people attend a church for years and never join because they are members of a church hundreds of miles away where grandma is buried. Dig grandma up or leave her there, and become a member of a gathered church where you are attending so God can bless you and your family. Living together isn't marriage and simply attending a church isn't membership.

The Gathered Church should be our Delight

"I was glad when they said unto me, Let us go into the house of the Lord" (Psalm 122:1).

A.W. Tozer called worship "the missing jewel of the evangelical church." Many churches have elaborate "acts" of worship without any "actual" worship. What misery! What hypocrisy!

Believers don't gather on Sunday for a church service. We don't show up to listen to a sermon. We don't get together for fellowship. We gather to meet God. We gather to humble our hearts before God. We gather to wait before God. We gather to listen to God. We gather to talk to God. We gather to obey God. We gather to honor God.

"One *thing* have I desired of the LORD, that will I seek after; that I may dwell in the house of the LORD all the days of my life, to behold the beauty of the LORD, and to enquire in his temple" (Psalm 27:4).

In the Bible, when people got themselves into God's

presence they were humbled, broken and changed. Job confessed, "**I have heard of thee by the hearing of the ear: but now mine eye seeth thee. Wherefore I abhor** *myself,* **and repent in dust and ashes**" (Job 42:5-6). The prophet Isaiah said, "**Woe** *is* **me! for I am undone; because I** *am* **a man of unclean lips, and I dwell in the midst of a people of unclean lips: for mine eyes have seen the King, the LORD of hosts**" (Isaiah 6:5). Daniel wrote, "**Therefore I was left alone, and saw this great vision, and there remained no strength in me: for my comeliness was turned in me into corruption, and I retained no strength**" (Daniel 10:8). It was a life-changing day when "...**Simon Peter...fell down at Jesus' knees, saying, Depart from me; for I am a sinful man, O Lord**" (Luke 5:8).

The Gathered Church evokes a sense of Duty

Churches have a lot of CEO's, who act as though they are doing the church a favor, showing up at Christmas and Easter only. Some professed Christians have the idea that they will come on special occasions. News bulletin: every Sunday is special!

Some people do not realize how many Sundays they are not in church. If they started marking a calendar they would see they are not attending church as much as they think. They are off to daddy and momma's one Sunday; on an extended weekend getaway; on vacation; out pursuing some hobby; at a sporting event; and a hundred other things. This isn't a *schedule problem*; it's a *heart problem*.

My question is, "If you don't need to attend every week, why does the person who sits next to you in church need to? And what about the ones in the front of you or who are behind you? Why does the whole section where you sit need to attend? Why does anyone in the church need to attend?"

I heard of a man who got up one Sunday and said to his wife, "I don't want to go to church today." She kindly said to him, "You should go." Then the husband said, "Tell me three good reasons why I should go to church today." The wife calmly said, "Well, for one thing, it's the Lord's Day. And, the second thing is you will feel better if you go." The man stopped her and said, "Okay. That's two. The third one has to be good." The wife finished, "Third, you're the pastor. Now get up you big baby, get dressed and get your Bible and let's get going!"

When you do not faithfully attend the gatherings of your church, you are in sinful disobedience to Hebrews 10:25 that commands believers to not forsake the "assembling of ourselves together." Some Christians stay in a perpetual state of discouragement because they neglect the gathering of the church.

Those who fail to gather with the church faithfully…

- Make evangelism harder
- Confuse new believers
- Discourage faithful attendees
- Misdirect the focus of the church on to themselves
- And frankly worry their pastor (Hebrews 13:17).

The Gathered Church requires the right Disposition

Church gatherings can be destructive, divisive and deadly when those who gather have the wrong spirit. If some people's attitude had an odor, we couldn't stay in the building for a minute.

Don't dare have an innocent visitor violate the "preferred personal seating" zone in some churches. The stares alone are enough to kill.

Some people say they are laying out of church because "somebody hurt my feelings." People at Walmart hurt my feelings all the time with their crummy carts and self-checkout but I keep going back. May I say very kindly, "Get over it, put on your big boy pants and grow up!"

Others don't attend with the right attitude because, they say, "I don't know anybody there." If that is so then, you are the problem. The Bible says, "He that hath friends, must..." do what? "...show himself friendly." (Proverbs 18:24) Quit being a knot on a log and shake somebody's hand and find out their name. Take somebody to the burger joint and get to know them.

Some don't go to church regularly saying, "I don't like our preacher." Neither does his wife a lot of the time. You make a big mistake when you fall out with the man of God.

The Gathered Church is about your Devotion

While the church at Ephesus was a remarkable church, they were a church in need of revival. The reason churches need revival is because Christians are not what they have been or what they ought to be. Christians need revival. When Christians are revived the church will be revived.

The epistle of Paul was not the final letter to the church at Ephesus. Christ has sent a final letter to that church in *Revelation 2* with this stern word, **"Nevertheless I have *somewhat* against thee, because thou hast left thy first love. Remember therefore from whence thou art fallen, and repent, and do the first works; or else I will come unto thee quickly, and will remove thy candlestick out of his place, except thou repent"** (Revelation 2:4-5). Jesus was talking to church-going people. It's too easy to go through the motions. Jesus had previously said, **"And**

**because iniquity shall abound, the love of many shall wax
cold"** (Matthew 24:12). That's our day – iniquity abounds!
And it has affected our love for God. Our love for the church,
our love for our fellow Christians, our love for God's work –
all of it must grow out of our love for the Lord.

Jesus lays down a plan for personal and cooperate
revival. He told them to "remember," "repent," "return" (do
the first works), "or else" He would "remove" the candlestick.
It's either *revival* or *removal*. When I was a boy and my dad
or mom gave me an "or else" proposal, I knew they meant
business and that I has better start meaning business.

God's gathered church needs to get back to *making much
of Jesus.*

"Return unto me…and I will return unto you"
(Malachi 3:7).

"Draw night to God…and He will draw nigh to you"
(James 4:8).

**"For thus saith the high and lofty One that inhabiteth
eternity, whose name *is* Holy; I dwell in the high and
holy *place*, with him also *that is* of a contrite and humble
spirit, to revive the spirit of the humble, and to revive the
heart of the contrite ones"** (Isaiah 57:15).

At anytime, anywhere, there can be at least a one-person
revival; or a one couple revival; or a one family revival; or a
one church revival.

What if twenty individuals became serious about the
gathered church?

What if fifteen couples became serious about the
gathered church?

What if ten families became serious about the gathered
church?

A genuine revival will be the result.

Be a part of the gathering at church Sunday and start a revival!

CHAPTER 10

Who are independent Baptists?

To simply say a church is a "Baptist" church has lost meaning for most people, even to those who are Baptists. The question that usually follows is, "What *kind* of Baptist are you?"

There are American Baptists, Southern Baptists, Regular Baptists, Particular Baptists, Reformed Baptists, Seventh-Day Baptists, Primitive Baptists, Free Will Baptists, Missionary Baptists, Fundamental Baptists, World Baptists, Bible Baptists, independent Baptists,[1] and more.

Before Baptists churches organized into denominations, they were all separate, independent churches. Baptist historian H. Leon McBeth (1932-2013) believed early Baptist churches were hampered by what he called "exaggerated independence."[2] No doubt Baptist churches probably had limited contact with sister churches, but they likely remained independent because of biblical convictions.

Baptist associations began in the early 1600's but they were not organized. They originally merely fellowshipped and cooperated on matters of common concerns. But by midcentury, they took the form of an organization.

The first Baptist association in America was founded among General Six-Principle Baptists[3] in 1690 in Providence, Rhode Island. A more widely known association was organized in 1707, in Philadelphia, when five Baptist churches from Pennsylvania and the Jerseys

---

1   The intentionally use of the lower case "independent" is as an adjective, not a noun.
2   H. Leon McBeth (1932-2013), *The Baptist Heritage*, p. 95.
3   Hebrews 6:1-2.

joined together in a formal organization of the *Philadelphia Association.* A third Baptist association was formed in 1751 in Charleston, South Carolina. *Warren Baptist Association* in New England was formed in 1766. By 1790 there were 35 Baptist associations, and approximately 560 ministers, 750 churches and 60,000 members in the U.S.[4]

Are churches free to do what the Bible does not clearly instruct them to do?

Do Baptist Organizations Outside the Local Church Serve or Subjugate Local Churches?

One historian believed some independent-minded Baptists "fear the concept of denominationalism almost as much as the apostasy."[5] If that is so, there was a good reason. Historically, all Christian denominations eventually move closer and closer toward apostasy. An organized, gathered group of pastors and churches inevitably requires reasonable concessions, if not outright compromises.

Bigness

There is not a single Scripture that commands or instructs local churches to organize into a denomination. The decision to do so often comes from pragmatism or flawed human logic. "Is it important *how* something is done for the Lord as long as it is done?" "Think how much more we can do together." That's kind of thinking is a flashback to the tower of Babel. **"Go to, let us build us a city and a tower...and let us make us a name..."** (Genesis 11:5). The sin for which God most severely judged King David was

---

4   http://www.abc-usa.org/what_we_believe/our-history/
5   H. Leon McBeth (1932-2013), *The Baptist Heritage*, p. 768.

when he numbered Israel (2 Samuel 24:1-10). King Uzziah **"was marvelously helped, till he was strong. But when he was strong, his heart was lifted up to his destruction..."** (2 Chronicles 26:15-16). Bigness is intoxicating and few survive it.

Sameness

In the end of the days of the judges, the nation of Israel wanted a human king to judge them "like all the nations" that surrounded them (1 Samuel 8:5). God declared to Samuel that in this the nation of Israel had "rejected him" (1 Samuel 8:7). God's churches have Christ as their Head, the Bible as their Law, and the Holy Spirit as their Guide. To create man-made organizations, no matter the reason, is a rejection of God's stated will to do His work inside and through His churches. Man-made organizations cannot claim God's institutional promises and they demand more and more grease (money) to keep their organizational machine running smoothly. Those who justify them by saying, "You don't find Sunday Schools or Wednesday night meetings or bank accounts in the Bible" are failing to see those things are the decisions and ministries of the "inside" workings of a local church and do not require giving up any of their authority or responsibility to have them. Man-made organizations are clearly "outside" the church.

At best, denominational organizations are *unnecessary*.
At worst, denominational organizations are *unscriptural*.

Togetherness

The issue of the Nicolaitians, their *"deeds"* (Revelation

2:6) and their *"doctrine"* (Revelation 2:15), had already intruded into the churches of the first century. A man by the man of Nicolai influenced churches to establish a new ecclesiastical order. Nicolaitanism seems to have been an effort to set up bishops to rule over groups of churches. *"This unscriptural idea, which causes the local church to become enslaved by one man or a small group of men whose spiritual life can determine the spiritual success of the church. Another evil of this practice is that it causes the local church to look to human beings for the solution to their problems rather than the Holy Spirit."*[6] Jesus hated this intrusion into His place as the church's Head. *"Would to God that the Church of Jesus Christ could learn the valuable lesson that it is not by ecclesiasticism or organization or promotion or administration, but 'by my Spirit, says the Lord.' When human beings get control of the spiritual training of other people and are in a position to dominate the church, their theological position will eventually dominate that church."*[7]

When asked about the current state of the Southern Baptist Convention, one man answered, "The Southern Baptist convention only exists two days a year during its annual meeting. So, in that sense, the state of the Convention varies from year to year."[8] While that was the man's sincere answer, it does not reflect reality. In fact, over-reaching denominationalism is on display at their annual convention and 363 other days. Even though they have an annual meeting where delegates from their churches attend, nothing of consequence is done except for electing their president. The annual meeting seems to be nothing more than a vacation for some and a time to connect with old friends because

6   Tim LaHaye (1926-2016), *Revelation Unveiled*, p. 47.
7   Ibid, p. 47.
8   Trevin Wax, SBC Voices Interview, August 2, 2010.

the denominational machine moves on without their input or control. Here is why. The SBC's Executive Committee, the North American Mission Board, the International Mission Board, LifeWay Christian Resources, Guidestone Financial Resources, and the SBC's six seminaries are all governed by trustee boards, and not by the convention or by their churches. It's like the national parks in America. The National Parks Service has more than 400 sites covering an enormous 84.6 million acres. Americans are told we own them and are obligated to keep them maintained, but we are not free to use them. We have access to them for a fee, but only at limited times and places.

Here is just one illustration of the far-reaching power of just one trustee board. On May 13, 2015, the International Mission Board of the SBC, meeting in Louisville, Kentucky, changed guidelines away from long-held Baptist positions for its 4,800 missionaries. One, they now allow divorced people and parents with teenage children to serve in more positions, including long-term mission assignments. Two, after decade-long resistance, the Southern Baptist Convention will admit missionary candidates who speak in tongues, a practice associated with Pentecostal and charismatic churches. The IMB said it will still end employment for any missionary who places *"persistent emphasis on any specific gift of the Spirit as normative for all or to the extent such emphasis becomes disruptive."* And three, the most disturbing, missionaries will now recognize baptisms performed by other Christian denominations so long as they involved full-body immersion. Previous rules required would-be missionaries to have been baptized in an SBC church, or in a church that held SBC-like beliefs about baptism. Candidates baptized in a church that did not believe in eternal security—the idea that true Christians can't lose their salvation even if they sin—or a church that views baptism is a sacrament were previously rejected. The new rules allow those who were simply immersed and who are members of an SBC church to be candidates.[9]

What the trustee board failed to understand or deliberately denied is one's baptism is an expression and affirmation of the church authorizing the baptism. While baptism is personal, it is not private. One's baptism underscores the doctrine of the church who carries out the baptism. The vagueness of this change means that the baptisms of an Orthodox Greek Catholic church that immerses babies, a Methodist or Holiness church that immerse but teaches you can fall from grace, any individual who has been full-body immersed by a friend, and the strict immersion of a believer upon profession of one's faith in Jesus Christ as Saviour by a doctrinally sound Baptist church are all seen as equal.

> If a Baptist congregation decides to join an association or convention, does it remain a truly independent congregation?

It is sometimes represented by some that independent Baptist churches have "an exaggerated emphasis upon local church autonomy"[10] and refuse to be identified among mainline denominational Baptists because they cannot get along. But just look at the history. Most of present-day

---

9   Charisma News, Greg Horton and Yonat Shimron, *Southern Baptists Change Policy on Speaking in Tongues*, May 15, 2015; Christianity Today, Bob Smietana, *International Mission Board Drops Ban on Speaking in Tongues*, May 15, 2015.

10   H. Leon McBeth (1932-2013), *The Baptist Heritage*, p. 461

organized Baptists groups now exist after "splitting" from a Baptist group with which they were at one time affiliated.

- In 1814, Baptists in the North and South met at the *Triennial Convention* which would eventually become the *Northern Baptist Convention* (Headquarters: Valley Forge, PA-renamed the *American Baptist Convention* in 1950).

- In 1845, the *Southern Baptist Convention* (Headquarters: Nashville, TN) was organized at a meeting of 310 delegates in Augusta, Georgia when it pulled out of the *Northern Baptist Convention*.

- In 1899, the *Baptist Missionary Association* (Headquarters: Texarkana, TX) pulled out of the *Southern Baptist Convention*.

- In 1905, the *American Baptist Association* (Headquarters: Little Rock, AR) pulled out of the *Baptist Missionary Association*.

- In 1920, the *Fundamental Baptist Fellowship, International* (Headquarters: Taylor, SC) pulled out of the *Northern Baptist Convention*.

- In 1932, the *General Association of Regular Baptist* (Headquarters: Schaumburg, IL) pulled out of the *American Baptist Convention*.

- In 1932, the *World Baptist Fellowship* (originally named World Fundamental Baptist Missionary Fellowship) (Headquarters: Arlington, TX) pulled out of the *Southern Baptist Convention*, led by J. Frank Norris (1877-1952).

- In 1950, the *Bible Baptist Fellowship International* (Headquarters: Springfield, MO) pulled out of the *World Baptist Fellowship*, led by G. B. Vick (1901-1975).

- In 1956, the *Southwide Baptist Fellowship* (Headquarters: Chattanooga, TN) was organized by Lee Roberson (1909-2007) after leaving the *Southern Baptist Convention* and now goes by *Southwide Independent Baptist Fellowship.*
- In 1984, the *Independent Baptist Fellowship International* (Headquarters: Fort Worth, TX) pulled out of the *World Baptist Fellowship,* led by Raymond Barber (1932-).
- In 1987, the *Alliance of Baptist Churches* (Headquarters: Washington DC) pulled out of the *Southern Baptist Convention.*
- In 1991, the *Cooperative Baptist Fellowship* (Headquarters: Atlanta, GA) pulled out of the *Southern Baptist Convention.*
- In 2000, the *Global Independent Baptist Fellowship* pulled away from *Bible Baptist Fellowship International.*
- In 2004, the *Nationwide Independent Baptist Fellowship* (Headquarters: McDonough, GA) pulled out of the *Southwide Independent Baptist Fellowship.*

It should be noted that those who pulled out did not seem to be opposed to their Baptist organization, just that the organization had become too liberal, or in a couple of cases, too conservative. So, when they pulled out they created an organization much like the one they just left. These new organizations installed presidents, hired employees, drafted by-laws, scheduled national meetings, created a mission agency, appointed missionaries, established retirement benefits, began owning vast properties (seminaries, schools, camps/conference centers), and owed, on some occasions, massive debts.

Independent Baptist pastors and churches need to be careful in their loose associations and fellowships that they do not end up becoming quasi-denominations, especially those who have pulled out of an organized denomination to become independent. When J. Frank Norris (1877-1952) was fighting with the Southern Baptist Convention, he exposed what he saw was the evil of *conventionism*, as he called it. Yet, upon leaving, he organized a group along the very same pattern, only much smaller. He gathered a following of pastors and churches, founded a seminary and mission agency, published a widely circulated newspaper, and began the *World Baptist Fellowship*.

Norman H. Wells (1918-1978) sadly observed that *"independent Baptists have* (often) *bound themselves together in the same kind of organizational ties that they so bitterly fought."*[11] The fatal pattern is to build extra-church organizations around a biblical cause led by strong personalities (1 Corinthians 1:12; 3:3-5).

All honest Bible scholars and students agree that churches in the New Testament were all independent congregations with no organizations beyond individual churches.

Some refer to independent Baptists as a "movement." Jesus and the apostles did not start a movement – they started local, visible, independent churches. Generally, independent Baptist pastors and churches fellowship around the gospel with other pastors and churches that share their emphasis and convictions, but there are many other sound

---

11   Norman H. Wells (1918-1978), *The Church that Jesus Loved*, p. 21.

independent Baptist pastors and churches beyond our knowledge.

A few independent Baptists do not speak for all
independent Baptists.

Independent Baptists are by no means alike. Their positions differ on ministry philosophy, methods of evangelism, attention to personal appearance, size of congregations, Bible translations, Christian college preferences, styles of music, public/private/home schooling, mission support, and some details about the second coming of Christ. As you can see, independent Baptist congregations vary vastly from church to church.

Baptist churches that are independent are similar when it comes to major Christian doctrines. They are often advertised as believing in "the Bible, the blood and the blessed hope." Independent Baptist churches make no apology that they are also strong in their stance in what they are against - infant sprinkling, female preachers, charismatic gifts, liberalism, ecumenicalism, evolution, abortion, aberrant sexual conduct (fornication, adultery, homosexuality), and drinking alcohol as a beverage.

Possibly the most famous independent Baptist was Charles H. Spurgeon (1834-1892). In 1887, he withdrew from the Baptist Union of Great Britain which had formed in 1813, with forty-six ministers as charter members. The "Down Grade Controversy," the doctrinal deterioration of their organization's membership, was more than Spurgeon could take. He charged the denomination with *"moral and doctrinal decay which resulted in prayerless churches, indifferent laity, and unbelieving pastors who spent their time in worldly pursuit like the theater rather than in Bible study and fervent preaching...*" Affirming that doctrinal conditions were ten times worse among Baptists than he first thought, Spurgeon lamented, *"A new religion has been initiated, which is no more Christianity than chalk is cheese.'"*[12] Spurgeon's conclusion was *"Fellowship with known and vital error is participation in sin."* For Spurgeon's efforts to stand for the truth he was censured by the Union with two thousand standing against him, and only seven with him. *"Though leaders in the Baptist Union professed loyalty to the faith, Spurgeon's instincts proved to be absolutely accurate in the matter of encroaching apostasy. Only thirty-eight years later an out-and-out liberal was elected to the highest office of the Baptist Union"* when Dr. T. Reaveley Glover became President.[13] By choice and at great price Charles H. Spurgeon was an independent Baptist for the last five years of his life.

In 1979 the conservatives of the Southern Baptist Convention began the struggle to change and correct the direction their denomination was headed toward liberalism. Paige Patterson, one of the leaders involved in the turnaround, said, *"I was astonished at how the Southern Baptist Convention controversy mirrored the Downgrade Controversy, even to the selection of language and method. I took heart from Spurgeon's courage and faith."*[14] The conservatives in the SBC saw it, not as a "take over," but as *"a take back to where our spiritual forefathers founded it -- on the cross of Jesus Christ and the absolute infallible Word of God. Our ecclesiology saved us,"* Richard Land (1946-) said. *"We believed in the autonomy of the local church and that all of our boards and agencies ultimately are accountable to the*

---

12   H. Leon McBeth (1932-2013), *The Baptist Heritage*, pp. 301-303.

13   Earnest Pickering (1928-2000), *Biblical Separation*, p. 91.

14   Tom J. Nettles (1946-), Russell D. Moore (1971-), *Why I Am a Baptist*, p. 72.

messengers from the local churches."[15] While we thank God for the good that was done, don't overlook the obvious. One, there will always be a downward slide of all man-made organizations away from truth. Everybody knows where two Baptists come together there will be three opinions. Two, it was the SBC's denominational structure which exposed that they had many hiding in their ranks who were very liberal and barely "Baptist." It was because of this "take back" that the less than conservatives (call them moderates or liberals if you like) split and organized their own mini-denominations - *Alliance of Baptist Churches* (1987) and the *Cooperative Baptist Fellowship* (1991). Three, it was probably the years of little to no teaching or understanding of New Testament ecclesiology among Southern Baptist churches that was exposed.

And it is still happening today. The modern trend of large, successful and popular Baptist churches having satellite campuses flies in the face of each church assembly being autonomous and independent. These celebrity pastors are now bishops over churches bearing their powerful brand. The multi-services of Baptist churches on Saturday nights and Sundays defies the simplest understanding of "ecclesia," the "gathered" church. Baptist churches who are embracing the Presbyterian form of "elders" government or pastors who see themselves as the church's CEO do not seem to notice that the long-held Baptist position has been congregationalism.

What are independent Baptist Churches?

As I have mentioned in a previous chapter, when I have been asked, "What kind of Baptist are you?" I answer them,

---

15   Richard Land (1946-), President of the Ethics & Religious Liberty Commission, *The Baptist Press*, June 15, 2004.

"Do you know what Baptists were two-hundred years ago? That's what we still are. And we are neither angry or ashamed of it."

It is often misunderstood or misrepresented that independent Baptist churches are independent to do as they please. Nothing could be farther from the truth. No Baptist church is free to do as they please. Churches exist for the glory of God to do the will of God. Individually and corporately believers are to do what pleases God. Churches that are unaffiliated are free to obey God without the overt or subtle influences that come from being in man-made organizations.

So, what are independent Baptist churches?

New Testament Churches

They are churches modeled after the pattern of the churches of the New Testament. A distinction held by all the churches of the New Testament was that they were all truly independent congregations.

Baptist Churches

They are churches who adhere to the principle doctrines of Baptist churches.

Historical Churches

Baptist churches that are independent are what congregations were before they organized themselves in associations, conventions and fellowships. While some churches joined Baptist organizations, others have remained independent.

Local Churches

The churches of the New Testament ministered where they were to reach their cities and communities with the gospel of Christ. Wayne Hardy (1963-) reminds us, *"We believe strongly in the local church, as opposed to the universal idea. 'Local' is more than a hot-button phrase to draw passionate 'amens' in preaching, though. The passion is better served in emphasizing the practical ramifications of a church's being local. It means that a church exists in a very specific context, first and foremost tied to its community. It demands that a church spend its majority passion on reaching the people around it."*[16] Independent Baptist churches assume the privilege and responsibility of being God's gospel light where they assemble and from where they do ministry.

Unaffiliated Churches

While some colleges and camps attract certain pastors and churches, independent Baptist churches are not affiliated with any human organization believing the only organization established and commissioned in the New Testament is the local church.

Bible-Centered Churches

Time hasn't left independent Baptist churches behind because they are anchored to the timeless Word of God. They understand one of the functions of a scriptural church is to both guard and proclaim the message of the Bible (Jude 3; 1 Peter 3:15; 2 Timothy 2:15; 2 Timothy 4:1). This is done through Sunday morning Bible classes, discipleship groups, one-on-one mentoring, and thorough expository preaching.

---

16   Wayne Hardy (1963-), *The Global Baptist Times - Reaching Our Jerusalem*, March-April, 2017, p. 7.

The Baptist pulpit is still central to the independent Baptist worship gathering.

Missionary Churches

Baptist churches that are independent are evangelistic at home and partner with other independent Baptist churches in global gospel missions. Many independent Baptist congregations strictly follow the Acts 13 model of the church at Antioch that sends out, supervises and supports men directly out of their congregation. This "direct-missions" approach is not only biblical, but financially it means one-hundred percent of support given to missions is received by the missionary on his field of service. Norman H. Wells reminds us, *"The greatest missionary effort the world has ever known took place during New Testament times. The only organizations used were local churches."*[17] If gospel work requires extra organizations, what did churches do for seventeen hundred years? They did quite well, actually!

Fellowshipping Churches

Independent Baptists pastors and churches voluntarily fellowship with other churches of like faith without the need for any structural organization. Churches can associate without an association; they can fellowship without an organized fellowship; the can convene without needing a convention.

Pastor Rick Washburn Jr. says, *"Our differences are not liabilities to get rid of; they are assets, blessings and benefits that we need to celebrate. In fact, the entire message of the Gospel is about all different genders, nationalities, ethnic groups, cultures,*

---

17   Norman H. Wells (1918-1978), *The Church that Jesus Loved*, p. 77.

languages and generations brought together by the Cross of Jesus."[18]

The Dangers Faced by independent Baptist Pastors and Churches

Alienating Attitudes

Are independent Baptists truly "contending for the faith," or are we sometimes just plain contentious? It is regrettable that many independent Baptists are on occasions ungracious and angry. It is difficult for many to balance between being narrow and being neurotic, having the right position held with the right disposition. Independent Baptists need to understand that every trivial disagreement in our undesignated ranks is not equal to the sin of Korah or the betrayal of Judas. Tongue and pen should be principally used to praise God and encourage brethren.

Radical Railer

Much of what we stand for as independent Baptists can become virtues taken to the extreme. Dave Hardy (1945-) wisely points out that "there is a ditch on both sides of the road."[19] Obviously, we need to stay on the road of truth and righteousness and avoid the extremes on either side.

Some of our independent Baptist brethren would do well to change their literary style and not punctuate every word with bold or capital letters or underlining or italics and by not ending every sentence with an exclamation mark!!!!!! (SORRY, I <u>couldn't</u> **help** *myself.*) How many people in some independent Baptist churches starve for lack of solid Bible

---

18   Rick Washburn Jr., *The Fundamentalist*, Summer 2016.
19   Dave Hardy, *Do Independent Baptists Think?* Baptist Times, September 2012.

food while their pastor spends most of their time ranting about some obscure issue? Is it possible to disagree without being disagreeable? Usually not.

Spoon Feeding the Saints

While the media is force-feeding society its humanistic soap, too many pastors are content to tell their people how to live by following a short list of "dos" and "don'ts" – usually the ones of their own making. In many independent Baptist churches, there is a short list of hot topics that are treated almost like the Ten Commandments. To keep the people in line they are regularly preached. This is why some independent Baptist church members leave after hearing the same list for the umpteenth time.

Wayne Hardy (1963-) believes pastors would better serve their people by teaching them how to think – biblically.[20] Instead of shallow self-help sermons, pastors should be regularly serving up some "strong meat" to help their people "discern both good and evil." Instead of thinking for the people, pastors should be equipping members to think for themselves. Paige Patterson has been quoted as saying, "Expository preaching is simply helping your people read their Bibles better."

Extreme Isolation

It will take the resurrection for many precious Baptists to finally understand you don't have to be twins to be brothers! We are at war, but it is not with our brethren. Fight the good fight of faith, but don't fight those in the faith. We would all be much better off if we invested in some positive

---

20   Wayne Hardy (1963-), *Do Independent Baptists Think?* Baptist Times, September 2012.

friendships with a few people who could encourage and/or challenge us in our walk with God. The Bible is still true, "It is not good that man (or woman) should be alone" (Genesis 2:18). Don't try to go at the Christian life alone.

Doctrinal Compromise

What you *believe* will determine what you *become* and how you *behave*. The pressure is always on to stifle or silence the voice of truth. After studying again what our Baptist forefathers stood for and stood against, we should be willing to treasure the truth at whatever cost. The modern-day privileges we enjoy as independent Baptists has been paid for by the blood of martyrs. Surely, we can at least add our sweat and tears by keeping the faith.

Heroes and Haloes

This is a touchy matter, and the fact that it is touchy reveals there is a problem. There is not much difference between an independent Baptist and those in a convention or fellowship when it comes to our love of preachers with big personalities. Admittedly, there are some men who have greater intellect, greater abilities, greater responsibilities, and greater opportunities, but there are no great men, only a great Saviour of men. We should have all discovered by now that the ground at the cross is level.

Obviously, I have honored some of the men of my past in the dedication of this book, but they would join me in giving all praise to our Lord and Saviour whose name is above all names.

It needs to be said that in some circles of independent Baptists, their attachment and adulation of certain men, dead or alive, borders on a "personality cult." The apostle

Paul identified for us that such behavior is base carnality, not biblical spirituality (1 Corinthians 1:12-13; 3:1-3). The ranks of independent Baptists have been shamed and soiled by some of its most prominent pastors and leaders whose names are not mentioned here to protect the guilty. It is probably more than coincidental that Psalm 118:8 is the middle verse of the Bible. "***It is* better to trust in the LORD than to put confidence in man.**"

The truth is, those who praise other men may have a secret desire to be praised.

What Can independent Baptist Churches do?

Independent Baptist churches can do anything any other Baptist church can do. They can assemble. They can worship. They can sing. They can pray. They can preach the gospel. They can win the lost. They can baptize believers. They can disciple baptized believers. They can give their tithes and offerings into God's storehouse. They can be generous. They can manage God's resources responsibly. They can fulfill the Great Commission. They can send missionaries out of their church. They can plant churches. They can voluntarily partner with other churches in the work of the gospel, at home and around the world. They can preach and teach the Bible. They can affirm biblical doctrine. They can expose false teachers. They can esteem their leaders. They can maintain doctrinal purity. They can publish study materials and books. They can take short-term mission trips. They can train preachers. They can ordain ministers and deacons. They can create opportunities for fellowship. They can attend summer church camps. They can conduct Vacation Bible Schools. They can equip their people to serve in their communities. They can help those in need. They can model morality. They can show compassion. They can hold before their people the pattern of biblical marriage. They can assist in building strong families. They can mentor young people. They can honor the elderly. They can assist families at the time of death. They can glorify God. They can do what Baptist churches have done for hundreds of years.

The identifying mark of a New Testament church is not to whom they *belong* but what they *believe* and how they *behave.*

"*If I am a Baptist and if I am proud of it, I want that it shall affect me not in the way of making me narrow and bigoted and intolerant, but humble, patient, loving towards those who differ from me, and hearty, generous, energetic and persevering in the use of my time, talents and means for the furtherance of the good cause. Let us show our devotion to our principles, not by boastfulness and arrogance, but by a watchful attention to the needs of the cause we love. Thus shall we best show to men our fidelity and zeal; and thus best help the truth in its onward march to complete and final victory.*"[21]

---

21   Richard M. Dudley (1838-1873), *Baptist Why and Why Not,* 1900.

285

Postscript

Keeping the "Baptist" Name

You may have heard the story of a woman who was involved in a bad accident. It looked for certain she would die. Suddenly an angel appeared and promised that regardless of how bad things looked she would live another 25 years. Well, she was in the hospital for weeks but made a full recovery. While in her last days in the hospital she decided to take advantage of her promised new life, so she stayed a little longer having a face lift and some body sculpting. On the day of her release she had on a beautiful new dress to show-off her new figure, a stunning make-up job on her new face, and a spring in her step as she walked out of the hospital feeling great about herself. She stepped off the curb onto the street just outside the hospital and was hit by a huge truck and killed on the spot. She immediately arrived at the Pearly Gates and angrily asked her guardian angel how this could have happened since she had been promised another twenty-five years. The embarrassed angel said, *"Well, the truth is, I didn't recognize you."*

When it comes to twenty-first century Baptist churches, most of us can hardly recognize them. In the past few decades, many Baptist churches have gone through radical make-overs and, in many ways, the surgeries have been botched.

In this book, I have not presumed to speak for other Baptists; and many of them do not speak for me. While I have no desire to speak *for* modern-day Baptists, I feel a deep need to speak *to* them.

As the title of this book declares, I am *STILL A*

BAPTIST... *and neither angry nor ashamed of it.* I will admit at times I do border on anger about what is happening to Baptists. To maintain the integrity of the title, let's just say from time to time I am on edge.

What if you were the curator of a famous, world-class museum. One morning you arrived to discover the most priceless piece of art in the collection had been stolen. There were no locks broken. The alarms had not been tripped. Your immediate evaluation? It was an inside job.

The demise of many Baptist churches has been an inside job.

"Take heed therefore unto yourselves, and to all the flock, over the which the Holy Ghost hath made you overseers, to feed the church of God, which he hath purchased with his own blood.

For I know this, that after my departing shall grievous wolves enter in among you, not sparing the flock. Also of your own selves shall men arise, speaking perverse things, to draw away disciples after them. Therefore watch, and remember, that by the space of three years I ceased not to warn every one night and day with tears" (Acts 20:28-31).

"Beloved, when I gave all diligence to write unto you of the common salvation, it was needful for me to write unto you, and exhort *you* that ye should earnestly contend for the faith which was once delivered unto the saints. For there are certain men crept in unawares, who were before of old ordained to this condemnation, ungodly men, turning the grace of our God into lasciviousness, and denying the only Lord God, and our Lord Jesus Christ" (Jude 3-4).

Baptist History

When it comes to the history of Baptists many may respond, *"What difference does it make? I am not interested in the people who were before me and what they did. I just want to do ministry today."* The otherwise brilliant Henry Ford I agreed, stating, *"History is bunk,"*[1] believing it is only the history we make today that matters.

Children with no family history would not agree. Some have spent their life and considerable money trying to find their biological father and mother. A family's history is a testimony of God's providence and purpose.

After having visited the historic sites of Valley Forge, Gettysburg, Arlington National Cemetery and Pearl Harbor, it is hard for me to understand those who would not appreciate the sacrifices that have been made, the blood that was shed and the lives that were given for our freedom. Even those who apply for United States citizenship are required to pass a one-hundred question test about United States history and government.

God required His ancient people, Israel, to make annual trips to Jerusalem to celebrate major historical events – Passover, Pentecost, and Tabernacles. Consider the following Scriptures about how they were to view their history.

"And the people served the LORD all the days of Joshua, and all the days of the elders that outlived Joshua, who had seen all the great works of the LORD, that he did for Israel. And Joshua the son of Nun, the servant of the LORD, died, *being* an hundred and ten years old. And they buried him in the border of his inheritance in Timnathheres, in the mount of Ephraim, on the north side of the hill Gaash. And also all that generation were

---

1   From the Dutch *bunkum*, meaning rubbish or nonsense.

gathered unto their fathers: and there arose another generation after them, which knew not the LORD, nor yet the works which he had done for Israel" (Judges 2:7-10).

"Give ear, O my people, *to* my law: incline your ears to the words of my mouth. I will open my mouth in a parable: I will utter dark sayings of old: Which we have heard and known, and our fathers have told us. We will not hide *them* from their children, shewing to the generation to come the praises of the LORD, and his strength, and his wonderful works that he hath done. For he established a testimony in Jacob, and appointed a law in Israel, which he commanded our fathers, that they should make them known to their children: That the generation to come might know *them, even* the children *which* should be born; *who* should arise and declare *them* to their children: That they might set their hope in God, and not forget the works of God, but keep his commandments: And might not be as their fathers, a stubborn and rebellious generation; a generation *that* set not their heart aright, and whose spirit was not stedfast with God" (Psalm 78:1-8).

"This shall be written for the generation to come: and the people which shall be created shall praise the LORD" (Psalm 102:18).

"Praise ye the LORD. Blessed *is* the man *that* feareth the LORD, *that* delighteth greatly in his commandments. His seed shall be mighty upon earth: the generation of the upright shall be blessed. Surely he shall not be moved for ever: the righteous shall be in everlasting remembrance" (Psalm 112:1-2, 6).

"**Great *is* the LORD, and greatly to be praised; and his greatness *is* unsearchable. One generation shall praise thy works to another, and shall declare thy mighty acts**" (Psalm 145:3-4).

"**Remove not the ancient landmark, which thy fathers have set**" (Proverbs 22:28).

"**Hearken to me, ye that follow after righteousness, ye that seek the LORD: look unto the rock *whence* ye are hewn, and to the hole of the pit *whence* ye are digged**" (Isaiah 51:1).

"**Thus saith the LORD, Stand ye in the ways, and see, and ask for the old paths, where *is* the good way, and walk therein, and ye shall find rest for your souls. But they said, We will not walk *therein***" (Jeremiah 6:16).

There are good reasons for Baptists to know their history.

The history of Baptists provides for us real people who were faithful *examples* of those who loved biblical truth in ancient and recent Baptist churches. We should, at the very least, become somewhat familiar with American Baptists like Dr. John Clarke (1609-1676), Isaac Backus (1724-1806), John Gano (1727-1804), John Leland (1754-1841), J. L. Dagg (1794-1884), John Jasper (1812-1901), John A. Broadus (1827-1895), B. H. Carroll (1843-1914), and a host of others. Present-day Baptists stand on their strong shoulders.

The history of Baptists *encourages*. Reading the accounts of those who faithfully stood for truth against great opposition and seeing how God was with them through it all gives us courage and hope. We should be encouraged when we read of the first century pastor of the church at Smyrna, Polycarp, who willingly gave his life for Christ. When given the opportunity to recant his faith in Christ, he said, *"Eighty-*

six years I have served him, and he never did me any wrong.
How then can I blaspheme my king and Saviour?" Such men
and women were willing to *die* for the Lord in their day. The
question for us is, "Are we willing to *live* for the Lord in our
day?"

Baptist history also *exposes.* The New Testament is the
record of the person and work of Jesus Christ – who He
is and what He alone accomplished. The New Testament
is "His story." This did not occur in a vacuum. At first it
was through "the Acts of the Apostles" – the supernatural
working of God the Spirit in the lives of believers who
constituted the churches of the living God by the identifying
mark of baptism.

The New Testament is the written record of the faith of
the church Jesus founded and from the apostolic churches
that followed. It is history that exposes the shifts away from
the apostolic pattern.

- At first there were only sound churches sharing and
  representing the gospel of Jesus Christ, after there
  were groups who embraced a corrupted gospel who
  established corrupt congregations.
- At first baptism was by immersion of believers
  only upon profession of their faith in Christ, then
  it was reduced by some churches to pouring or to
  sprinkling of infants.
- At first New Testament churches were understood
  as local and visible, then the church became viewed
  as universal and invisible.
- At first New Testament bishops were pastors only
  of individual congregations, then some pastors were
  installed as overseers over several congregations.
- At first New Testament Scriptures were viewed as

the church's only authority, then some churches joined Scriptures with traditionalism, paganism, mysticism and ritualism.

- At first New Testament ordinances were viewed only as symbolic, then they were believed to be saving.
- At first New Testament churches recognized Jesus as their only Head, then a human leader was installed as the earthly head over churches.

Many modern Baptists who do not know, appreciate or learn their history may be afflicted with what C.S. Lewis (1898-1963) called *"chronological snobbery,"* the belief that anything of a prior time is inherently inferior to that which is known in the present.[2] J.I. Packer (1926-) added that the heretical spirit of our age holds that *"the newer is the truer, only what is recent is decent, every shift of ground is a step forward, and every latest word must be hailed as the last word on its subject."*[3]

Baptists without a knowledge of their Founder, their origin, their past, their doctrines, and their heroes are like trees without roots.

Baptist Distinctives

In the previous chapters I have attempted to delineate the biblical distinctives and the blood-bought history of Baptist people and their churches.

As noted in chapter 6, there is no one doctrine or position that marks Baptists as a unique people. Rather, it is

---

2   C. S. Lewis, *Surprised by Joy*, pp. 207-208.
3   J.I. Packer, *Doing Theology in Today's World: Essays in Honor of Kenneth S. Kantzer*, p. 21.

a composite of beliefs practiced from the time of Christ that identify Baptists as New Testament Christians, committed to New Testament principles. The following limited acrostic identifies some of the Baptist distinctives. It is admitted that other Christian groups have held some of these, but only Baptist people have held them all and held them consistently.

Biblical authority

The Bible is our final authority in all matters of faith and practice. We hold to no creeds, confessions, or any other works of man that supersede the Bible's authority. (2 Timothy 3:15-17; 1 Thessalonians 2:13; 2 Peter 1:20-21; Matthew 24:35; 1 Peter 1:23)

Autonomy of the local church

The local church is an independent body directly accountable to the Lord Jesus Christ, who is the "head of the body, the church." All human authority for governing the local church resides within the local church itself. Thus, the church is autonomous, or self-governing. No religious hierarchy outside the local church may dictate a church's beliefs or practices. However, we can and do enjoy fellowship with other like-minded churches and individuals. (Colossians 1:18; 2 Corinthians 8:1-5,19,23)

Priesthood of all believers

"Priest" is defined as "one authorized to perform the sacred rites of a religion, especially as a mediatory agent between humans and God." Every believer today is a priest of God and may enter His presence in prayer directly through our Great High Priest, Jesus Christ. No other mediator is needed between God and man – we all have equal access to God. (1 Peter 2:5, 9; Revelation 5:9-10; 1 Timothy 2:5)

Two ordinances

The local church practices two ordinances: (1) baptism of believers by immersion in water, identifying the individual with Christ in His death, burial, and resurrection, and (2) the Lord's Supper, or communion, commemorating His death for our sins. (Matthew 28:19-20; Acts 2:41-47; 1 Corinthians 11:23-32)

Individual soul liberty

Every individual, whether a believer or an unbeliever, has the liberty to choose his own beliefs. Baptists have always been opposed to the use of violence, coercion, and religious persecution. However, this personal liberty does not exempt one from responsibility to the Word of God or from accountability to God Himself. (Romans 14:5,12; 2 Corinthians 4:1-2)

Saved church membership

Local church membership is reserved for those who have in repentance and faith trusted Christ as their Saviour and have been baptized by immersion in a church of like faith and practice. (Acts 2:41; 2 Corinthians 6:14)

Two offices of the church

The scripture gives two distinct offices for each local church – pastors (synonymously referred to as elder and bishop) and deacons (servants). (1 Timothy 3:1-7; 1 Timothy 3:8-13; Titus 1:6-9)

Separation of Church and State

This belief does not come from the American Constitution. The concept came from a letter Thomas Jefferson wrote to the Baptist Association in Danbury, Connecticut, January 1, 1802, where he mentioned a "wall of separation." The fear was not that the church would one day take over the government, but that the government would take over the church. They had come from England that had a State church. The First Amendment of the Constitution states, "Congress shall make no law respecting an establishment of religion, or prohibiting the free exercise thereof…" The founding fathers did not view America as being free from religion, but a place where people were free to practice religion. Baptists have consistently believed that if people want to be Mormons, Buddhists, atheists, etc., they have the American right to be that; understanding they will ultimately face God with their choice. That doesn't make them right; it only means they have the right. There is no record in history of Baptist people persecuting others for their religious beliefs or non-beliefs. The "free exercise" clause is a Baptist belief. (Matthew 22:15-22; Acts 5:29)

Modern-day Baptists who do not distinguish themselves from Protestants have joined them.

The Baptist Name

It is a sign of courtesy to introduce one's self to others. My name is "Jerry." "Jerry" is one of those names that can go either way. One of my first girlfriends in grade school was also named Jerry. She was about a foot taller than me with flaming red hair. We were an odd couple, if ever so briefly. I am the third boy of Al and Mary Locke. When my mom

was alive, I would introduce myself to her friends at her
retirement home, "I'm the girl my mom never had." Anyone
could figure that out. She never denied it. After two boys, I am
certain my dad and mom were hoping for a girl, not another
boy. I'm okay with it. My brother, David, says I am the reason
why he didn't have a sister. I remind him he is the reason they
had me! I am named after a Baptist preacher, Jerry L. Davis
(1863–1956), one of my dad's spiritual mentors and the
founding pastor of Lake Worth Baptist Church, the church I
served as pastor for 33 years.

Imagine a world without names. What if every person
was just a man or a woman? "Hey, you" would be the regular
statement. What if you had to go into each building to find
out what they offered – shoes, car parts, food, sporting
goods? What if you had to open every container to see what
it was? Things would be a royal mess! The simple reason we
have names for people and places is to identify them so life
can be more orderly.

Names tell you a lot.

What about the people and churches who go by the
name "Baptist"?

The first man to bear the name Baptist was John the
Baptist (Matthew 3:1). The public ministry of Jesus Christ
began with him. He was a man "sent from God" (John
1:6) as the forerunner of Messiah (Matthew 3:3) and was
a New Testament prophet (Matthew 11:13) who baptized
with the authority of heaven (Matthew 21:25). The chapter
headings of S.E. Anderson's (1900-1977) book, *The First
Baptist*, gives us a brief insight into the person and work
of John the Baptist. John the Baptist was (1) Divinely
Praised, (2) Clearly Prophesied, (3) Richly Endowed, (4)
Thoroughly Prepared, (5) Widely Heard and Seen, (6)

Surprisingly Believed, (7) Cruelly Martyred, (8) Tragically
Ignored, (9) Hopefully Reviewed and (10) Rewardingly
Followed.[4] While we are to admire the unique place John
the Baptist filled in God's plan to prepare the material from
which Christ started the church, we need to be careful in our
adulation. I agree with Darrell W. Sparks who cautions us,
*"It is inaccurate, and frankly, hurtful to our cause to claim that
John was a Baptist in the same way that we are Baptists, that he
started the church, or that he was a member of Christ's church. It
amounts to equivocation. It seems to me that it is a feeble attempt
to give our name some Biblical authority. If true New Testament
churches get their name from John, then why are churches not
identified with the name 'Baptist' in Acts or the Epistles?"*[5]

While there have been baptistic churches since the
time of Christ, the first churches and Christians to bear
the name Baptists were "Anabaptists" in Europe in the
early 1500s. "Ana" (from the Greek *ana*) means "again."
"Baptist" (from the Greek word *baptizo*) always refers to
immersion. While many of these new believers in the 1500's
had been sprinkled as unbelieving infants in a ceremony
by the Catholic church, they understood the Bible spoke
of believers who were immersed upon profession of their
faith in Christ. Anabaptists rejected the idea that theirs was a
"second baptism," believing rather that their immersion was
the true and first baptism. *"The Anabaptist movement was the
continuation of that unbroken line of Christians and churches
from Christ forward. Throughout the centuries, these believers
had been called Anabaptists, not because they constituted a
movement, but because of their practice of requiring proper
baptism of those who came to them."*[6]

---

4   S.E. Anderson (1900-1977), *The First Baptist*, p. 3.
5   Darrell W. Sparks (1956-), *What's in a Name?* p. 26.
6   Lester Hutson (1941-), *The History of the Churches*, p. 371.

"*The simplification of the name 'Baptist' appears to have occurred in Holland and England as a result of these separatists' churches calling themselves, 'The baptized church of Christ worshipping at…' The records of the early English Baptist churches show this.*"[7]

Baptist Detractors

Those who are currently criticizing and attacking Baptists charge us with all kinds of evils - "sectarian prejudice," "denominational bigotry," and/or "cultural irrelevance." One of their biggest presumed threats is that if old-time Baptists don't get with the current trends they will end up being "on the wrong side of history."

The evangelical bandwagon is calling, not just Baptists, but, all denominations to join together for the greater good. Ecumenical pressure is mounting as the world moves toward a one-world religion predicted in Revelation 13. Popular gospel singer, Steve Green (not a Baptist) added his influence with the song, "Let the Walls Come Down."

All throughout the spirit realm a fearsome battle rages
The fates of men and nations hang suspended in the fray
Walls designed by Satan in the twilight of the ages
Now stand as great divisions all across the world today

Walls not born of government nor strife amid the nations
But walls within our churches and between denominations
Stones of dry tradition carved in fear and laid in pride
Become a dismal prison to those withering inside
The body weak and powerless, crippled by division
The victim of a tragic and most cruel civil war

---

7   Jack Hoad, *The Baptist*, p. 6.

Brother fighting brother over culture and tradition
While countless lost and dying lie as casualties of war

It's time to end the foolishness of warring with each other
And kneel in true repentance that our union be restored
May we then as brothers rally round the cross of Jesus
And carry on with diligence the mission of our Lord

Oh children of God
Oh soon to be bride
Let us humble ourselves
And crucify pride
Throw off the flesh
And its pious facade
And unite in the name of God
Let the walls come down
Let the walls come down
Let the walls that divide us
And hide us come down
If in Christ we agree
Let us seek unity
Let the walls
Let the walls come down[8]

Though these words are not historically accurate, they have become the convenient theology for many of today's churches and only add fuel to an unnecessary fire.

There was a day when all Baptist churches stood alone, only accepting Baptist baptism for membership and allowing only their members to participate in the Lord's Supper.

---

8   Jon Mohr, 1991.

Baptist Defectors

The trend of established Baptist churches removing the name "Baptist" from their church name has become a more than twenty-year epidemic. Removing a church's long-standing "Baptist" name is about as subtle as a massive coronary. It is apparent that churches that remove the "Baptist" name are doing so because they no longer want to be openly identified as "Baptist."

The greater percentage of current startup churches out of Baptist denominations, while led by Baptist people, educated in Baptist seminaries and funded with Baptist money, do so without taking the Baptist name.

The Minneapolis, Minnesota newspaper, the *Star Tribune* (April 15, 2017), published an article by Jean Hopfensperger entitled, *What's in a Name? Churches Trade Old Names for New, Younger Members.* In her research, Ms. Hopfensperger found *Maple Grove Evangelical Free Church* just converted to *"The Grove," First Lutheran Church* in White Bear Lake is now *"Community of Grace,"* and *Trinity Baptist Church* in Maplewood became *"LifePoint Church."* About 160 of the 253 Baptist churches in Minnesota and Iowa don't have the word "Baptist" on their doors, said the Rev. Dan Carlson, executive minister at *Converge North Central* — previously called the *Baptist General Conference.*

Who is leading this charge to discard the Baptist name?
Who are these defectors?
What are they saying?
Do they have their facts straight?

Assertion: *"We want to reach unchurched people so we don't want to have additional barriers."*
Fact: According to a 2015 study from the Nashville-

based *LifeWay Research,* a church's name isn't going to drastically change the way the public perceives it.[9] Their study found about half of Americans view denominational names favorably, while the other half feel either negatively or indifferently toward it. If dropping the "Baptist" name from a church's sign and advertisement was the deal maker then the logic is all non-Baptist churches would be growing. That's not the case. The viability and survivability of all church startups is that barely over 50 percent will still be going after just four years.[10] Since identifying or not identifying doesn't matter to the general population of the unchurched, there must be other reasons for discarding the Baptist name.

Assertion: *"I don't see why putting the name Baptist on a church matters."*

Fact: Amazingly, the ones who have this opinion are usually the young men who have been trained in Baptist churches and seminaries. It certainly exposes some deeper issues than the absence of a name. This must be said. The younger generations seem to have less and less appreciation for all of God's institutions: marriage/family, government and church. If they would read just a little Baptist history and see what their spiritual forefathers lived and died for, they would know the name matters. The seeds of relativism that have been sown among Christians for several decades has produced a harvest of people who tout that one church is no better or worse than another church. Ignorance or indifference are no excuse for not carrying on as Baptists.

---

9   Morgan Lee, *Christianity Today, Leaving Baptist in Your Church Name Won't Scare People Away,* June 3, 2015.

10 Ed Stetzer (1966-), *Church Planting and Survivability, Research Reflections,* Center for Missional Research, North American Mission Board, February 2007.

Saying nothing says everything!

Assertion: *"We are still identified as 'Baptist' in our legal documents and our associations."*

Fact: This seems to be done to retain their legal status as a church which is connected to a main denomination for their non-tax purposes and to reap the benefits of the denomination. On the face of it, this seems to be dishonest. Should we assume that those who gather in churches that say they are Baptist but do not choose to identify as Baptist are consistently being taught the doctrines that make Baptists distinctive? That's seems unlikely. It behooves those who no longer openly identify as Baptists to declare exactly who they are.

Assertion: *"Denominational names aren't positive anymore; they are negative."*

Fact: The word "denomination" only means "the act of denominating." It comes from the Latin word *nomen* which means "to name." As it relates to churches, it refers to differing branches of Christianity. What is wrong with identifying differences in beliefs and practices in churches that call themselves Christian? To assume or assert there are no differences in churches is both naive and dishonest. At least only a few decades ago churches were honest enough to put a sign in front of their buildings that let people know what they were. Now it takes a private investigator and a search warrant to discover what a church really is and what it believes. A *Grey Matter Research* project in 2013 discovered that churches with no denominational references in their name were less than twice as likely to be perceived as "honest" and almost five times more likely to be perceived as "trying to hide what they believe."[11]

Assertion: *"We are trying to reach people who might be offended by what 'Baptists' in the past have said, been or done."*

Fact: There is no denying there are people have been offended by people who have represented themselves as Baptists. Nobody I know wants to be identified with Westboro Baptist Church. In my personal, family history there was an unsubstantiated story in the late 1800's that my grandmother's brother was shot and killed by another family member who was angry at being accused of cattle rustling. There would be little benefit from changing my family name because there was a nut or two hanging from some distant limb in my family tree. Just how far are Baptist churches willing to go to not offend potential attendees? Should churches be "safe zones" where people are never confronted with truth – the truth of the existence of God, the truth of creation, the truth of the gospel, the truth of exclusive salvation in Christ alone, the truth of natural marriage, the truth of basic morality, the truth of the church, the truth of eternity? Certainly, a church would not want to run the risk of offending the unchurched or new members by teaching something as uncool as old-fashioned Baptist doctrine. Putting "rear ends" in a church building on Sunday might improve a church's "bottom line" (pun intended), but there is no way of avoiding offending the lost on some level. Jesus did it quite often (Matthew 13:20, 57; 15:12).

---

11   Christianity Today, article by Jeremy Weber, Grey Matter Research, *Denominational Names Are Not a Widespread Liability as Often Thought*, February 22, 2013.

When you refuse to be openly identified as something,
you will be closer to being identified as nothing.

Assertion: *"A lot of people think of 'Baptists' as the 'no'
denomination — no drinking, no dancing, no playing cards, no
fun."*

Fact: Churches of any denomination should not
apologize for having moral standards and biblical
convictions. Sadly, on too many fronts churches have become
far too worldly. Someone has said, "The church has become
so worldly, and the world has become so churchy, you can't
tell them apart." Instead of confronting the culture, many
Christians are accommodating the culture. For centuries,
the world and the church have been at odds. Attempting to
be relevant, churches have lost their edge and, in turn, have
lost their respect. What good has saying "yes" to drinking,
dancing and playing cards brought people?

Assertion: *"We would rather spend our time explaining
Christ to people than explaining 'Baptist'."*

Fact: Baptized Christians in New Testament churches
are the God-ordained means of explaining Christ. Whether
people inside or outside the church like it or not, scriptural
churches are the principle means God choses to do His
work. The Great Commission[12] was not given to Christians
in general, but to churches in particular. Churches are
responsible for the threefold work of evangelizing, baptizing
and maturing believers in the faith.

Baptist Defenders

There are still some things worth fighting for – the Bible,

---

12   Matthew 28:18-20.

natural marriage, basic morality, national and religious freedom, and, for me, openly being identified as a Baptist. And remember, I am neither angry nor ashamed of it.

KEEPING THE BAPTIST NAME AS A MATTER OF HISTORY

Every born-again modern-day "Baptist" who is ashamed of the name "Baptist" will meet their faithful ancestors in eternity. What might they say to us? Will they be shocked that we valued our desire to be accepted by the culture over the truth of salvation in Christ alone and baptism of believers by immersion alone? Homer G. Lindsay, Jr, (1927-2000) long-time pastor of the First Baptist Church of Jacksonville, FL, wrote, *"The name 'Christian' was first applied in ridicule to the followers of Christ by their enemies at Antioch. The name 'Baptist' was first given in ridicule by opponents of Christians who rejected the baptism of babies. Both names, like the cross, have been changed from marks of shame to badges of honor... Although the name 'Baptist' was not used to designate a particular group until a few centuries ago, and though it may not be possible to trace Baptist history back to the apostle without a break, it is true that Baptists are a Bible-made people, and Baptist principles and practices have lived through the centuries."*[13]

KEEPING THE BAPTIST NAME AS A MATTER OF TRANSPARENCY

If you are a Baptist, stand openly, biblically, intelligently, graciously and boldly. If your church is a Baptist church, someone looking on the internet or driving by your building should be able to know that. And you should not be angry or

---

13   Homer G. Lindsay, Jr. (1927-2000), *Spiritual Helps for New Members*, pp. 54-55.

ashamed of it.

A question to those who are not transparent about who they are and what they believe might be, "What other matters are you not transparent about?"

The label on the outside tells you what you will find or not find on the inside.

To cover all the bases, Pastor George Ragsdale suggested a church might call itself *The First NazerMethodist Bapticostal Seventh-Day Organized Luthertarian Non-Denominational Church of Our Lady of the Mind?*[14]

KEEPING THE BAPTIST NAME AS A MATTER OF IDENTITY

Recently, my wife and I went through the arduous and somewhat expensive task of establishing a revocable living trust. It has very specific names that establish it as an official document.

For centuries, the name "Baptist" has identified congregations that held to a core of New Testament doctrine. H. Boyce Taylor, Sr. (1870-1932), for more than thirty years pastor of First Baptist Church, Murray, KY, wrote, *"The name Baptist is a differentiating name. It differentiates and distinguishes all who hold it from all other sects and denominations. It marks out the people who wear it. God said His people are a peculiar people. The name Baptist marks out the peculiarities of those who wear it. It distinguishes those who practice immersion only from all those who do not. It distinguishes those who are baptized Christians from those who are not. It distinguishes those who have Baptist baptism from those who have not. It distinguishes those who reject infant baptism from those who follow Rome and receive it. The name Baptist is so distinguishing*

---

14   George Ragsdale, http://www.westmarionbaptistchurch.com/
      faq5.html

a name, that heretical Baptist sects, such as Hardshell Baptists or Free Will Baptists or Seventh Day Baptists have to use a prefix of some kind in front of their name to mark them as 'sick' Baptists who are following a stranger. The only sheep that will follow a stranger is a sick sheep. So with Baptists. The prefix Baptist is a sick Baptist or his prefix is a nickname. Like the Israelites in Old Testament days, Baptists have had many names; but they have always been the same people."[15]

It is the role of sound pastors and the responsibility of informed congregations to know and stand for biblical doctrine and their Baptist history.

A Baptist church is not obligated to acknowledge the baptism nor receive members from a congregation that will not identify as a Baptist church. This is not a petty, narrow-minded, bigoted position. Follow this simple line of thought: The gospel of Jesus Christ is pictured by baptism; baptism is carried out with church authority; a church's authority to baptize is founded upon its doctrine.

"I will keep the name 'Christian' – it identifies me with the One I follow. I will keep the name 'Baptist' - it identifies me with how I follow Christ."
- Evangelist Dave McCracken (1955-)[16]

KEEPING THE BAPTIST NAME AS A MATTER OF MINISTRY

Maybe those of us who are Baptists should pay closer attention to our name. The word "Baptist" comes from what word? Baptism. Baptism in a Baptist church is only conducted after a person has come to personal faith in Jesus Christ.

---

15 H. Boyce Taylor, Sr. (1870-1932), *Why Be a Baptist?* p. 34.
16 Dave McCracken (1955-), Personal correspondence, May 26, 2017.

Baptistm conducted by a church presupposes people who have been saved by the power of the gospel and as an act of obedience have submitted to baptism. Too many Baptist churches are hardly living up to their name. Instead of being fishers of men, many churches are only keepers of the aquarium. Instead of churches growing by conversions, they are often reduced to swapping or stealing sheep. Too many sound churches are just plain sound asleep.

By 1869 the missionary-explorer David Livingstone (1813-1873) had advanced so far into Africa that everybody presumed he was either dead or lost. James Gordon Bennett, Jr. (1841-1918), the owner and publisher of the *New York Herald,* sent a telegram to one of its correspondents, Henry M. Stanley (1841-1904). Bennett was in Paris, and Stanley at Gibraltar. The telegram summoned Stanley to come to Paris at once. Stanley went, reached Paris at midnight, knocked at the great newspaper-man's door, and asked what was wanted. *"Find Livingstone,"* was the short, blunt reply. *"How much money do you place at my disposal?"* asked Stanley. *"Fifty thousand dollars, or a larger sum. Never mind about the money; find Livingstone."*

Stanley went. It took two years' time to get ready. It required a specially planned campaign and thorough preparation. The planning was done, and the world was thrilled when the bold missionary leader was eventually found in 1871.

Our Master has sent a message to His churches. It is written down in a Book and is repeated constantly. He says, *"Find my world, and bring it back; never mind about the expense of money and lives. Find my world and win it back."* God's churches have the winning power to do it.[17]

"*Jesus Christ called out His church while He was here on earth, commissioned it to go into all the world with the gospel message, and promised it His presence through it all, assuring them that the gates of hell would not prevail against what He had begun. That faith is here today, and has been here through all the ages in between, and will be here when our Lord returns to gather us home. No amount of rewriting church history can change the heavenly record, and when we get there we may well find that those whom the modern historians rejected as 'sects' are those whom the Lord will reward as the faithful, while the rest of us look on with wonder.*"[18]

---

17 Adapted from S.D. Gordon (1859-1836), *Quiet Talk with World Winners.*

18 I.K. Cross (1917-2008), *The Battle for Baptist History*, pp. 178-179.

Bibliography

Donald F. Ackland, *Joy in Church Membership*, Convention Press, Nashville, TN, 1955.

John Quincy Adams, *Baptists the Only Thorough Religious Reformers*, Sheldon & Co., Revised Edition, New York, NY, 1876.

Sam Allberry, *Why Bother with Church?* The GoodBook Company, 2016.

S.E. Anderson, *The First Baptist*, The Challenge Press, Little Rock, AR, 1972.

Louis Franklin Asher, *John Clarke (1609-1776)*, Dorrance Publishing Co, Pittsburg, PA, 1997.

Charles Austin, *The Bergen Record (New Jersey)*, October 12, 2000.

Robert Baker, *The Baptist March in History*, Convention Press, Nashville, TN, 1958.

William Barclay, *God's Young Church*, The Westminster Press, Philadelphia, PA, 1970.

Thomas W. Bicknell, *Story of Dr. John Clarke*, Providence, RI, 1915.

William H. Brackney, *Historical Dictionary of the Baptists*, The Scarecrow Press, Lanham, MD, 1999.

Jerry Bridges, *The Discipline of Grace,* NavPess, Colorado Springs, CO, 1994.

Patrick R. Briney, *The Local, Visible Church*, Mission Blvd. Baptist Church Publications, Fayetteville, AR, 1995.

D. Stuart Briscoe, *The Communicator's Commentary – Romans*, Word Books, Waco TX, 1982.

John A. Broadus, *Commentary on the Gospel of Matthew, An American Commentary of the New Testament,* The American Baptist Publication Society, Valley Forge, PA, 1886.

Kenneth T. Brooks, *Why Cumbereth It the Ground*, Danbury Baptist Press, West Redding, CT, 2008.

F.F. Bruce, *The Church of Jerusalem*, Christian Brethren Research Fellowship, Journal 4, April 1964.

Ergun & Emir Caner, Editors, *The Sacred Desk*, Broadman & Holman Publishers, Nashville, TN, 2004.

B. H. Carroll, *An Interpretation of the English Bible*, Baker Book House, Grand Rapids, MI, 1948, reprinted 1973.

J. M. Carroll, *The Trail of Blood*, Ashland Avenue Baptist Church, Lexington, KY, 1931.

John T. Christian, *Close Communion, or Baptism as a Prerequisite to the Lord's Supper*, Baptist Book Concern, Louisville, KY, 1892.

John T. Christian, *A History of the Baptists*, Sunday School Board of the Southern Baptist Convention, Nashville, TN, 1926.

Robert Coleman, *The Master Plan of Evangelism*, Fleming H. Revell Company, Old Tappan, NJ, 1981.

J. B. Cranfill, *Baptist and Their Doctrines*, Fleming H. Revel, New York, NY, 1913.

W. A. Criswell, *The Doctrine of the Church*, Convention Press, Nashville, TN, 1980.

I. K. Cross, *The Battle for Baptist History*, Brentwood Christian Press, Columbus, GA, 1990.

John L. Dagg, *A Treatise on Church Order*, Southern Baptist Publication Society, Charleston, SC, 1858.

A. A. Davis, *Sermons on The Trail of Blood*, Christian Printing and Publishing, Inc, Houston, TX, 1952.

Mark Dever, *A Display of God's Glory*, IX Marks Ministries, Washington DC, 2001.

Mark Dever and Paul Alexander, *Deliberate Church*, Crossway Books, Wheaton, IL, 2005.

Mark Dever, *Polity: Biblical Arguments on How to Conduct Church Life*, Center for Church Reform, 2001.

Mark Dever, *The Church-The Gospel Made Visible*, B & H Academic, Nashville, TN, 2012.

Jason G. Duesing, Thomas White, Malcomm B. Yarnell III, *Upon This Rock*, B & H Academics, Nashville, TN, 2010.

Louis Entzminger, *The New Testament Church*, The Manne Company, Fort Worth TX.

Tony Evans, *God's Glorious Church*, Moody Publishers, Chicago, IL, 2003.

Mike Gendron, *Preparing for Eternity*, The Northhampton Press, Orlando, FL, 2011.

Gene A. Getz, *Sharpening the Focus of the Church*, Moody Press, Chicago, IL, 1974.

Everett Gill, *A.T Robertson: A Biography*, MacMillian, New York, NY, 1943,

Miss L.F. Greene, *The Writings of Elder John Leland*, 1845 (1986 reprint).

Norman Grubbs, *Continuous Revival*, Christian Literature Crusade, Fort Washington, PA, 1977.

William C. Hawkins and Willard A. Ramsey, *The House of God*, Hallmark Baptist Church, Simpsonville, SC, 1980.

Edward E. Hindson, *Glory in the Church*, Thomas Nelson Publishers, New York, NY, 1975.

Edward T. Hiscox, *Principles and Practices for Baptist Churches*, Kregel Publications, Grand Rapids, MI, 1980.

Jack Hoad, *The Baptist*, Grace Publications, Hertfordshire, England, 1986.

H. H. Hobbs, *The Baptist Faith and Message*, Convention Press, Nashville, TN, 1971.

Charles L. Hunt, *The Body of Christ: Separating Myth from Metaphor*, Grace Baptist Church Printing Outreach, Florence, KY, 2006.

Lester Hutson, *The History of Churches*, Amazon, 2013.

F. J. Huegel, *The Cross Through the Scriptures*, Bethany Fellowship, Minneapolis, MN, 1970.

W.A. Jarrel, *Baptist Church History (1894)*, Delmarva Publications, 2014.

W. Glenn Jonas, *The Baptist River*, Mercer University Press, Mason, GA, 2008.

Adoniram Judson, *Christian Baptism*, Audubon Press, Laurel, MS, 2000.

Buell H. Kazee, *The Church and the Ordinances*, The Little Baptist Press, Lexington, KY, 1965.

Bob Kauflin, *Non-Christians on the Worship Team?*, May 22, 2008, www.worshipmatters.com

Homer A. Kent, *The Pastoral Epistles*, Moody Press, Chicago, IL, 1958

Tim LaHaye, *Revelation Unveiled*, Zondervan Publishing House, Grand Rapids, MI, 1999.

Clarence Larkin, *Why I Am A Baptist*, American Bible Publication Society, 1902.

J. Stanley Lemons, *First, the First Baptist Church in America*, Providence, R.I. 2001.

C. S. Lewis, *Surprised by Joy*, 1966.

Homer G. Lindsay, Jr., *Spiritual Helps for New Members,* 1969.

Paul E. Little, *How to Give Away Your Faith,* Intervarsity Press, Chicago, IL, 1966.

J. Howard Marshall, *Acts, the Tyndale New Testament Commentary,* William B. Eerdmans Publishing Company, Grand Rapids, MI, 1992.

Roy Mason, *The Church That Jesus Built,* 1923.

Victor I. Masters, editor, *Re-thinking Baptist Doctrines,* The Western Recorder, Louisville, KY, 1937.

Peter Masters, *Do We Have a Policy?,* The Wakeman Trust, London, 2002.

William MacDonald, *Ephesians, the Mystery of the Church,* Harold Shaw Publishers, Wheaton, IL, 1968.

George W. McDaniel (1875-1927), *The People Called Baptists,* The Sunday School Board of the Southern Baptist Convention, Nashville, TN, 1919.

John C. Morgan, *Independent Baptist,* The Challenge Press, Little Rock, AR, 1970.

Ray C. Morrow, *What is a New Testament Church?*

R. Larry Moyer, *21 Things God Never Said,* Kregel Publications, Grand Rapids, MI, 2004.

Tom J. Nettles & Russell D. Moore, *Why I Am a Baptist,* Broadman & Holman, Nashville, TN, 2001.

Joe T. Odle, *Church Member's Handbook,* Broadman Press, Nashville, TN, 1962.

Joe T. Odle, *Why I Am a Baptist,* Broadman Press, Nashville, TN, 1972.

Stephen F. Olford , *Committed to Christ and His Church*, Baker Book House, Grand Rapids, MI, 1991.

J. I. Packer, *Keep in Step with the Spirit*, 2nd ed., Grand Rapids: Baker, 2005.

Jonathan & Judith Pearl, *The Chosen Image*, McFarland & Company, Inc, Publishers, Jefferson, NC, 1999.

Bob Pearle, *The Vanishing Church*, Hannibal Press, Garland, TX, 2009.

John Phillips, *Exploring Acts, Vol. 1*, Loizeaux Brothers, Neptune, NJ, 1991.

John William Porter, *The Baptist Debt to the World*, Baptist Heritage Press.

Paul Powell, *Basic Bible Sermons on Handling Conflict*, Broadman Press, Nashville, TN. 1992.

Earl D. Radmacher, *The Nature of the Church*, Portland, Oregon: Western Baptist Press, 1972.

Willard A. Ramsey, *The Nature of the New Testament Church on Earth*, Hallmark Baptist Church, Simpsonville, SC, 1973.

D. B. Ray, *Baptist Succession*, The King's Press, Rosemead, CA, 1949.

A.T. Robertson, *Word Pictures of the New Testament, Vol IV*, Broadman Press, Nashville, TN, 1931.

Wendell H. Rone, Sr., *What is the Church?*

Charles R. Ryrie, *Ryrie Study Bible*, Moody Press, Chicago, IL, 1978.

Robert J. Sargent, *What? I Must be Re-baptized*, Bible Baptist Church Publications, Oak Harbor, WA, 2001.

C. I. Scofield, *The Scofield Reference* Bible, Oxford University Press, New York, NY, 1909

Bailey Smith, *Real Evangelism*, Broadman Press, Nashville, TN, 1978.

Colin S. Smith, *Unlocking the Bible Story Vol. 4*, Moody Press, Chicago, IL, 2002.

Steven W. Smith, *Dying to Preach*, Kregel, Grand Rapids, MI, 2009.

Darrell W. Sparks, *What's in a Name?* Theophilus Books, Dearborn, IN.

Charles H. Spurgeon (1834-1892), *C. H. Spurgeon's Autobiography*, Passmore & Alabaster, London, 1897.

Charles H. Spurgeon, *Metropolitan Tabernacle Pulpit*.

Andy Stanley, North Point Church in Atlanta, sermon February 28, 2016.

Ray C. Steadman, *God's Unfinished Book*, Discovery House Publishers, Grand Rapids, MI, 2008.

Ray C. Stedman, *Reason to Rejoice*, Discovery House Publishers, Grand Rapids, MI, 2004.

Augustus Hopkins Strong, *Systematic Theology*, Fleming H. Revel Co., Westwood, NJ, 1963.

H. Boyce Taylor, Sr., *Why Be a Baptist?* Ashland Avenue Baptist Publication, Lexington, KY, 1963.

Gary Thomas, *Authentic* Faith, Zondervan, Grand Rapids, MI, 2002.

Stephen Tomkins, *A Short History of Christianity*, William B. Eerdmans Publishing Company, Grand Rapids, MI, 2005.

George W. Truett, *The Supper of Our Lord*: A Sermon preached at First Baptist Church, Dallas, TX, 1907.

J. Clyde Turner, *The New Testament Doctrine of the Church*, Broadman Press, Nashville, TN, 1951.

Leonard Verduin, *The Reformers and Their Stepchildren*, The Baptists Standard Bearer, Paris, AR, 1964.

Jerry Vines, *The Corinthians Confusion*, 2005.

C. Peter Wagner, *This Changes Everything*, Chosen Books, Bloomington, MN, 2013.

Trevin Wax, *Counterfeit Gospels*, Moody Publishers, Chicago, IL, 2011.

Webster's New World Dictionary of the American Language, World Publishing Company, Cleveland/New York, 1964.

Norman H. Wells, *The Church That Jesus Loved*, The Challenge Press, Little Rock, AR, 1973.

Donald S. Whitney, *Spiritual Disciplines for the Christian Life*, NavPress, Colorado Springs, Co, 1991.

Warren W. Wiersbe, *From Worry to Worship*, Victor Books, Wheaton, IL, 1983.

Joseph Foulkes Winks, Editor, *The Baptist Reporter and Missionary Intelligencer*, London, January 1853.

John D. Woodbridge and Thomas Edward McComiskey, Editors, *Doing Theology in Today's World: Essays in Honor of Kenneth S. Kantzer*, Zondervan Publishing, Grand Rapids, MI, 1991.

Other books by the Author

Cross Examination
24 intensive investigations of the greatest event in human history

The Gospel Truth
An evaluation of 18 "modern gospels" in contrast to the gospel preached and believed in the New Testament

Pardon Me ... Please
Discovering the joy of a forgiven and forgiving life

What's Next?
A layman's guide for 21st Century Bible prophecy

Believers in Babylon
A biblical strategy for surviving in an anti-Christian America

What Kind of Love is This?
An honest evaluation of our love for God

9 Holy Habits
Shaping, strengthening and sustaining our daily walk with God

NO DOUBT about it
For those who struggle with assurance of salvation

Now That You've Believed
A discipleship guide for spiritual growth

LWBC PUBLICATIONS
4445 Hodgkins Road
Fort Worth TX 76135
817-825-8991
jdlocke@lakeworthbaptist.org
www.lakeworthbaptist.org